PERTH

A guide for the curious

IN MEMORIAM

Fanny Balbuk

George Seddon

Geoffrey Bolton

For their contributions
to the imagination of Perth.

PERTH

A guide for the curious

EDITED BY

TERRI-ANN WHITE

CITY *of* PERTH

LORD MAYOR'S FOREWORD

Perth: a guide for the curious honours our city's richness and celebrates our diversity in 24 very personal perspectives of what Perth means. And has meant, to its people. Certain themes clearly resonate throughout – a sense of place: of where we have come from, what drives us into the future, and a love of living in such a fabulous part of our world.

Having had the honour of being Lord Mayor of Perth since 2007, my vision has been to create a vibrant capital city where 'care' is paramount for its citizens. A city made through progressing important projects and programs, and inspiring communities to think about their surroundings in different ways. The Council has collectively driven some major developments and changes across our City.

In recent years Perth has been enlivened by activities that encourage visiting the city and using space more effectively. With strong and continuing growth in the inner city residential population and the development of many new commercial buildings, our business and retail sectors have flourished.

Having lived and worked in the City all my life I am so proud of having played a part in this growth at a time when people were not appreciative and, at the start, somewhat fearful of the changes that they have now been wholeheartedly embraced.

Perth is recognised as the western gateway to the nation of Australia; a city of some 2.3 million which annually ranks as one of the top ten cities in the world in The Economist's liveability index.

The opening of Elizabeth Quay and future developments already underway, such as Perth City Link and Waterbank, are exceptional projects that are practical, inject investment into the local economy, and will attract and keep visitors making return visits to Perth.

Through good planning, learning from others, and embracing sustainability we are seeing Perth develop into a global city of substance. I could not be prouder.

I hope you will enjoy reading the contributions contained in this book, and that it inspires you to discover areas you may not yet have discovered.

The Right Honourable the Lord Mayor Lisa-M. Scaffidi

CONTENTS

INTRODUCTION

A CITY AND HOW IT WRITES ITSELF

Perth, Western Australia, is an urbanised capital city that hasn't produced much fiction and poetry about itself by local writers or guest observers. It has unrolled its distinctiveness largely within the constraints of formal history and anthropology. It's hard to nominate contemporary books to visitors—in non-fiction too—that capture the contours of the streets, the urbanity (or its disavowal) lurking in laneways and intersections, those features of a city that were somewhat overlooked in the 1980s when key streets turned into one-way mazes and people stopped visiting the CBD after six at night. The way it had always been used by citizens was forgotten: going to 'town', by day and night, where all types of initiations and transgressions could be conducted. It become a 'town' that carried the traces of memories of street photographers outside grand department stores, bunches of boronia sold on the street, an ecoculture of bookshops and music stores where serious staff members could provide an education in, say, jazz music since bebop or international fiction in translation to eager customers (like me).

The 1980s boxed up these memories of what the city once was and made a less appealing version that, in various lean times, wasn't worth bothering with as a *destination*. Described

pejoratively as a knock-off version of a provincial English city—all beige and prefab shopping complexes—it looked like a town centre where civic pride may have once resided. An insult better or worse than the mantle of *backwater*?

What a difference decades can make. Ten years ago you could fire a rocket down many of the main CBD streets and only hit rubbish bins. I recall an epiphany in around 2011 when I walked along St George's Terrace with sophisticates from Sydney from cocktail bar to restaurant on a Thursday evening and the streets were teeming with people. Miraculously, there was now choice, diversity, and people on the streets.

All of these streets are now reinstated to two-way and the city of Perth has lost its contentious slogan that *Your car is as welcome as you are*. It isn't that I'm fixated with driving a car through the city but those one-way streets made for transit routes to get you out of the city as fast as possible. And now, after all of the enlightened decisions have been applied from those changed planning priorities, small and often artist-led interventions have made new spaces in which to eat, drink, meet and these efforts have been matched with large imaginative developments in key city sites that had sat neglected for decades. I am thinking of the State Treasury building complex and Brookfield Place, both of them with open access and the most heartening approach to urban renewal and beauty. After some years of a boom time in the mining and exploration industries this city has filled with new people in large numbers (in 1960 the population was 409,000; in 1980 898,000; in 2015 we were 2.02 million, and projected for 2050 we'll be

4.9 million). There are people in the streets and a palpable appetite for renewal. Big city traffic jams, too, for the first time.

While we have a contemporary literary cohort, following a strong twentieth century literature in Western Australia that is distinctive and vibrant and noted for its relationship with both describing and projecting landscape and place, most of this current writing follows its antecedents and looks closely and lovingly at the bush, the flat plains, the coast and its dunes and white sand and buoyant water. And its suburbs. Has Tim Winton written about Perth city? Only in passing—it has not been his focus. And Winton has been the poster boy for a sense of Western Australian place for thirty years, particularly for readers from elsewhere. He has drawn visitors to this state. What do they make of Perth, usually the first destination when flying in?

Think about the yield of writing from this state with its over-abundance of talent. Katherine Susannah Prichard. Kenneth Seaforth McKenzie. Randolph Stow. Dorothy Hewett. Joan London. Gail Jones. Kim Scott. Stephen Kinnane. Marion Campbell. Stephen Daisley. A few of my favourites. But it is only the stray poem or short story or set-piece in a novel that occupies itself with that stretch of Swan River from Heirrison Island up to Kings Park and all that sits behind it up to Newcastle Street in what was renamed Northbridge in the 1970s. For those in the know, there are other examples. Gerry Glaskin, a Perth-born author, wrote and published novels in the UK in the 1950s and 60s that tracked love affairs and other congress between men in the Perth gay scene, but he anonymized the street names and places and fixed it into an encoded setting that you could only recognise if you belonged to that community at a particular moment. Randolph Stow, too, chose to set his novel *The Suburbs of Hell* (1984), formed around the years of fear that Eric Edgar Cooke instilled here in the 1960s, in a fictional city with contours that more closely resembled his adopted city of Harwich than Perth.

I'm not sure why Perth city has been so neglected by our creative writers. I scoured the pages of the vast range of anthologies published since the 1970s and found very little. The main literary writing to have tackled the site of the CBD, the focus of this book, has been memoir and non-fiction. Novelist David Whish-Wilson rehearses much of this writing in his narrative book *Perth* (2014), which belongs to a series of books by writers about their Australian cities. He illuminates the way it operates as a city, and describes it successfully to readers including life-long residents. Whish-Wilson certainly provides a vivid picture of the Swan river running through the city and all the way down to the port.

The most striking image from Whish-Wilson's book is the figure of Fanny Balbuk, trapped for some time in the writings of Daisy Bates but released in other writings—in interpretation and imaginative flight—in recent decades to be her own woman again. There are a number of contemporary accounts of Noongar and other Aboriginal people in the city. Stephen Kinnane's *Shadow Lines* (2004) is a standout: a portrait of care in an organised community in Perth that celebrated life and pleasure.

The most descriptive writing about Perth city, with a menacing historical soundtrack, can be found in the immaculate memoir of place by Robert Drewe, *The Shark Net* (2000). His is a coming of age narrative with a teenaged Rob occupying the city in the 1960s, on the loose from the suburb of Dalkeith and, a little later, as a cadet journalist at *The West Australian* covering, amongst other assignments, the trial of Eric Edgar Cooke, a man he knew through associations described in the book.

Recently, at Wendy Martin's first Perth International Arts Festival as artistic director she presented her opening event, outdoors and free, filling Langley Park with fifty or so thousand people. Two of our best writers, alongside performing artists and musicians, took to the stage and a lectern and actually read a short passage of luminous writing. As a literary colleague from Sydney said to me the week after: *who'd believe such a remarkable thing?* It was both surprising and deeply successful to see Kim Scott and Robert Drewe up there, unadorned aside from words on paper, as part of a joyous, honest account of how this place once was, how it was settled, and what has been made of it since then. I'm not sure I'll recover soon from this complex, political, courageous and very beautiful shadow play offered to Western Australians about what we are made of in this corner of a tremendous continent.

Our focus here in this book is a quirky one: we asked people with expert knowledge or deep experience to write in a more informal, or personal style, about the city of Perth. To take us through it, on a walking tour of what they know about the city and its history. We defined the city as starting at the Causeway and following the span to Kings Park and ending at Newcastle Street to the north. We've provided maps, and hope both visitors and residents will enjoy this illumination of the city of Perth. Don't forget your sunscreen!

Terri-ann White

COUNCIL HOUSE

Geoffrey London

Council House has been justifiably celebrated as the best example of modern architecture in the city of Perth. The history of Council House, however, has been marked by two periods of controversy: the first starting well before it was designed and then, during the mid-1990s, when the building was seriously threatened with demolition.

THE SITE

The decision to conduct an architectural competition for the design of Perth's New Town Hall, as the project was initially known, came while arguments were erupting about the site nominated for the building. The site selection controversy had bubbled along since the mayoral elections of 1901, but became more urgent and more rancorous once the project became real.[1]

---

1   After the site was finalised in the second half of 1959, the *West Australian* newspaper of 9 November 1960 reported:

"I am in favour of disposing of the present Town Hall site and of building a larger town hall on a central site to be selected by ratepayers" . . .<<AU: does the *West Australian* quote end here or does the entire quote go to the end of the endnote? Unclear>> This could have been a statement from a candidate in the last Lord Mayoral elections. But it was made 59 years ago. It was a plank in the platform of William Gordon Brookman, who was seeking election as Mayor of Perth in 1901. Even then, only 31 years after the completion of the Perth Town Hall, a new

The Crown Grant for the Council House site on St Georges Terrace was handed over on 21 July 1954 and the announcement of an Australia-wide competition for the 'planning and design of the new Perth Town Hall' was made public on the same date. The original plan was for a two-stage competition, with submissions due over a twelve-month period.

In the years leading up to the competition there was a fierce campaign to promote the selection of an alternative site on the river's edge. In particular, the Western Australian Chapter of the Royal Australian Institute of Architects (RAIA) asserted that the new Town Hall should be located on Perth's riverfront, taking advantage of the best setting for this long-anticipated piece of civic architecture. Before the competition was announced, the campaign gathered momentum and was given sustained exposure in the press, indicating a high level of public interest in the new structure.

In the face of spirited opposition and four and a half years after the first announcement of the competition, the Perth City Council issued a press release dated 15 December 1958 in which they launched the Australia-wide competition for the '...new Town Hall and municipal offices to be built at a cost not exceeding one million six hundred thousand pounds' on the St Georges Terrace site.

An editorial in the *West Australian* newspaper followed the press release, applauding the concept of architectural competitions for important buildings:

---

site had become a civic issue. . . Shortly before World War I a referendum on the siting question recorded a majority for the advocates of the present army headquarters site in Beaufort-street . . . Premier Collier in July 1934, suggesting three sites – Government House, Stirling Gardens and the Esplanade.

All big buildings – particularly those which will become landmarks – should make a distinctive contribution to the city's appearance. The only sure way of achieving this and guarding against dullness and mediocrity is to enlist the ideas of the best architects in all the schools of their profession. The imaginative conception of Sydney's proposed opera house, which was inspired by the waters of Port Jackson, is the result of an international competition.

But a regret was noted:

The architects entering for the town hall competition will be restricted by the setting for the new buildings. Even at this stage the council would do well to reconsider the proposed site of the civic group in favour of one on reclaimed land fronting the Esplanade. The building would then be uninhibited in style and would occupy a more dominant and pleasing position as a focal point of the proposed sweep of botanic features on the foreshores of Perth Water.[2]

Town Clerk Green, a past president of the WA chapter of the Royal Australian Institute of Architects, was resolute in his defence of the selected Town Hall site and equally resolute in arguing that there was no need to respond to the recommendation of the Institute. He believed that sufficient information was already available to show that the Institute's preferred riverfront site would prove very expensive because of the depth of silt, the requirement of a further reclamation of 15 acres from the Swan River, the difficult piling conditions and, in his view, the necessity for a retaining wall on the riverfront.

---

2   *West Australian*, 19 December 1958.

He argued that there were difficulties of access to the river site and advantages arising from a more central city location.[3] The town clerk's clear firmness of conviction later contributed very positively to the successful building of Council House. The influential English planner Sir William Holford, during a visit to Perth that coincided with the site debate, viewed the options and recommended that the Council remain with the site chosen. In his subsequent letter to the Institute, the town clerk wrote that the Council had been 'fortified' by the opinion of Sir William Holford. The *Daily News* then reported the headline: 'TOWN HALL, FILE CLOSED'.[4]

THE COMPETITION

The Council's expressed desire to have the building completed for the 1962 Empire Games in Perth, coupled with the time spent battling over the site, contributed to the decision to reduce the competition to a single stage. The appointed assessors, in addition to the chair, Professor Brian Lewis from The University of Melbourne, were all prominent architects: Harry Seidler, Leslie Perrot, and A E (Paddy) Clare. The decision to accept the role of assessor had provided a problematic choice for Harry Seidler, who wrote a letter to Town Clerk Green:

> Your recent visit to my office placed me in quite a dilemma. The forthcoming competition promises to be a most interesting project in which I would have very much liked to participate as a competitor.[5]

---

3   Memorandum by Town Clerk Green to the General Purposes Committee, 9 March 1959.

4   *Daily News* 13/7/59

5   Perth City Council Archive File 40/59, letter dated 2 October 1959.

The competition called for an office block and a public suite, which was to contain a main hall for 2,500 people, a lesser hall for 1,000 and a banquet hall for 1,200. The conditions of competition were bald, descriptive, and quantitative. There was no attempt to solicit a particular architectural approach or to urge any kind of representational or qualitative response. The conditions did, however, advise that the earth foundations would support a building of about 18 storeys and that the plot ratio was 5.

The competition was open to all architects who were corporate members of the Royal Australian Institute of Architects and was described as a competition for the selection of an architect rather than the final design of a Town Hall. The first prize on offer was £5,000 and 61 entries were received.

Professor Brian Lewis, chairman of assessors for the competition, was triumphant in his description of the winning entry:

> For Perth citizens, this is a milestone. It will be a magnificent building, giving something of grandeur to Perth and making it an even finer city. It will be the best building of its type in Australia. I congratulate Perth on this very fortunate design.[6]

Sections of the assessors' report were printed in the *West Australian*, reinforcing the public importance of the outcome:

> the awards made were unanimous and unqualified, and . . . the authors of the winning entry should be appointed as architects for the new town hall . . . The design No 19, premiated first, was immediately recognised as a direct and satisfactory solution. Detailed examination established

---

6   Assessors' report

it as being capable of development into a most dignified and efficient Town Hall.[7]

Design No 19 was by Jeffrey Howlett and Don Bailey, two young architects who worked together at Bates Smart and McCutcheon in Melbourne and entered the competition independently from that distinguished Modernist firm. Howlett had previously worked in Perth for a number of years after travelling there from England following the completion of his diploma at the Architectural Association.

The firm of Cameron Chisholm and Nicol of Perth was awarded the second prize, and the partnership of Anthony Brand, Gus Ferguson and Bill Weedon, also of Perth, awarded the third prize.

Howlett and Bailey moved to Perth from Melbourne to set up a new office and take on the appointment as architects for the new building. The third architect joining Howlett and Bailey in Perth from the Bates Smart and McCutcheon office was Lindsay Waller who described himself as the 'nuts and bolts man.'[8] During 1956 and 1957, Waller had been the project architect in Perth for the construction of the Methodist Ladies College building.

The winning design went through a number of changes and refinements before building began. The rather squat proposed building of 9 storeys increased in height to 11 and then to 12 storeys to allow for future expansion. Floors 8 to 10 were designed to take advantage of the views and house the reception areas for Council, including a staff cafeteria and councillors

---

7   *West Australian*, 2 September 1960

8   Interview between Lindsay Waller and the author, Perth, 10 October 1995

banqueting room on level 10.

The competition design had the columns going straight down to the ground, continuing the upper structural frame, but the design was changed at a late point to allow the opening up of the ground floor. Howlett had recognised the possibility of visually linking the St Georges Terrace entrance with the proposed Public Suite to the rear of the site. Lindsay Waller recalled how Town Clerk Green acted as the client and was prepared to make decisions on behalf of the Council. This streamlined the process considerably and, according to Waller, he made a significant contribution to the project through his receptiveness and decisiveness. In the instance of the changes to the ground floor, it was a case of Green enthusiastically agreeing with Howlett.[9]

Although the winning competition entry was designed as a reinforced concrete flat-plate structure, the building was converted to steel-framed, chosen as the most economical and speedy form of construction. It is unlikely that the building would have been ready for its part in the 1962 Empire Games if pre-ordered steel had not been used.

Construction began on the administrative block in 1961 at a contracted cost of £1,230,000. The first pour of concrete took place under floodlights on 10 November 1961. The Public Suite, the halls at the rear, were costed at £640,000 and the decision was not to proceed immediately with their construction. After some heated debate about the acoustic qualities of circular halls, this deferral of the Public Suite eventually became abandonment, leaving Council House as

---

9   Interview with Lindsay Waller

an incomplete version of the competition proposal. The Public Suite, however, was pursued in another form and, in 1968, Howlett and Bailey was commissioned by the City to design a new concert hall on a site to the east of Government House, the former Chevron-Hilton hotel site.

After a popular and well-publicised ceremony at the almost completed Council House during the Empire Games at which the Duke of Edinburgh officiated, Her Majesty the Queen opened the completed building on 25 March 1963.

THE BUILDING

Council House is a slab block with eleven storeys hoisted off the ground by massive marble-clad beams and columns. The ground floor originally had a glazed foyer to the eastern side with the western side open, offering a clear vista through to the gardens behind and a visual link to what was meant to be the Public Suite. The western side was glazed in 1978 to provide a display space for the Council.

The slab block plan provides a vast open office area with the service cores at the narrow eastern and western ends of the building. To the east, the core contains the four high-speed gearless lifts, the toilets, tea room, and main staircase. The escape stairs, risers, and air conditioning ducts are at the western end. The open space offers spectacular views to the north across the city, to the south across the Swan River, and to the west up to Kings Park. Council departments, together with some commercial tenants, occupied the first seven floors with the Council reception and Mayoral suites on the eighth floor and the Council suite on the ninth. The Council Chamber on the ninth floor is in the form of a 13-metre diameter glass cylinder with a white marble floor.

The window walls comprise floor to ceiling double glazed sealed units in aluminium frames. An innovative form of testing, a "typhoon test", was developed for the double-glazed windows planned for Council House. At the Perth airport, firemen hosed water into the slipstream of an aeroplane engine mounted on a truck to simulate a storm with torrential rain in wind gusts of 145 km per hour. It was the first time such windows had been used in Perth and Lindsay Waller stood behind the prototype during the testing as a sign of faith in the design.[10]

Howlett and Bailey required all their consultants to be established in Perth so that nothing about the building was handled through remote control. The committed team effort allowed for a high degree of coordination of structure, with services, with fabric, and with finishes.

Furniture was designed by the architects for the building and made in Western Australia. Specially designed door handles, taps, and smokers' stands, all made by local artisans, were incorporated into the building. Carpet, repeating the T-motif of the external window shadings, was designed by the architects. One of the most distinctive elements of the building is the pattern of T-shaped sunshades placed uniformly against the four glazed walls of the building. According to Lindsay Waller there was only one possible dimension that would allow the Ts to go around the corner and repeat themselves. This dimension was arrived at empirically and was set out by Waller after

---

10   Interview with Lindsay Waller

numerous geometric experiments.[11] The result is an apparently floating cage of Ts creating a continuous mat of a sunscreen which folds seamlessly around the corners of the building. They perform an additional role as fire-isolating spandrels between the floors.

As sunshades, the shallow Ts cannot be regarded as highly effective. However, as a modern filigree, a crisp carapace of sparkling abstract figures, the Ts bestow on the building a civic and celebratory demeanour that emphatically lifts the building from the banality of many contemporaneous office buildings. As the building progressed, Caliban, the wry and astute critic writing in the local chapter journal of the Royal Australian Institute of Architects, called Council House '...very sharp, very sharp indeed. If it had feet it would undoubtedly wear Italian pointeds.'[12]

At the time of its completion there was a widespread, almost natural assumption that the new would triumph over the old, that the modern city would take precedence over the colonial city. This view held such currency as to allow open discussion in the architectural press about the relocation of the adjacent Government House to Kings Park, or at least the demolition of the Government House ballroom, which was thought to be perilously close to the base of Council House.[13]

The *West Australian* published letters that advocated similar approaches to those found in the architectural journals, without raising any objections to the suggestions either through editorial comment or letters from others. The letter from F E McCaw of

11   Interview with Lindsay Waller

12   The Architect, Vol. 6, No. 72, June 1963, p. 48.

13   Architecture in Australia, Vol. 52, No. 4, December 1963, pp. 84–9

Perth suggested that '...the "antiquated" Government House be bulldozed for the purpose of creating the best possible site for the Town Hall.'[14] A J Hepburn, in speaking of the Council House site, stated that 'Its one drawback is that it will become cramped in time, because no encroachment on to Stirling Gardens should be tolerated. But the answer to this is to get the State Government to agree that Government House can some day be demolished.'[15]

The proposal to demolish the buildings of the colonial past extended at one point to the neo-classical Supreme Court building to the south of Council House. This great porticoed building was to make way for a new ceremonial drive, a western continuation of the Esplanade.

However, there were dissenters to those who were intoxicated by the modern and the new. A letter to the *Daily News* lamented that '...a little more dignity was not incorporated in the administrative block.'[16] And on the following day the same newspaper published a letter whose author was in no doubt about what constituted the necessary elements of a respectable town hall:

> Our proposed new Town Hall has no clock and no dome roof, both of which are essential civic building requirements.[17]

The New Review supported the modern forms of the winning scheme:

> Those few old fashioned rate-payers who are suggesting

---

14   *West Australian*, 24 March 1959.

15   *West Australian*, 22 May 1959

16   *Daily News*, 6 September 1960.

17   *Daily News*, 7 September 1960.

that the new scheme is before its time, should make a point of inspecting the City of South Perth and City of Subiaco new centres, converse with officials and citizens and learn, as they undoubtedly will, that these new modern structures have given their respective cities a great boost as well as meeting a very real necessity in their civic requirements and progress.[18]

Council House is a building that was emblematic of the young colonial city of Perth embracing with enthusiasm the promises of international Modernism. From 1963 until December 1993 Council House accommodated the Perth City Council administrative offices, the Mayoral and reception suites, the Council Chamber, the Council Library, and numerous other Council facilities of a less grand nature.

THE BUILDING UNDER THREAT

However, in the early 1990s, after just 30 years of life, Council House was earmarked for demolition by the State Government, its consultants, and the City of Perth, with the neighbouring colonial buildings proposed to remain in a newly refurbished 'Heritage Precinct' as part of Premier Richard Court's vision for Perth.[19]

The WA Chapter of the RAIA aggressively opposed the plan to demolish Council House. This may seem paradoxical after its predecessors argued equally forcefully that it not be built on its site. The issue for the RAIA moved on from that of site

---

18   New Review, April 1961.

19   Perth: A City for the People, brochure prepared as a summary of joint development initiatives between the Government of Western Australia and the City of Perth, 1994. The development proposals were prepared by consultants, Philip Cox, Etherington Coulter and Jones.

selection and became the protection and acknowledgment of a key part of Perth's recent past, its most celebrated modern building.

The RAIA joined with CityVision, a voluntary urban advocacy group, and other concerned citizens to argue against the demolition. Their arguments embraced a view of heritage which recognised that heritage buildings were not only from the distant past but were being created on a daily basis as the 'heritage of tomorrow' and were reliant on their distinctive qualities and cultural importance. Council House clearly had such qualities, as recognised by experts external to the state and local governments.

The Perth City Council commissioned Schwager Brooks and Partners Pty Ltd, the Sydney-based conservation and heritage consultants, to evaluate Council House and advise on its future. They reported that:

> Council House is a valid, if contrasting, component of a rich group of 19th and 20th century public buildings, all drawn together by the surrounding gardens and parkland.

Schwager Brooks argued that Council House was appropriate in its context as it represented a civic and cultural continuity and should be retained, refurbished and entered on the *West Australian* Register of Heritage Places. They recognised that the building survives in a relatively intact form, both externally and internally, with few modifications having been made to the building fabric throughout its life; that it was designed to utilise the most modern technological building systems of the time; and that it was a landmark building in this respect in Perth and Australia.[20]

The Western Australian branch of the National Trust of Australia recognised that Council House survives as a fine example of office design which featured the most progressive ideas of the time, reflecting influences of the major contemporary structures in Europe and America. The building is acknowledged by them as having national significance in this regard. The National Trust recommendation was strong in asserting that Council House should be conserved in accordance with the recommendations of the conservation plan prepared by Schwager Brooks.

In the face of this evidence the Western Australian Government and the interim Commissioners of the City of Perth publicly expressed the view that Council House should be demolished. They proposed an extension of Stirling Gardens on the site and the re-instatement of the colonial gardens surrounded by turn-of-the-century institutional buildings. While they did acknowledge that Council House has architectural merit, they argued that it should go because it did not 'fit' within a 'heritage precinct'. This view suggested that the saved past is more worthy than the present. Inevitably when such a past is reflected upon it is idealised and is, more often than not, in the words of the British critic, Patrick Wright, '. . . the historicised image of the establishment'.[21]

The Council House Urban Design Assessment Report prepared by the City Planning Department in May 1994 recommended the building should not be entered on the Heritage Register.

---

20   Ibid, Heritage Assessment and Conservation Plan, Council House, 1993, p. 5.

21   Cited in *A Heritage Handbook*, edited by G Davison and C McConville, Allen & Unwin, Sydney, 1991, p. 8.

And the State Government Heritage Minister Graham Kierath refused to place the building on the Heritage Register, despite calls from the Heritage Council and the National Trust to do so.[22] At one point in the often acrimonious debate over whether Council House should be retained, the construction of a 'heritage look-alike' in the place of Council House was mooted by Craig Lawrence, the Chair of the Commission then running the Perth City Council.[23]The term 'heritage' was used to advocate an historic style. This clearly demonstrated that the problem was not the fact that there was a building on the site earmarked for the colonial garden, but that it was a modern building.

Council House, once willingly and proudly embraced by the public and press as a civic emblem of Perth, its optimism, its modernity, and its future, had been abused and seriously threatened. Its modernity proved to be its vulnerability, its potential undoing.

It is now history that Council House was refurbished, enjoys widespread affection, is a source of local pride, and is the subject of respectful pilgrimages by architectural aficionados from other Australian cities.

This chapter has drawn on previous research and writing by the author, appearing in 'Council House, Perth' in Jennifer Taylor, *Tall Buildings, Australian Business Going Up: 1945–1970*, Craftsman House, Sydney, 2001, pp. 228–239. It was previously published by the City of Perth in a publication to celebrate the building's 40th anniversary entitled *Council House*.

---

22   Letter from Thomas Perrigo, CEO National Trust to the PCC CEO, 20 June 1994 and article 'Call for Council House review by National Trust', The *West Australian*, 25 June 1994..

23   *Business News*, 26 May–8 June 1994, p. 4.

1

OORL NGULLUCK KOORLINY
(COME WE WALK TOGETHER)

*Len Collard, with Clint Bracknell
and Angela Rooney*

Just as those old Nyungar have done since *nyitting* or *ngadamanong*, continuously, for eons upon eons, we stand here atop a place with many names; *Kaatagarrup, Kaata Koombar, Kaata Djianginy Bo*, or more recently, *Kings Park*. We soak up a shimmering panorama of the *Derbal Yirigan*, the Perth waters at the foot of the city. This place is indeed fit for kings, but there's a bigger story here. It's been here for the longest of times and is imbued in the language of the place, Nyungar language...so listen carefully...

Nyungar boodjar lies in the south-west corner of Western Australia. Our *boodjar* extends from eastward past Esperance on the south coast, moving in an arc north-west of Esperance across close to the small wheat-belt town of Nyoongah, and west-north-west towards Coorow to south of Geraldton on the west coast of Western Australia. Nyungar language has long echoed through this region. The language changes a little as you move through country and different Nyungar people have described their regional dialects using terms including Amangu, Yuat, Whadjuk, Binjareb, Wardandi, Balardong, Nyakinyaki, Wilman, Ganeang, Wirlomin, Bibulman, Kwetjman, Mineng, Goreng, Wudjari, Ngokgurring and Njunga, but it's all Nyungar language.[1]

From my point of view, whichever way you spell it, Nyungar,

1 N. Tindale, *Aboriginal Tribes of Australia: their terrain, environmental controls, distribution, limits and proper names*. Berkley, CA: University of California Press, 1974.

W. Douglas. *The Aboriginal Languages of the South West of Western Australia*. Canberra: AIAS, 1976.

C. Taylor, 'Vocabulary of the Ngokourring or Shell People', in E. Curr (ed.) *The Australian Race: its origin, languages, customs, place of landing in Australia, and the routes by which it spread itself over that continent*, Melbourne Government Printer, 1886, pp. 392–393.

K. Scott and L. Roberts, *Noongar Mambara Bakitj*. Crawley, WA: UWA Publishing, 2011.

Noongar, Nyoongar, Nyungah or Nungar is the generic term that means a human being or person and it describes the people whose ancestors originally occupied and continue to occupy the whole South-West boodjar or lands. The word Nyungar is not gender specific. It doesn't mean man or woman, it means a human being.[2] So in this yarn I'll spin to you mob I'll be focusing on the dreamtime events and some of the placenames in and around the boodjar that I know about, the place *wedjela* mob call the City of Perth.

Isn't it lovely? What do you see looking back across the river to the ranges from the top of *Kaata Djinanginy Bo*, that hill from which you can see a very long way? What feelings arise for you looking far across the city foreshore to *Mattagarup*, the place of the 'leg-holes' made by those old peoples' feet as they walked in the soft mud that has today solidified into a grassy island known as Heirisson?

This is an ancient land. This is Nyungar boodjar, Nyungar land. You are looking across country that our stories explain. The *Waakal* or Dreamtime Serpent created the landscape. You can almost imagine the huge Waakal weaving and turning as it made its way to the coast at *Walyalup*, Fremantle. Nyungar stories reflect these beliefs and the link between the physical and spiritual worlds, which may be why you feel the earth speaking to you from this place.

Let your eyes drift all the way across to the *Kaata Moornda*, the dark ranges of the Darling escarpment to the east. Gaze and wonder at the blue haze across the range, following the hills down to see the sun glisten on the river. The water shimmers

2   Noongar–English Dictionary, in A. Mountford and L. Collard, Nidja Noongar Boodjar Noonook Nyininy (This is Noongar Country You are Sitting In), Perth, 2000.

like scales; twisting, turning and weaving its bulky body across the plain, curving down to a wide path in front of the City of Perth, the bloated belly of a well-fed python. Leave yourself dreaming for now; you'll be back soon…

Yoorl ngulluck koorliny. Come, let us walk together. If you really, really want to know why I love Perth, it's a long story. It's a story that's still going on and a story sprawling out off these pages, far and wide in every direction – not just the points of the compass, but encompassing the cosmos and the clay beneath our feet too. I'll tell you just a little now, and I suppose I need to start from the very beginning.

Well, for kura kura or a long, long time, in accordance with Nyungar Cosmology within the Whadjuck Nyungar moort area around the City of Perth, there's existed a trilogy that I use to interpret and describe how Nyungar moort explain our worldview. In this trilogy katitjin, the knowledge, boodjar, the land and moort, the family, are utilised in wangkiny, informing us of the relationships between knowledge, people and places around the City of Perth.

Wangkiny is the Nyungar word for talking, speaking or telling depending on the context. This story of Nyungar boodjar, or country, follows oral traditions of storytelling handed down continuously through Nyungar moort for well over 40,000 years. Nyungar cosmology, worldviews, theories and ideologies have existed for all these years, and, in that time we Nyungar have occupied and managed the landscape and all its resources in the south-west of Western Australia.[3]

As you traverse the trails crisscrossing this city, you can

---

3   S. Hallam, S. 'The First Western Australians', in C. T. Stannage (ed.) *A New History of Western Australia*, Nedlands, WA: University of Western Australia Press, 1981, pp. 35–71.

think of the many feet of the folk whose footsteps you follow. Bidi or biirt is a Nyungar word for trail, track, sinew or energy. Many of our old people's paths are preserved by bitumen or concrete now, supporting a daily barrage of inner-city tyres, trainers and the click-clack of high heels. You can walk down here to the place we call kepa boodjarlup, land by the water. You can sit under the kwela or sheoak tree and listen to the mar or wind whilst catching your breath. That mar reminds me of a yarn Aunty Dorothy Winmar told me.4 Wardan is the ocean or sea, see?

Another story about the wardan told to me by my Pop, Tom Bennell, was that the wardan is a place where the *yorga mar*, the feminine easterly wind or land breeze, meets the *maaman mar*, the masculine south westerly or sea breeze. Nyungar Dreaming tells us that yorga mar and maaman mar were lovers and would chase each other back and forth over the wardan and across the boodjar, giving the Swan coastal region its daily easterly or southerly breezes. Anywhere in Perth, you can take a moment and listen to those two lovers whispering to each other as the mar blows between the leaves of the kwela.

There are a few Nyungar placenames around here like *Dyeedyallup, Kooyamulyup, Goodinup*, lots of –*up*s. If we were further east and inland, all the Nyungar place names would end in an –*ing*, like *Katanning, Nyabing, Duranilling* and so on. Both the –*up*s and the –*ing*s are suffixes denoting a place or location. Down river from *Kaata Djinaning Bo* or Kings Park, *Booladarlungup* is a Nyungar name for Pelican Point. In a rare instance where the wedjela name reflects the Nyungar name,

---

4   D. Winmar, Oral transcript, unpublished.

boola is a great quantity, *darlung* refers to a mouth, and–*up* is the 'place of'. Put that all together and you get the sense that old Nyungar saw some greedy pelicans at that place. A little way west, *Goordandalup* is a place where *goort*, lovers, husbands and wives get together. Its wedjela name is Matilda Bay, so maybe one of those young lovers was named Matilda...you'll never know.

When you follow the bilya or river westwards to the wardan past *Boorianup, Goordandalup, Mandyuranup, Dyundalup, Jenalup* and *Nierganup* you arrive at the *Walyalup* or the Fremantle coast. *Walyalup* is a place of crying. All these places have meanings but perhaps that is a story for another day. These place names remind us that the City of Perth is Nyungar *boodjar*. Many of them are written on street signs and used by people in the City every day. Nyungar language still rings in the air here and you can still see the path of the Waakal and its many resting places along the *Derbal Yirigan*. I said before I was going to tell you a story, didn't I? I guess I never properly began or ended, but there's lots of middle...and that's why I love Perth and that's why you'll get to love it too, *woolaa*.

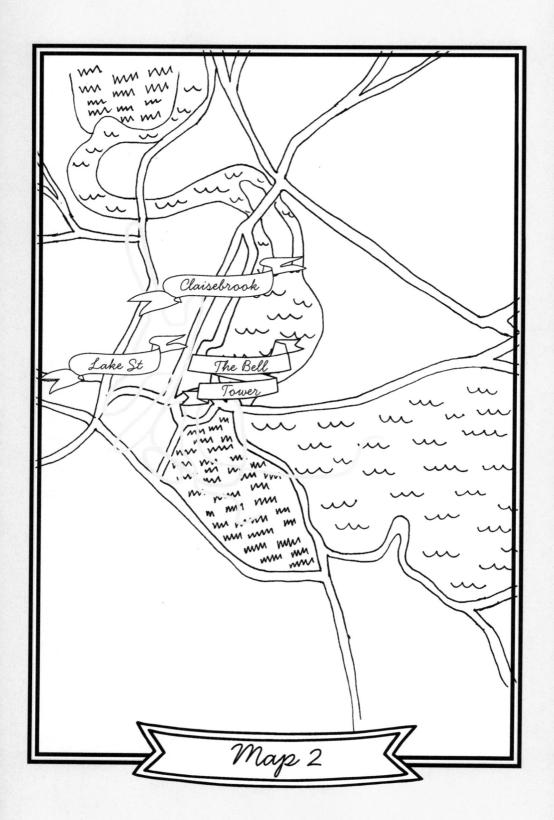

Claisebrook

Lake St

The Bell
Tower

Map 2

2

PERTH: GROWING UP

Malcolm Mackay

PLACE AND CHARACTER

"If you could describe yourself as a city, where would you be?" Me, I'd be Barcelona, but that's a conversation for another day.

Turning the old dinner party question around: "If Perth were a person, who would it be?" My first thought is a comment from Professor Peter Newman, a leading authority on urban sustainability, who reckoned that Perth is in a state of adolescence, midway between enjoying the youthful innocence of a country town and carrying the fears and responsibilities of a global city.

If Perth is an adolescent teenager, then what's the story behind this teenager: a troubled past or a sheltered upbringing? What emotional baggage is this teenager dealing with? What prospects lie ahead?

I love the idea of describing cities as people. Every city has character. Some have more than others. Some mesmerise you on the first date and never leave you, others grow on you over time, and some you couldn't care if you never saw them again. What's more, cities are complex. Think about it for a minute: millions of people living their lives, hundreds of thousands of buildings, constant movement, a hidden network of pipes and cables under the surface keeping the whole thing alive, and a complex set of abstract social commercial and cultural interactions between people and organisations. Yes, cities are complicated, just like people.

LOOKING BACK

John F Kennedy said, "Those who look only to the past or present are certain to miss the future." Whilst I appreciate the sentiment, I'm also guessing that he wasn't a rower. Anyone who has ever rowed a boat will know that you can move forwards by looking back, and a view astern gives a different perspective on your journey. Looking back tells you where you came from, and how accurate your course has been. As a rower, watching the receding shoreline gives a sense of how far you've come and it keeps getting better with each stroke.

In a similar vein, looking back at the history of a city helps us to understand its identity and character. Knowing what has gone before gives us an appreciation of the place we're in, not just physically, but also in time. With the past as a context, the present becomes part of a continuum rather than just the starting point for the future. It's no coincidence that the world's most interesting cities often have the longest histories.

To understand who Perth is, we need first to look back at its early life.

BABY

Perth was born in 1829. Like many other cities born before the end of the colonial era, Perth was the product of a military position. At the regional scale, Perth provided the British colonialists with a "we got here first" outpost on the far side of the continent as a warning sign to other potential colonialists; understandable, but perhaps not the most compelling reason for starting a city, particularly for the descendants of the indigenous people who were here first.

At the local scale, Perth was located on a long sloping ridgeline (it's under Hay Street if you look carefully) that dropped down to the Swan River on its southern flank and to a chain of lakes and wetlands on the northern flank. The lakes have long since been filled in to become Northbridge. The last clues to the lakes can be found in the name of Lake Street and in the vestige of the old Claise Brook trickling down to Claisebrook Cove in East Perth. The sharp bend in the river at East Perth provided the fledgling settlement with protection on two sides, and the availability of a lookout position on Mount Eliza helped to make Perth readily defendable.

However, Perth was almost born further down river on the knoll above the junction of the Swan and Canning rivers where the old wards of the former Heathcote hospital now stand. With its northerly aspect over Melville Water (the widest stretch of the Swan River) and a sheltered beach at its feet, Heathcote would have been a more logical place for a city in the eyes of today's planners, for whom lifestyle is an all-important driver. Ultimately, the long-gone Northbridge lakes as a nearby source of water meant that Perth is where it is.

TODDLER

Perth found its feet in the late 1890s following the establishment of the goldfields around Kalgoorlie. Perth and its little sister, Fremantle, provided miners with a port and a railhead, as well as a source of water, services, governance and labour. As such, Perth went from makeshift to 'made it' and became the 'ride in, ride out' hub for Western Australia's first resources boom.

Perth and Fremantle were rewarded handsomely for their efforts and the fossilised remnants of that newfound wealth can still be seen in the elegance and adornments of the remaining buildings of the era. Culturally, Perth had rapidly evolved from a colonial outpost to a large county town with a sense of purpose.

CHILD

The era of post-war expansion and the arrival of migrants such as the 'ten-pound poms', literally by the boatload, brought a new chapter in Perth's growth. The 1950s and 1960s was an era of optimism where growth was good, and Australian cities competed with each other to show off their shiny new toys:

> "Look at me I've got a freeway";
> "Ah, but I've got an oil refinery and a fancy bridge";
> "Yes, but look at the height of my office towers".

It becomes quite apparent, browsing through the media of the time, that Perth's proudest achievement was filling in Mount's Bay, and the building of the Narrows Bridge and the freeway interchange that lies in the middle foreground of the hero image of the city from Kings Park. Interestingly, filling in the river has been a common theme of Perth's history. The whole of the city centre foreshore was a massive 'work for the dole' land reclamation project in the 1930s, although now part of it is being rightfully returned to the river in the form of Elizabeth Quay. The Burswood Peninsula, Perth's casino playground and the home of the soon-to-be-built football stadium, was once little more than a sand bar in a swampy bend of the river.

Along with the unbridled optimism and the big-city toys of the post-war era came a smaller shiny new toy for the ordinary family: the motorcar. The advent of motoring affordability propelled people outwards in search of the suburban dream. More than anything else, this has defined the current pattern, extent and character of Perth, and the lifestyle of most Western Australians.

ADOLESCENT

The dominance of the motorcar brought Perth's residents a sense of freedom for half a century or so, but as with all car-dominated cities, there comes a point where the growth of traffic outstrips the capacity of the road infrastructure to carry it. That point has finally arrived for Perth. Where cars once brought the pleasure of freedom, they now bring the pain of congestion.

The expansion of Perth has triggered other growing pains. The need to consolidate the inner suburbs and enable people to live close to jobs, services and education, and thus avoid the daily grind along the freeways, means that the inner suburbs are becoming more urban. But, for a city that has pushed relentlessly into the landscape in pursuit of the suburban dream, urbanism is confronting. For the generation of postwar migrants, urbanism was one of the reasons they left Europe in search of the clean, green open spaces. And, now urbanity has followed them half away around the planet.

Urbanism is essential if Perth, ranked as the least sustainable city in the country in 2010 in the Sustainable Cities Index compiled by the Australian Conservation Foundation, is to become more sustainable. The conundrum for city planners is that the reason for Perth's inability to sustain itself in the future – the sprawling suburban lifestyle – is the very reason that people love it. Western Australians can see that the city they've known is not working the way it used to. The pace of life, prices and congestion are increasing, whilst backyards and time with the family are decreasing. Deep down, they know that at some point the way they live has to change. But, Perth residents are so used to the suburban life. For many, it's the only life they know.

Perth's recent growth spurt, courtesy of the resources boom in the Pilbara and a subsequent 'fly-in fly-out' workforce has brought further growing pains. House prices are now comparable to major global cities as demand for housing has outstripped supply. In fact, the prices of most things have risen as Perth businesses compete with the resources sector for workers.

Yet, amid the present anxieties, there is a feeling of optimism as Perth realises that it has a bigger role to play on the world stage. Closer than most of the developed world to the emerging nations of Central and Southern Asia, and in a state bulging with tradeable commodities, Perth has exciting possibilities.

So, here is Perth, caught between a comfortable past and an uncertain future, like a rower certain about what's behind but only catching an occasional peripheral glance of what lies ahead.

LOOKING AROUND

The uncertainty of who Perth really is manifests itself in many ways. For example, some people argue that the Bell Tower in the centre of Barrack Square is too small. "We're a big city now so we need a BIG tower" they say. However, the tower is the height it is for a good reason. The spire is exactly the same height as the spire of St Martins-in-the-Field, the London church from where the bells came. In the design process for the, meaning was more important than size.

Next door, at Elizabeth Quay, a similar debate has raged for years. The first master plan was a confronting display of gaudy excess that was rapidly christened 'Dubai-on-the-Swan'. The design was subsequently toned down. It's still a brave project because, more than any other by virtue of its scale and location, it will be a measure of who Perth is. It could be a bold, confident, welcoming and engaging space, or it could equally be a sterile, vacuous civic statement. The jury is still out and may have to wait for another ten to fifteen years until all the surrounding buildings are completed and brought to life.

Whilst Perth wants to be its own city, driven by the fierce parochialism of being the place on 'the other side' of the country, it can't help drawing comparisons with other places, particularly its older cousin Melbourne. A recent viral clip on YouTube proclaimed "everything's better in Melbourne". It might be an exaggeration, but Melbourne is a city that can teach Perth a thing or two about urban design.

Melbourne is regularly ranked as one of the world's most live-able cities so it's clearly not a bad role model. The current lesson being learnt from Melbourne is the value of city centre laneways as a place for small bars and restaurants with a funky urban edge. It's early days, but city lanes such as Wolf Lane in the Perth CBD are transforming from utilitarian back-of-house spaces to the new places to be. Lanes are often seen as the 'naughty spaces' where people shouldn't be, which is why they're so appealing to the growing band of urban hipsters. To a teenage city, a laneway culture is the equivalent of having a drink or getting a tattoo.

A less appealing aspect of Perth's search for identity,

and one that is largely driven by insecurity, is the perceived need for 'Woo-hoo-look-at-me' architecture. Architects fall over themselves to draw something weird and wacky to be different, but if they're all being different, then really they're all being much the same. Furthermore, being different does not automatically equate to being better. The wild geometry of the new Perth Arena might superficially echo the patterns of Melbourne's Federation Square, but Federation Square is a more sophisticated architectural response that weaves together a place from ideas about organic growth, the enclosure of space, European plazas, community building and the interaction between people and architecture, as well as harmonies of patterns and textures. The new Perth Arena might be visually arresting on first sight but, to my eyes, is the architectural equivalent of a fat bloke in a loud shirt standing alone on a street corner.

Looking around the world, the architectural strength of confident cities lies in restraint and elegance, with buildings that are comfortable in their skin and are happy to work together as a team to enclose and define urban spaces. They also stand the test of time.

LOOKING AHEAD

Perhaps the original question could be rephrased: "If Perth were a person, who would it *want* to be?" Perth is in a fortunate position where the benefits of the Asian century and a place on the Indian Ocean coincide. Perth sits a temptingly short distance from the growing economic powerhouses of Central and Southern Asia, and shares the world's most populous time zone. Much has already been made of Western Australia's abundant commodities, but Perth could be more than just the administration centre for the resources industry. With its clean, dry air and a near-perfect climate, Perth is the ideal respite from the choking smog of Beijing or the sapping humidity of Jakarta or Kolkata. Combined with clean beaches and great local food and wine, Perth has the capacity to become Asia's sophisticated playground.

To pull it off, Perth needs to develop a mature and sophisticated attitude to engage its residents and visitors. Casual is fine, as long as it's done well. If Perth is to evolve into a sophisticated city of choice, a greater emphasis needs to be placed on the value of good urbanism and architectural maturity. Urban design is now on the agenda of most planning departments in the Perth metropolitan area and the City of Perth has released an urban design manifesto – the Urban Design Framework – to guide new development.

Perth needs to grow up rather than grow out. And, that's starting to happen too. Despite community opposition, the process of urban consolidation is taking hold in the central city and the inner-city suburbs, with new residential towers and apartment living emerging from the ground almost on a monthly basis.

The Perth city centre needs to be more than just the tall bit in the middle. In a mature and sophisticated city there is no line between the city centre and the rest of the city – it's seamless. The sinking of the railway line and the redevelopment of the railway land between central Perth and Northbridge is removing a long-standing barrier to the city centre that dates back to the original chain of lakes.

Finally, Perth needs to continue to embrace diversity in its people, culture, businesses, social activities and architecture. Diversity is what makes places interesting. After all, the opposite of diversity is monotony. The choice of food and entertainment has never been greater, nor has the number of languages overheard on a walk down Hay Street. Perth now has housing options that simply didn't exist ten years ago…it's definitely a sign that Perth is getting better at embracing diversity.

REFLECTION

As a professional with portable skills in urban design, architecture and town planning, I could have chosen to live in an older and more mature city, but my role would have been more of a custodian than an agent for change. Perth is an exciting city for someone who does what I do. I'm here because I enjoy the challenges of the confusion, the contradictions, the optimism and the opportunities, both real and imagined, that an adolescent city has. That's why I love Perth.

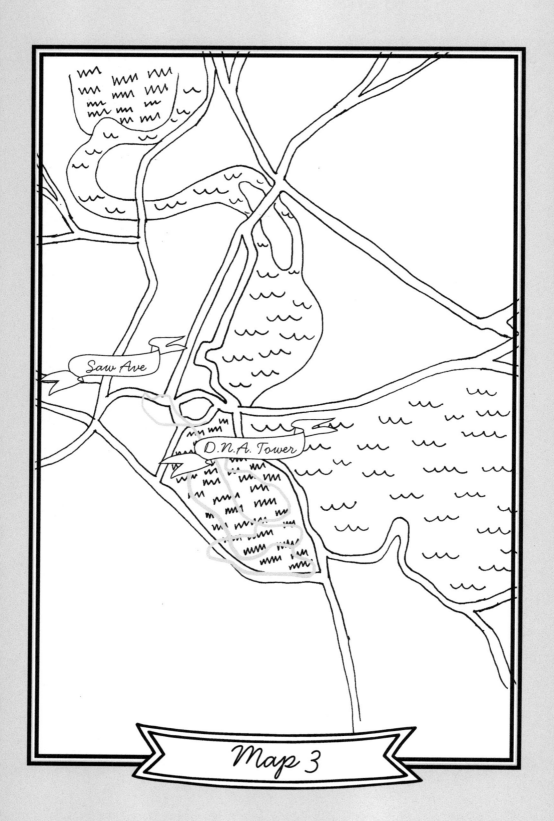

Saw Ave

D.N.A. Tower

Map 3

3

KNOWING LANDSCAPES

Helen Whitbread

Set aside as a public park by Perth's Governor Weld in 1872, Kings Park attracts millions of visitors each year, both first-time visitors to Perth and locals who return, often ritually, for public and private occasions. This chapter provides a landscape architectural review of place. The review is informed by the ideas of Swiss landscape architect Christophe Girot who describes how the French word for landscape, *paysage*, incorporates qualities that are both visible and invisible, including a sense of identity and cultural belonging.[1] The observations of place are thus initially concerned with what Girot describes as Landing, the first impressions of a place, and Grounding, an understanding of place developed through deeper research and repeated site visits. Almost inevitably, through the process of Landing and Grounding, a further progression occurs, that of Knowing. Knowing Kings Park is further enriched by an understanding of how the immediate landscapes of the Freeway Interchange and John Oldham Park provide a physical and metaphorical link to the broader city landscape.

LANDING AND GROUNDING

The landscapes of Kings Park and the Freeway Interchange are populated with lines (pathways) and nodes (places). Travelling some of these lines with the reader will give a sense of landing, while residing in and exploring the nodes will allow the reader to become grounded in the landscape. This rhythm then, of travelling through and residing in the landscapes of Kings

---

1 C. Girot, 'Four Traces in Landscape Architecture', in J. Corner (ed.) *Recovering Landscape*, Princeton Architectural Press: New York, 1999, p. 59.

Park, forms the temporal journey of the chapter.

LINES

The landscape lines of Kings Park and the Freeway Interchange are formal roads and pathways, informal tracks and 'sweeping' lines. Sweeping lines are experienced when the eye follows a line of sight and then, without shifting location, drifts to subsequent views. Such a line is a significant landscape element of Kings Park and a formative influence in the development of the city of Perth.

The formal roads in Kings Park are experienced as sweeping lines, both physically as serpentine movements through the landscape and visually as the vista, which is at times revealed and then concealed. Entering the park from any of the three major avenues, Saw, Poole or Fraser, one is struck by the thin veneer of formalism expressed first by the road and then by the lines of memorial trees. The trees form a living guard of honour to all who pass through the park, an unobtrusive symbol of a life for a death. By coincidence rather than design, the trees also form an ordered permeable edge between the urban landscape of the road and the mythologised 'other' in the Australian psyche, the bush. And herein lies some of the contradiction of the landscape of Kings Park, at times tranquil and civilised and at others, raw and dark.[2]

A broad walking line has been carved through Kings Park linking the nodes of the Synergy Playground in the west to the DNA Tower and Western Australian Botanic Garden to the east.

---

2   Kings Park's secluded urban bushland has at times posed a fire threat to surrounding areas and at others made it a place of choice for suicide and/or burial.

Cut as a swathe through the bushland, this grassy promenade was designed by Dr John Beard, the foundation Director of Kings Park and Botanic Garden in 1966, and alludes to the original vision of Kings Park as a vast public park and recreation ground featuring lakes, grand vistas and carriageways all set in a landscaped parkland.[3] Walking this promenade, however, one does not recall the formal elements of French Renaissance gardens from which it is derived; rather, there is a sense of a cultured landscape boldly charging through the vast Australian bush. At the end one encounters a folly.

The folly, perhaps more a pause than a node, was commissioned by Beard after being inspired by a set of interlocking spiral staircases he had seen at the French Chateau Blois. Intended as an architectural punctuation, a viewing platform and, through its articulation including stone donations from Western Australian towns and shires, a symbol of the broader Western Australian landscape, the folly was colloquially dubbed the DNA Tower.[4]

Anchoring the west end of the Broadway, the Synergy Parkland node contains landscapes that reveal and conceal layers of history. Synergy Parkland, formerly known as Lakeside Parkland, was initially laid out by Beard who, although not a professional designer, nonetheless brought a conscious and reflective approach to the naturalistic design of the parkland. Site sensitivity is apparent in the use of a natural low point to create the lake, retention of mature indigenous tree clumps,

---

3 J. Considine and P. Griffiths, Kings Park Conservation Plan for the Developed Areas, 1999, p. 210.

4 The viewing tower, now known as DNA Observation Tower, has a double helix structure similar to deoxyribonucleic acid. Ibid., p. 207.

and use of existing bushland to define an edge to the site. Located within Lakeside Parkland was Perth's first adventure playground, designed by Kings Park Superintendent, Arthur Fairall. Considered innovative in its day, Fairall made use of tree stumps harvested during construction and maintenance work within the park for play equipment. The structures were intentionally of the place and included bush poles, wooden stepping-stones and log bridges crossing to an island in the lake. While the philosophy of this adventure playground stemmed from Fairall's horror of children's exposure to military and warlike toys as playthings, his recognition of the importance of unstructured play with natural materials anticipated the contemporary environmental sensory playgrounds of today.[5]

Forty years later, with Kings Park under a revitalised management structure called the Botanic Garden and Park Authority (BGPA), a proposal to refurbish and re-badge Lakeside Parkland was endorsed. The new design by Plan E is a testimony to contemporary landscape design perimeters, including integration of heritage, environment, and sponsor and typology requirements. Sponsored by Western Power, now known as Synergy, the new playground was informed by a creative synthesis of energy (Western Power) and biodiversity (BGPA's vision) as the key metaphor for thematic design. These themes were integrated into a range of landscape elements, such as planting, furniture, and play equipment creating a narrative, that is both didactic and experiential. Commenting on these themes, Chief Executive Officer of the BGPA, Dr Steve Hopper, wrote:

The Western Power Parkland's theme of energy and fossil

5   T. Scalzo, 'The Arthur Fairall Adventure Playground', Friends of Kings Park Magazine, Winter Edition, 2001, p. 9.

biodiversity through time is consistent with Arthur Fairall's original concept for the Adventure Playground. He aimed to keep children of the technological age in touch with nature by using natural play elements constructed of timber and stone. The Western Power Parkland's theme of the basic sources of energy and of Western Australia's plants and animals through history will similarly reinforce connections with nature in an enjoyable play environment.[6]

Notwithstanding the different level of sophistication between the rustic Adventure Playground of the 1960s and the themed directed play design of the new Western Power (Synergy) Playground, there are still those who remember crossing the lake to the island on slippery stepping logs, and falling in. Getting wet was not considered an issue; indeed, it was a playground rite of passage for Perth children.

On that point, getting wet is embraced in Kings Park's most recently designed landscape for play and learning, the Rio Tinto Naturescape. Also designed by Plan E, the landscape is a series of mini environments such as wetlands, creeks, bush shelters and the bush itself. As someone who recalls a childhood spent in creeks and the bush, it is apparent that as Perth becomes increasingly urban and suburban, valuable unstructured play in leftover spaces and remnant bushland is becoming less available. Naturescape, which releases the urban dweller into a carefully choreographed bush landscape, is Kings Park's scientific and social antidote for this inevitable outcome of progress and development.

The fusion of science and art, architecture, landscape and

---

6   S. Hopper, 'An Extra Ordinary Journey Through Time', *Friends of Kings Park Magazine, Winter Edition*, 2001, p.11.

engineering found in the Lotterywest Federation Walk (the Walk) is equally choreographed. Borrowing from the tradition of the Japanese stroll garden and the English picturesque, this line leads the visitor through a celebration of the diversity of Western Australian flora in the Botanic Gardens to an elevated walkway and a glass-edged bridge thrust into the treetops by massive corten steel trunks.[7] Spanning a valley said to be created by the passage of the Aboriginal dreamtime serpent, the Wagyl, the bridge physically and metaphorically connects past with present, making the indigenous narrative of the Kings Park landscape visible and celebrated. Here, the visitor experiences nature ordered, tamed, named, and known through the centuries-old tradition of the Botanic Garden. Amongst the Indigenous canopies of Karri, Marri, Tingle and Jarrah trees, the visitor finds that strangers such as the Kimberley Boab tree have been invited to share the Mount Eliza scarp, causing one to ponder the botanical temerity of such a feat. And it is here that the invisible is experienced; the sense of slight insecurity as the Fremantle Doctor[8] buffets the glass-edged bridge, looking out and engaging in the picturesque tradition of knowing the landscape through framed views, and similarly borrowing from the Romantic tradition of landscape, feeling the choreographed exertion as one encounters the steep topography of circuitous pathways.

Knowing the landscape through framed views is a foundational ideology underpinning the development of the City of Perth and, more broadly, Australia itself. Captain James

7   Designed by a project team headed by Donaldson and Warn Architects in 2003.

8   The Fremantle Doctor is a colloquial term for the afternoon sea breeze experienced in Perth, primarily in the summer months.

Stirling (1791–1865), founder of the settlement of Western Australia, described the view from Mount Eliza thus:

> THE BANKS BECAME EXTREMELY BEAU-
> TIFUL AND PICTURESQUE. THEIR BEAUTY IS
> ADORNED BY THE LOFT TREES, WHICH OCCA-
> SIONALLY ADORN THEM AND BY THE BRIGHT
> GREEN PENDULOUS FOLIAGE WITH WHICH
> THE SHRUBS ARE COVERED.[9]

Understanding the landscape as picture is almost a natural consequence of gazing out from the scarp of Mount Eliza, a phenomenon that has been commented on by academics such as George Seddon and Hannah Lewi. In his text, *A City and its Setting*[10], Seddon traces the evolution of the city as it developed from a settlement camp into a colonial town and then city, from the vantage point of Mount Eliza. Drawing our attention to the importance of the view from Mount Eliza, Seddon describes a persistent design idea, the picturesque, that underpinned the cultural landscape of Perth.[11] Lewi equally recognised the formative significance of the Mount Eliza scarp, describing it as a 'viewing edge'.[12] Interestingly however, Lewi criticised Seddon's complicity in perpetuating naturalistic interpretations of the view from the summit, noting that Seddon's description of Mount Eliza insinuates a primacy of the natural landscape over the constructed landscape:

---

9   G. Russo and H. Schmidt, *Swan River Mania, A Colonial History of Western Australia*, Lynwood Enterprises, Perth, 1987, p. 32.

10   Seddon and Ravine, 1986.

11   Ibid., pp. 260–272.

12   H. Lewi, post terra nullius: The remaking of antipodean place; University of Western Australia Thesis, 1999, p. 128.

ACCOUNTS HAVE TENDED TO TREAT ANALYSIS
OF THE COLONIAL SETTING IN OVERLY NATURAL-
ISED AND NON-CONSTRUCTIVE TERMS. WITHIN
THIS 'NATURAL ATTITUDE', THE LANGUAGE OF
MODERN ARCHITECTURE HAS OFTEN BEEN
CAST AS AN UNNATURAL INTRUSION.[13]

As noted later in this chapter, Lewi's observations are borne
out through the difficulty experienced over the years in introducing change to the Perth Foreshore, and thus scenic view
from Kings Park.

It is useful to dwell a little in this spot, as from here you
are able to see the Freeway Interchange landscape which has
more than just visual links to the site. The Freeway Interchange
Park (1956–1973), now known as the John Oldham Park,[14] was
designed by architect and planner Lord William Holford and
landscape architect John Oldham. A curious mix, this landscape is one of Western Australia's most significant modernist
landscapes and yet it has a picturesque heart. The modernist
structure is evident in the way in which the built landscape
of the Narrows Bridge and Kwinana Freeway ties seamlessly
back into the natural grade of the surrounding landscape.
This was Holford's contribution. Oldham, Western Australia's
first landscape architect, was initially vehemently opposed to
the construction of the freeway, which involved dredging and
filling the Reflecting Pool in Mounts Bay:

13   Lewi, p.128.
14   The Freeway Interchange Park, now known as the John Oldham Park, forms part of the
Narrows Bridge and Freeway Interchange landscape. The history of this project is protracted
and complex with construction of the bridge landscape commencing in 1957, the interchange
landscape commencing around 1964 and the whole project being completed by 1973. The
Narrows Interchange, Main Roads Department of Western Australia, 1973, p. 9.

WE [JOHN OLDHAM AND HIS WIFE RAY] STRONGLY OPPOSED WHAT WE CONSIDERED TO BE THE RAPE OF A RIVER ESTUARY BY THE FREEWAY BUILDERS.[15]

Relative to this opposition, the Reflecting Pool, a poorly flushed bend in the Perth Water, was malodorous and of low physical amenity, therefore it was not a loss of the physical that was lamented but rather the view. The picturing of Mounts Bay, the viewing pleasure it afforded, the way in which it defined the city landscape, all recall a romantic ideology where landscape design sought to construct or retain landscape for its picturesque and sublime qualities. Oldham later agreed to help the Main Roads Department make the Narrows Interchange attractive;[16] however, this was conditional on the Interchange landscape being part of his greater long-held vision: that of stretching the Botanic Garden of Kings Park along Perth's foreshore.

While the gaze offers a visual link between the Kings Park and the city landscapes, one of the few pedestrian links from the scarp to its base is Jacob's Ladder. Located adjacent to Kings Park at the end of Cliff Street this humble landscape element is so called because the real estate at the top of the scarp was once likened to a slice of heaven. Comprising 242 concrete steps and use-polished galvanised railing, Jacob's Ladder is as much a social phenomenon as physical structure. Its utilitarian aesthetic stands in stark contrast to the elegant land art of the Lotterywest Federation Walk; however,

15   J. Oldham, 'Early landscape architecture in Western Australia 1954–1967 Part Two', Landscape Australia, vol. 3, no. 85, 1985, p. 219.
16   Ibid., pp. 219–220.

notwithstanding its lack of elegance, the Ladder along with much of Kings Park and the surrounding foreshore landscape has been appropriated as a free outdoor gym. With this there is an unspoken but clearly understood Ladder etiquette. And so for the visitor who is just strolling and wishes to slip between the panting exercise faithful, the stair rules are: stay to the left and you will safely reach your destination, be it Kings Park at the top of the scarp, or Mounts Bay Road at the base.

The gaze or view form an important element in the final three nodes in this chapter – the Place of Reflection, the State War Memorial, and the Bali Memorial. Only recently completed in 2011, the Place of Reflection does not capture an event or identity, but rather is a dichotomy of a universal and yet intensely private space. The existing landscape is artfully borrowed in scale, texture and geomorphology to lend weight to the notion of a light embrace. The meandering path leading to a contemplation space is lightly dressed by the bush landscape allowing views through and glimpses of other spaces. The pavilion is one of the most exquisite built forms in Kings Park. Constructed of stone, steel and timber, it is structural poetry capturing the light and movement of a eucalypt forest.

The State War Memorial and the Bali Memorial are also places of reflection; however, they also express a memorial syntax. Memorial landscapes require that identity, of an individual, a political entity or a country, be integral to the design. Implicit also is an expectation that the design capture a moment in history and express this in an enduring manner. Noted American landscape historian Professor Marc Treib suggests that the German word for monument denkmal, translated as 'a means to a thought'[17], best captures the essence of commemoration. Memorial design often relies on text to capture the moment, but words of a memorial inscription can reveal more than simply identity and an historical event. The State War Memorial[18], for example, captures both an event and a change in sentiment. While earlier Kings Park memorials such as The Fallen Soldiers Memorial[19] acknowledge Australia's imperial allegiance, the State War Memorial inscription reads:

ERECTED BY GRATEFUL CITIZENS IN REMEMBRANCE OF MEN OF THIS STATE WHO AT THE CALL OF DUTY GAVE THEIR LIVES FOR FREEDOM AND HUMANITY IN THE GREAT WAR 1914–1918.[20]

That is, whilst the men who volunteered were members of the Australian Imperial Forces (AIF), the memorialisation was not on behalf of the Empire but rather on behalf of freedom and humanity and, implicitly, a sense of self as a nation.

Embedded in the process of memorialisation are the concepts of memory, the act of remembering, and identity – who

---

17   M. Treib, 'The Landscape of Loved Ones', in J. Wolschke-Bulman, (Ed.) Places of Commemoration: Search for Identity and Landscape Design, Dumbarton Oaks Research Library and Collection, Washington, D.C., 2001, p. 82.

18   Cenotaph monuments are modelled on the Cenotaph, Whitehall London, 1919, by Sir Edward Lutyens. Lutyen's monument is an 'empty tomb' mounted on a pylon inscribed simply 'The Glorious Dead'. The empty tomb represents the tomb of all soldiers, missing or killed. The Western Australian War Memorial is in the form of an obelisk. The obelisk, an Egyptian form, represents a shaft of sunlight descending from the Gods.

19   Now known as the South African Memorial, J. Considine and P. Griffiths, Kings Park Conservation Plan for the Developed Areas, 1999, p. 10.

20   K. Inglis, Sacred places: war memorials in the Australian landscape, Melbourne University Publishing, Melbourne, 2008, p. 288.

or what is remembered. The State War Memorial uses particular and universal iconography and symbolism to codify space. The State Cenotaph, a universal memorial symbol, is embellished by icons: a Cross of Sacrifice, laurel victory wreaths, and the AIF badge. The Eternal Flame of Remembrance, a more recent addition to the memorial assembly, is a neo-archaic symbol of life. Additionally, the location of the State War Memorial on the scarp of Mount Eliza enables it to employ the rising sun as a symbol of eternity and reinforce a strong sense of place from its view. The Western Australian State War Memorial, by virtue of its location on Mount Eliza, inextricably links the landscape to the act of memorialisation and a sense of local and national identity.

Located slightly north of the State War Memorial is one of Kings Park's most recent memorial landscapes, the Bali Memorial. Erected to memorialise the sixteen Western Australians who lost their lives in the 2002 terrorist bombing on the Indonesian island of Bali, the site of the Bali Memorial on Kings Park's viewing edge equally exploits the symbolism of site. The memorial, which is more sculptured place than object, frames the iconic view of the city, the river, and fortuitously, the national flag. Moreover, on the dawn of the anniversary of the bombing, the design perpetually captures a shaft of sunlight in the interior of the memorial, thus linking the place and the moment to an ethereal non-secular spirituality. Describing the initial difficulty in realising the design, architect Geoff Warn stated:

> When we turned our back on the park and looked out from the site we found that the view resolved many problems.

The families (of the victims) had spoken strongly about a need to bring 'our' children home. With the families coming from a range of locations spread across the metropolitan area, home was disparate. It was up to us to nominate home, and the framed view of the city, the Swan River and the Darling Scarp seemed to represent a shared sense of home. The memorial was to be secular, in no way representing any religion, so capturing the sunrise added a spiritual dimension without compromising the families' wishes.[21]

By virtue of its location and its intent, The Bali Memorial reinforces a sacralisation of the Mount Eliza landscape while ingraining the view of Perth as home.

Let us conclude by returning to the moment when Stirling stood on Mount Eliza and looked out. For him the prospect seemed a fine location for a town and, in time, a home. By selecting the site for the city of Perth from this scarp, Stirling embedded the idea of landscape as view, a perception that now forms and informs a Western Australian sense of identity and cultural belonging.

---

21 Interview by author with architect Geoff Warn of Donaldson and Warn, Bali Memorial architecture team, June 2009.

Map 4

4

ENDURING PERTH

Kate Hislop

PICTURED: PANORAMA FROM KINGS PARK, NEAR THE STATE WAR MEMORIAL, ACROSS PERTH WATER, SOUTH PERTH PENINSULA (POINT BELCHES) AND MELVILLE WATER 2010 (PHOTOGRAPH K. HISLOP)

Like all colonial cities Perth was founded at a particular time and with particular aspirations. And like all cities the founding acts of settlement leave permanent marks and impressions on the form of the city that last for the ensuing centuries.

TODAY

Behold…Fraser Avenue in Kings Park: a lofty, leafy, lemon-scented arcade of gums (*Corymbia Citriodora*) framing one of Perth's most memorable civic experiences. Closing the avenue is the State War Memorial, crowning the outcrop of Mount Eliza. Here an eternally flickering Flame of Remembrance dwells in the Court of Contemplation: a shrine to fallen soldiers, at the same time extending a magnificently unfolding panorama of the riverside city. From this spot one enjoys the best view of the city and the sweep of the vast water basin that is the raison d'être of Perth. Add the bush surrounds of the Park plus – to the east, far beyond the city and coiling river – the backdrop of scarp, and all at once Perth crystalises as a classic garden city, or rather bush capital. Many tourist encounters start here, and for local residents this place forms life-long memories of an expanding metropolis. Surely, too, it was encountering this spot during the 1827 British expedition that inspired the very establishment of the Swan River Colony in Western Australia, and Perth its capital city, in this remotest of places.

The unique colocation of bush park, river and city domains – remarkably equivalent in area – makes Perth an unforgettable urban setting. Here a visitor or resident can enjoy one of the world's biggest inner city parks (surpassing New York's Central Park), on the doorstep of the largest body of water along the Swan River and overlooking the sunniest and windiest city in Australia (and among the most blowy in the world).

Viewing Perth city from Kings Park is one of the most popular and quintessentially Western Australian experiences. From here the modern city is at its showy best – tall, slender and gleaming. It is a product of nineteenth-century vision, colonial planning, twentieth-century innovation (particularly driven by the car) and abundant mineral wealth. The scene is captivating. Dawn sees the city solidify against the hazy glow rising over the Darling Ranges to the east, back-dropping the glinting glassy towers and the river that is a lustrous mirror on all but the gloomiest of mornings. At day's end the city lights up, buildings dematerialise and from the Park a buzzing light display enacts upon the freeway interchange and Narrows Bridge in the foreground.

1827

Imagine…The glittering promise of this view greeting a weary band of British explorers on a balmy March day in 1827. Unfurling before them was the far-reaching prospect that would come to be the site for Western Australia's capital city. Royal Naval Officer James Stirling and his party had spent a fortnight tracking the Swan River from mouth to source and back again, assessing soil quality and other features of the region that two years later would become the Swan River Colony. On the return leg of the expedition the group scaled the high promontory of Mount Eliza, named by Stirling after Lady Darling, wife of the then-Governor of New South Wales. The climb was a gratifying one.

From their elevated vantage point beside the Swan River they looked south across a narrow neck of water to Point Belches, Melville Water and the Canning River, and east across the lagoon of Perth Water to Point Fraser and Heirisson Island. Even further east the encompassing ridge of the General Darling's Range held their view. Downstream to the west, beyond where they could see, lay the river mouth (which would become the port of Fremantle) and the Indian Ocean. In their minds' eyes, the glance westward carried them overseas to Britain and, as well, to a potentially more immediate trading relationship with India; the eastward glance transported them over the gently undulating grassy coastal plain and the Swan Valley, and across vast inland Australia to the established penal colony of New South Wales.

This was a land of promise, a southern Eden; a place Stirling wanted to name (after the mythological Gardens of Hesperides) 'Hesperia'. The party's botanist, Charles Fraser, later reported that "The view from this point of the meanderings of the river and the Moreau, with the Surrounding country and distant mountains, is particularly grand".[1] Expedition artist, Frederick

---

1 Charles Fraser cited in B. Chapman, *The Colonial Eye: a topographical and artistic record of the life and landscape of Western Australia 1798–1914*, Perth: Art Gallery of Western Australia, 1979, p. 76.

Garling, recorded this view and its promise, deftly capturing in watercolour a glow that matched Stirling's enthusiasm for the spot. Stirling had, in 1827, found not only the place for a new British colony, but evidently the site upon which, as founding governor, he would build its capital city.

1839

Ten years after Europeans settled at Swan River a manual for British emigrants was produced by Nathaniel Ogle with the express aim of attracting greater migrant numbers to the colony. The book opens with an image of the emerging township of Perth as seen from Mount Eliza, an enticing expansive and romantic overview. Though devoid of colour, Charles Wittenoom's lithograph conveys the same sense of a glowing prospect as had Garling's watercolour view from almost the same location a decade earlier, prior to colonisation. Wittenoom's image became the first of many such views of Perth and Perth Water from this spot. It has indeed become the favourite position from where to watch and record the city unfold and evolve on a daily, yearly and generational basis. Wittenoom's image depicts the logic in Stirling's choice of this site for the capital and illustrates that Perth's uniquely elongated town plan may have been at least partly determined by the fact that the town would be visible from this high point.

There were, of course, many factors influencing the layout of the town of Perth. Geographic features such as the 'saddle' topography, a narrow ridgeline running east–west (now marked by Murray Street) and, beyond that to the north, the swampy terrain, together seemed to dictate a linear plan bordering the river. British planning policy also shaped the town, defining minimum lot sizes and general precinct patterns for example. These aspects, alongside the special topographic qualities afforded by the relationship between Mount Eliza and Perth Water, led Stirling and Surveyor General John Septimus Roe, along with other officials in the first settlement, to lay down a plan that was more significantly stretched than any other in Australia.

At six chains (120 metres) Perth had easily the longest town lots among Australian capital cities, exceeding Melbourne's at 95 metres, and greatly stretched compared to those in Brisbane and Adelaide. Perth also had large street blocks (averaging 300 metres in length) exceeded only by Adelaide's at 523 metres. But overall Perth's first town plan was narrow: in 1832, at only three city blocks deep, it was about half the depth of Melbourne's plan and about a third as deep as Adelaide's. This slender plan resulted, in the early decades, in a thinly-spread, modestly-scaled town with buildings and occupants scattered the length of the river frontage from Point Lewis, beneath Mount Eliza in the west, to Point Fraser in the east.

The earliest plan shows a division of the town into three parts. A commercial sector to the west end and a residential area to the east bookended a central government domain. All had river access, though the government and residential sections were set back beyond a promenade-like strip. This template has informed city development for almost 200 years; however, to the great benefit of civic vibrancy there has been significant cross-over of the zones in more recent decades.

In the catalogue of Australian cities Perth is distinctively thin. Stretched some three kilometres east to west, the city stands on the northern bank of a great belly in the Swan River known as Perth Water. From river's edge to the rail line that skirts the cosmopolitan Northbridge precinct measures only about 750 metres. Mostly, however, the central city has a depth not much more than 600 metres. Narrower still is the main strip of tall office buildings flanking St Georges Terrace. This twentieth-century canyon of steel, concrete and glass abuts the north-bound Mitchell Freeway at the city's west end, swells at the core business district between Mill and Barrack Streets and undulates along what becomes Adelaide Terrace to the east.

The city's linearity is perhaps the most compelling and long-lasting feature of the founding design strategies. Generations of commercial, public and retail construction only reinforced the linearity through increasing consolidation and verticality. CBD high-rise towers along the Terrace are now visible from many reaches of the metropolitan area (as well as from Rottnest Island). The primary street grid is little changed though buildings (rather than ground) now dominate the undulating terrain, framing corridor views to (and funneling stiff breezes from) the river. Despite significant building activity in the twenty-first century the city's form has remained a firmly entrenched legacy of topography, romantic aesthetics, colonial planning and modern zoning.

Beyond the plan itself, very little has survived of colonial building stock, as Perth experienced waves of demolition and growth sponsored largely by mineral wealth. Here is a fascinating corollary: Stirling had predicted such mineral richness upon his 1827 expedition, and plugged this as one among many of the region's natural attractions to the British government. Western Australia was founded as a result of his persuasions but, to begin with, only under a provisional act limited to five years. How fitting that the city commanding the country's most abundant store of natural resources, heading the state established on provisional terms, has had the means to renew itself multiple times in its short lifespan. In Perth, the provisional has seemed a permanent sensibility.

From the early settlement period only one building still stands in the city: the diminutive 1836 Perth Court House, designed by Civil Engineer Henry Reveley. Over its lifetime it has functioned as courthouse, church, school house and theatre/concert hall; later serving as immigration depot, Supreme Court and store. Nestled within the Supreme Court Gardens, this building is testament to the permanence of the colonial plan, as well as to the provisional forces that have continued to reshape Perth city. Once sitting close to the river's edge, successive stages of land reclamation to manufacture a public foreshore and support a freeway interchange have distanced this building (along with the city behind it) from the river.

Debate has flowed for decades about the benefits and ways of linking central Perth both to its river heart and to the cultural life of Northbridge, long separated from the CBD by the Midland-Fremantle railway line. Two major state government projects currently under construction are set to achieve these goals. The Elizabeth Quay development, bordered by Barrack Street and the Swan River, has controversially (though perhaps quite logically) excavated the reclaimed but nonetheless fiercely protected apron of green known as 'The Esplanade', replacing turf with an artificially constructed inlet around which mixed-use development will be clustered. This project is not the first to significantly tamper with the Swan River's northern shoreline, but it represents the most significant move towards uniting city with river through activating the river's edge. The Perth Link Project is another major initiative, this time activating the strip of land between the CBD and Northbridge that has become available thanks to the sinking of major bus and rail transport infrastructure. These projects together will enhance the original Perth plan by working across its slender linearity to allow residents, workers and visitors alike to experience the special and enduring qualities offered by the riverside garden city of Perth.

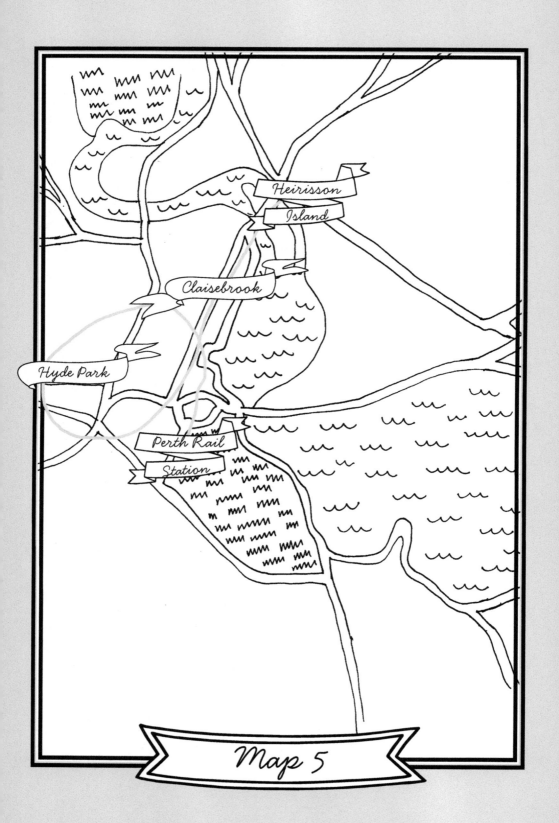

Heirisson Island

Claisebrook

Hyde Park

Perth Rail Station

Map 5

DAMP FEET IN PERTH

Felicity Morel-EdnieBrown

THE WETLANDS OF PERTH

Perth is a dry and sunlit city, yet its formative influences are ancient wetlands. The central city is built on their drained beds; its inner suburbs are shaped around and over them.

Even the lineal development of the greater Perth metropolitan area mimics Aboriginal use of an extended chain of wetlands dotted some three hundred kilometres north–south down the Swan Coastal Plain from Yanchep to Dunsborough.

To get a sense of the Perth wetlands, imagine an arc nine kilometres long – fat in the west and narrowing to the east – splayed in an almost unbroken fan across the top of the city. These are the rough boundaries of the wetlands which, prior to European occupation, traversed the modern suburbs of Leederville, West Perth, North Perth, Highgate and lower East Perth.

Immediately to the north of Perth were the 'central' wetlands: Lakes Sutherland, Irwin, Kingsford, Thomson, Henderson, First Swamp, Second Swamp and Third Swamp. Further out to the north-west was 'The Great Lakes District' comprising Herdsman Lake, Lake Monger and Lake Georgiana. To the north-east was Stone's Lake and to the east were Tea-Tree Lagoonstet and Claise Brook, which served as the drainage point of the wetlands to the Swan River.

For Noongar people, lakes, wetlands, rivers and estuaries are sacred. They believe the landscape was formed by the Waugyl (Waakal, Waugal, Wagyl, Wargal), a large snake-like creature created in the Dreaming. The Waugyl's body created the serpentine meanders in the Swan and Canning Rivers; where his body rested lakes and wetlands formed.

His back created the adjacent hills; his skin, the hollows and vegetation.

Unlike the deep, still, permanent lakes of England, the Perth wetlands were seasonal. In spring, blue flowers, green grasses and cooling glints of water enticed picnicking, paddling and play. In summer, the fierce sun scorched their shallow pans of flat sand to blinding whiteness, the water little more than tea-tree stained brackish puddles smelling of dying crustaceans and baked mud. In winter they flooded, joining in large, flat rushing sheets of water, sweeping away branches, twigs and the unwary to Claise Brook in the east, flooding the homes of colonists en route.

From dry puddles to rushing torrents, the wetlands formed the shape and sense of Perth, but within one lifetime of European arrival the Perth wetlands were drained, parcelled and sold as exclusive property. By 1989, it was estimated that some eighty per cent of the wetlands on the Swan Coastal Plain had been drained. Whilst there has been increasing recognition of the importance of wetlands as habitat for global biodiversity and for the health of waterways, wetlands continue to be drained and filled, primarily for urban development. Some have been rehabilitated in a growing awareness of the importance of wetlands to the ecology of the Swan River, but most are but mere hints in the landscape, detectable as a few flat playing fields, grassed over, ringed by introduced trees and framed by roads.

Together we will rediscover key sites of the Perth wetlands.

CENTRAL WETLANDS: LAKE KINGSFORD

(Perth Railway Station and Forrest Place)
Aboriginal name: Goologoolup

The Perth Railway Station and Forrest Place are situated on the bed of the former Lake Kingsford. As the deepest of the central Perth wetlands, Lake Kingsford divided the northern part of town from the south, and was pivotal in creating the form of Perth and the structure of its streets. Saint Georges Terrace is deliberately aligned so that Stirling Street, a broad street the same width as Saint Georges Terrace, could stretch northward on a narrow ridge of land between Lake Kingsford and its unnamed extension to the east. Thus, even the most important street in Perth and the most prestigious parcel of land in town was sited in a subtle and now largely unremembered response to this wetland making the streets of modern Northbridge different from those of the rest of Perth.

In 1853, convict labour dug deep drains all the way to Clause's Brook (Claisebrook) in the east. When sold as small plots of 'rich garden' ground in 1854, Lake Kingsford was some of the most expensive land in Perth. Nonetheless, it continued to flood through the nineteenth century until the construction of the railway in 1881 and growth of the city during the gold boom led to better drainage. Aboriginal use of the wetlands is commemorated in the wall of the railway station entrance from Barrack Street Bridge. A 1994 artwork depicts the former indigenous connection with the area and shows swamps, kangaroos and some of the wildlife and bird life that lived in the wetlands. The trees growing near the railway bridge are of the type that would have grown in the wetlands.

Forrest Place occupies the south-eastern extension of Lake Kingsford. Today, Forrest Place features an interactive water sculpture *Water Labrinyth* by artist Jeppe Hein, which playfully recreates the waterscape. Few know that the area actually once sat within the central wetlands and that small freshwater crayfish ('gilgies') could be caught in an old drain near the railway station.

The Cultural Centre likewise sits above the bed of this former wetland, located where Mooro Whadjuk people would sit to share culture and tradition and pass on knowledge to their young people. Next to the Art Gallery of Western Australia a reconstructed 'swamp' references the wetlands upon which the gallery sits. Opposite it is the Urban Orchard, a free urban garden with fruits and vegetables grown by volunteers. The orchard is a modern initiative to revitalise the area but it, too, references the past, reflecting the horticultural pursuits undertaken in the same spot over a hundred years ago.

Although technically having its northern boundary at Newcastle Street, Northbridge is colloquially broadened to reach as far north as Brisbane Street, incorporating the wide shallow basin of the central wetlands: Lakes Irwin, Kingsford, Poulett, Henderson and Thomson, Stone's Lake and Second Swamp. It is no accident that Northbridge, Perth's cosmopolitan, quirky, bohemian and vibrant entertainment precinct, is on the bed of the former swamps. It follows the tradition of Aboriginal communities past and present who use it as a meeting, eating, greeting and gathering place.

CENTRAL WETLANDS: FIRST SWAMP

(south-west corner Beaufort and Bulwer Streets)
Aboriginal name: Chalyeding

North of Northbridge, this broad expanse of park marks the site of the unimaginatively named First Swamp, later called Lake Poulett in honour of British Cabinet member Poulett-Thomson.

Lake Poulett was drained in 1838 to unsuccessfully grow Zante currant. By 1855, it was sufficiently drained to allow an extension of Brisbane Street to cross Beaufort Street between the south-eastern boundary of Lake Poulett and the north-western boundary of Stone's Lake. By 1872, Lake Poulett was being used as a rubbish dump.

The 1890s rapid gold boom led growth put pressure on Perth's food supplies. Lake Poulett (along with other Perth wetlands) became a market garden growing vegetables, tubers and citrus. Tilled by Chinese men in their traditional wide-brimmed hats, the market gardens they leased became known as 'Chinese Gardens' which supplied a fresh market opposite the Chung Wah Association building in James Street.

After motor transport opened up alternative market garden areas south and north of the city, the Perth City Council, influenced by the City Beautiful movement in which green recreational spaces were seen as the 'lungs of the city' and an 'antidote' to increasing urban consolidation, began resuming the Chinese Garden leases with the intention of transforming them into parks. In 1913, Lake Poulett was transformed into Birdwood Square, complete with a curved, raised terrace (Baker Avenue) and named after Lieutenant-General Birdwood, a Commander in the Gallipoli campaign.

CENTRAL WETLANDS: SECOND AND THIRD SWAMP

(Second Swamp: intersection William and Bulwer Streets; Third Swamp: North-west corner William and Glendower Streets) Aboriginal names: Boodjamooling (place of initiation and nose-pegging, young men's initiation), Boojamaeling, Bidjabooling, Bidjabunda

Second Swamp was a small swamp notorious for its quicksand, which was said to have swallowed a cow.

A block north, Hyde Park is the former Third Swamp. One of the largest of the central Perth wetlands, at fifteen and a half hectares, it was a favoured camping ground and initiation site for Aboriginal people. Known for its good water supply, plentiful ducks and large paper bark trees, it was a popular picnic, camping and duck shooting site until the 1890s and was occasionally used by drovers bringing sheep into the city.

During the gold boom, the City of Perth allowed Third Swamp to be used as a temporary camping ground for prospectors en route to the goldfields. Overcrowding led to fears of disease from poor sanitation and, shortly afterwards, work began to transform the wetland into a formal park in the English vein. Complete with a three- tiered decorative fountain and renamed Hyde Park, in honour of the London Park of the same name, six hundred introduced trees were planted, rushes removed, annuals planted and a central lake formed.

CENTRAL WETLANDS: LAKE HENDERSON

(bounded by Palmerston, Fitzgerald, Stuart and Randell Streets) Aboriginal name(s): Goongarnulayarreenup, Goongarulnyarreenup,

Goongarnula (place of the stinking spring with moss), Yarreenup, Little Boojoormelup, Danjanberup Danjanberu (place of shallow lake; three island lake where Zamias and byers grow; name also attributed to Smith's Lake)

For Aboriginal people, the wetlands were a place of gathering, sharing and dissemination of knowledge. Throughout the nineteenth century, local newspapers identified Lake Henderson as a popular site for Aboriginal corroborees and gatherings. By the end of 1873, the wetland had been drained sufficiently to grow vegetables and run dairy herds. Despite drainage, the wetland continued to flood until construction of a new drain in 1908, by which time the area was surrounded by small house lots, some of which overlooked the 'lake'. During the 1890s gold boom, parts of the wetland were leased by Chinese market gardeners; one of the structures to survive from the era is Lee Hop's house at the south-western corner. From 1913, the City of Perth incrementally resumed the market garden leases to create parkland. In February 1929, parts of the park were converted to municipal tennis courts, with the thump of the tennis balls echoing the thump of feet from the corroborees seventy years earlier.

Continuing the connection between wetlands and ceremony and learning, a small synagogue was established on the north-east corner of the wetland in 1918 not far from a larger synagogue in Brisbane Street. A young 'Ladies College' (later Presbyterian Ladies College, one of Perth's most prestigious schools for girls) was established in Ormiston House at the edge of Lake Henderson and, in 1939, a building at the corner of Fitzgerald and Stuart Streets was converted into a children's library and learning centre and touted as the first of its kind in Australia and New Zealand.

CLAISE BROOK

(situated on the western bank of the Swan River, above Heirisson Island)
Aboriginal names: Mardalup, Mandalup (place of the small marsupial)

Originally called Clause's Brook after Frederick Clause, the Ship's surgeon in Captain Stirling's first expedition of Western Australia in 1827. By 1838, the name had been anglicised to Claise Brook and land at its mouth reserved for government purposes. Although this reserve was subsequently shown as 'Public Gardens' as late as 1918, its fate was somewhat different.

Luxuriant in its foliage until the 1860s, Claise Brook was gradually used for light and noxious industries, brickworks, scrap yards, warehouses, rail yards, stables, gambling dens and brothels. It was also the site of the town abattoir, Perth Gas Company (later Perth Gas Works), and the East Perth Power Station. Unsurprisingly, the area's soil was badly contaminated with heavy metals and hydrocarbons.

In 1992, the Claisebrook Redevelopment Authority initiated the Claisebrook Village Project and began significant environment rehabilitation on both sides of the former brook to convert 146 hectares of land into a vibrant inner urban mixed-use precinct. Capitalising on its proximity to the river and broad views to the east, the area was converted from derelict industrial sites to a prestigious housing and recreational area featuring parkland, bush gardens, walkways and public art. Black swans and inquisitive dolphins now glide in Claisebrook Inlet and egrets, pelicans and cormorants dive for dinner at the edges of the river or sit sunning themselves on piers.

The wetlands of Perth still empty into the river by subterranean drains as part of the 'Claisebrook Catchment Area'. The pumping station is disguised as a large hill – popular for grass-tobogganing – and the drain exits at a small inlet slightly to the south of Claisebrook Cove which often has herons perched nearby.

Aboriginal connections to the area are recognised, celebrated and interpreted though numerous public artworks including an interpretive water brook and artwork depicting the flora, fauna and traditional uses of the area. A series of narrative plaques and a mural explain the evolution of the area from Aboriginal to European use.

HEIRISSON ISLAND

(an island in the eastern bend of Swan Water)
Aboriginal names: Matagarup, Mattagerup, Kakaroomup, Boodjar-Gorden (statue of Yagan)

Heirisson Island was originally a series of isles named after French Ensign Antoine Heirisson who led an exploration party of the Swan River from the *Naturaliste* in 1801. The isles were one of the few places Aboriginal people crossed the Swan River, and their name for the area reflected the isles' deep sticky mud; a roughly translation is 'knee deep in mud'. The mud proved an impediment to European navigation and, after settlement, channels were cut in a curve of the river and the river dredged near the isles, causing a permanent change to the freshwater nature of the river above. The first bridge was constructed across the river in 1843 and amalgamation of the isles began by infill and naturally occurring silt deposits. This process was completed by the time the two Causeway Bridges were constructed in 1947 and 1952.

Today, Heirisson is a single island populated by a mob of introduced western grey kangaroos. There are walking trails and small beaches with rush lined shores and public art reflecting the history of the area. It is home to a statue of the Noongar warrior Yagan commemorating his resistance to European settlement in the 1830s; the island has also been the site of protest against proposed destruction of places of significance, for land rights and for Native Title negotiations.

POINT FRASER

(Eastern end of Swan Water; bounded by the Swan River, Riverside Drive, Plain Street and Adelaide Terrace)
Aboriginal name(s): Boorla, Boorlo, Beabboollup (place of many fish)

By the 1950s, increasing urbanisation caused an annual occurrence of algal bloom in the Swan River. Caused by the over abundance of nutrients washing into the river, it choked the river, killing fish and diminishing birdlife. From the late 1990s, the City of Perth has undertaken a programme of rejuvenation at Point Fraser to combat the effects of pollution and run-off. It has re-established the riverine environment with plantings of sedges, rushes and other wetland plants which filter nutrients and contaminants from the water and also provide habitat for animals and waterbirds. Today, Point Fraser is home to over thirty species, including the common sandpiper and the musk duck.

CONCLUSION

We have walked over the changing topography of the city understanding the land as it used to be before asphalt and concrete. We have stood where the swamp waters flowed and have seen how the city still echoes the wetlands to its north. We have heard in our mind the echoes of the thump of the corroboree on the dry, sunbaked wetlands in the entertainment venues of Northbridge.

Who would have thought that Perth, the capital of the driest third of the driest continent, would still bear so many traces of its damp, wetland past? From seasonal wet to dry; abundant to scarce; from loved to despised, abundant to drained, the wetlands of Perth are part of the fabric of the city and its culture. The wetlands fashioned the landscape and shaped the streets, creating first the form of the town, then a physical barrier that, later, formed a psychological and social divide. The former wetlands define the ebb and flow of the city, manifesting in its rhythm and pulse, shaping its daily activities and creating its sense of place.

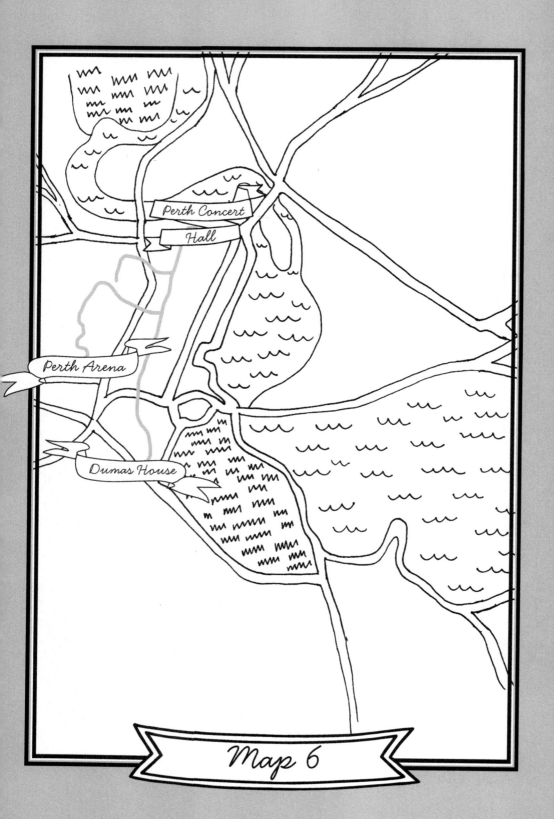

Perth Concert Hall

Perth Arena

Dumas House

Map 6

6

THE BUILDINGS OF PERTH

Michal Lewi

I've selected for this chapter buildings that serve as visual reminders of successive epochs in Perth's relatively short architectural history. The Town Hall, St George's Cathedral, the Old Court House, the Supreme Court and Government House comprise Perth's foremost heritage precinct. It includes one outstanding modern heritage building – Council House. A surprising number of other heritage places has survived the widespread demolition in the sixties and seventies of the city's older building stock. The wholesale demolition made way for the high-rise buildings that form the wind tunnels of the twenty-first century.

Many of the buildings I've chosen are 'firsts' in one way or another. They range from Perth's first boys' school, its first court house, cemetery and concert hall, to its first reinforced concrete building and first aluminium-clad tower. The period I've covered in this survey ends with some very good examples of Perth's modernist architecture of the mid-twentieth century. Of course, like other cities, Perth suffers from a few architectural and planning failures, like the Perth Convention and Exhibition Centre.

THE OLD COURT HOUSE

This was the city's first public building, built in 1836 by Henry Reveley in the so-called Greek Revival style. In the early days of the Swan Colony it doubled as the Court of General Quarter Sessions and also as the only place of worship until St George's Church was built. It was also the first school in Perth, and it often served as a place of assembly for public meetings and musical and theatrical performances. In 1846 the first Abbot of the Benedictine monastery of New Norcia walked the 100 km to Perth and gave a brilliant recital to a packed audience to raise funds for his mission.

6.1 The Old Courthouse

The newly constituted Supreme Court occupied the Old Court House from 1856 to 1863. In 1974 the Old Court House became the Francis Burt Law Education Centre, a law museum and education centre under the aegis of the Law Society of Western Australia.

In many ways this simple, small building is a key to Perth's history: it shows, by its juxtaposition to the imposing Supreme Court building of today, the tiny beginnings from which Perth grew.

ST BARTHOLOMEW'S CHURCH AND EAST PERTH CEMETERY

This was Perth's first proper cemetery, with the first recorded burial in 1830. Many early pioneers and their families are buried there. The building known now as St Bartholomew's Church began as a mortuary; it was converted and extended by R. R. Jewell in 1871 to become a chapel. It's now vested in the National Trust. The tombstones survived intact until the mid-twentieth century, when they became popular targets for vandals. In response, the

6.2 St Bartholomew's Church and East Perth Cemetery

Trust had to fence the cemetery and lock it up; previously it had been enjoyed by the local community as public open space in an otherwise urban residential environment.

6.3 MEMORIALS IN THE OLD PERTH CEMETERY

MEMORIALS

These ornate memorials of early Perth worthies were erected in Perth's first period of affluence at the turn of the nineteenth and twentieth centuries. They nicely frame the markers of Perth's next age of affluence in the second half of the twentieth century: office towers in St George's Terrace

OLD PERTH BOYS SCHOOL

6.4   OLD PERTH BOYS SCHOOL

The Old Perth Boys School was designed by W. A. Sanford, Colonial Secretary and an amateur architect, in an early Gothic Revival style, and looks like a small church. It was completed in 1854 and was the first purp ose-built school building in Perth.

The building is extremely important in the streetscape of St George's Terrace. Situated amongst the huge contemporary office towers, it's a potent reminder of Perth's tiny colonial origins. It's now vested in the National Trust

ST GEORGE'S CATHEDRAL

This building, the successor to a previous Anglican cathedral, was designed by the Sydney architect Edmund Blacket and built in 1888.

In their book *Western Heritage* (1961) Ray and John Oldham claim that "architecturally speaking, St George's is probably the best of the colonial buildings in Perth". In particular, they praise the interior: the jarrah hammerbeam roof and the warm, rosy brickwork are quite beautiful, and the nave and transepts have elegant proportions.

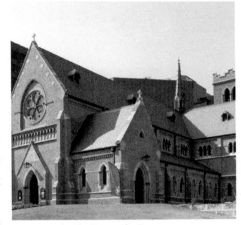

6.5 St George's Catherdral

The building is in the Gothic Revival style, which was popular in the nineteenth century for important church buildings. The exterior has a pleasing combination of stone and mellow, deeply coloured brickwork. There's some beautifully carved stonework, particularly on the west front. Altogether, the cathedral forms an important feature of Perth's heritage precinct.

CATHEDRAL SQUARE

This delightful urban space used to lie between the Diocesan

Trustees' building (since demolished), St George's Terrace, the Lands Department and St George's Cathedral. The space was ruined when the oversized office block (shown on the right in image

6.6 St George's Cathedral, exterior

6.7) replaced the old Diocesan Trustees' building, creating an uninhabited 'Cathedral square' which is in permanent shadow.

This is how Cathedral Square looked after it was overwhelmed by the bulk of the Law Chambers' office block. As I write in 2015, the Square is being redeveloped and it is hoped that sunlight will once again enliven what should be one of Perth's congenial spaces.

6.7 Cathedral Square

FORMER LANDS DEPARTMENT

The east wing of the Old Treasury Building, with its wonderful Italianate facade, was designed by George Temple-Poole and completed (though never finished) in 1896. This rare view of

6.8 The former Lands Department

the entire facade was revealed briefly during the demolition of the old Diocesan Trustees' building and the Public Trustees' building

HIS MAJESTY'S THEATRE

The theatre, designed by W. G. Wolf in the Federation Free Classical style, was built in 1904. It was the first reinforced concrete building in Western Australia, and probably in Australia. In its day it was the largest theatre in Australia.

According to the entry in the State Heritage Register, it "demonstrates the ebullient decorative form and style favoured by successful developers within the central business district of Perth during the goldrush period". Standing on the corner of Hay Street, it dominates King Street, giving it a landmark quality.

6.9 His Majesty's Theatre

It's become the home of the West Australian Opera, West Australian Arts Orchestra, and the West Australian Ballet Company.

FORMER PENSIONERS' BARRACKS AND ARCH

This arch stands like a triumphal arch at the top of St George's Terrace, but it commemorates no triumph; rather, it symbolises Perth's greatest loss of heritage.

Ray and John Oldham wrote in *Western Heritage* (1961): Beautifully terminating the vista of St. George's Terrace at its western end is a dignified old three-storeyed building, whose wings gently enclose the hill behind it. The softly mellow colours of the bricks have been skilfully used in decorative patterns, to add richness of texture to the plain wall surfaces, and to emphasise the basic lines in the design of the building. It forms the keystone in the group of decorated brick buildings which give the city its personality...[1]

The Oldhams were referring to the Pensioners' Barracks, and Image 6.10 shows where the Pensioners' Barracks stood till 1966, when they were heedlessly demolished to make way for the Mitchell Freeway. When the proposed demolition of the Barracks was announced there was a public outcry and, as a compromise, the Arch alone was retained. This photograph was taken from in front of Parliament House.

The Barracks were designed by R. R. Jewell and built in 1863 to house soldiers of the Enrolled Pensioner Forces, which guarded the convicts who were being shipped to the colony after 1858.

GOVERNMENT HOUSE

The building is in Stuart or Jacobean Revival style, with what's described as Fonthill Gothic arcading. It reminds

6.10 THE FORMER PENSIONERS' BARRACKS AND

---

1   R. and J. Oldham, *Western Heritage*, Perth: Lamb Publications, 1961.

me of a toy soldiers' castle. The present Government House was completed around 1864. It has served as an impressive representation of gubernatorial power, but whether it will have relevance when Australia eventually becomes a republic remains to be seen. In the future the expansive grounds, in the form of an English garden, could be opened up to the public, permanently, as valuable parkland in the city centre.

6.11 GOVERNMENT HOUSE EXTERIOR

THE OLD OBSERVATORY

Although called The Old Observatory, this place was actually the luxurious residence and offices of the Government Astronomer. Originally three buildings comprised Perth's first observatory, which occupied this site on top of Mount Eliza: the Transit Observatory, the Astrographic building and dome, and this lovely building. They were designed by George Temple-Poole and completed in 1896. It's beautifully detailed, combining nineteenth-century Classical and Colonial elements.

Accurate astronomic observations were important in colonial days. They were used to determine the exact latitude and longitude of the colony and to establish the time of day with greater accuracy (announced by firing a cannon located on the site). Before this, clocks could vary by up to half an hour.

6.12 THE OLD OBSERVATORY

The real observatory buildings were demolished (according to rumour, in the dead of night) in 1965 when the astronomical equipment was moved to the new State Observatory at Bickley. The ensuing protests saved this remnant, an important heritage place, which is now the headquarters of the National Trust of Australia (WA).

Both these buildings, styled in what's been colloquially described as Ballarat baroque, are typical of the attractive low-rise buildings that formed the St George's Terrace streetscape until the 1960s. Then most of them (including the Bank of Adelaide and Perpetual Trustees' buildings in image 5.17) were demolished and replaced with concrete and glass towers (see image 6.13).

6.13 ST GEORGE'S TERRACE BEFORE THE SKYSCRAPERS TOOK OVER

SUPREME COURT

John Grainger, father of composer Percy Grainger, designed the present Supreme Court in what's officially called the Federation Academic Classical style. It was completed in 1906. The tiny Old Court House, just visible on the left, stands in contrast to the later, purpose-built court which boasts several courtrooms, judges' chambers and cells for prisoners.

Unlike court precincts in many other cities, this building

occupies unrestricted public open space between Supreme Court Gardens and Stirling Gardens. These are Perth's oldest gardens and its first botanical gardens.

6.14 THE SUPREME COURT

GENERAL POST OFFICE

At Federation in 1901 the Commonwealth took control of postal and telecommunication services throughout Australia. Thereafter, it established impressive General Post Office buildings in the State capitals.

The Perth GPO was designed by the Western Australian Principal Architect, Hilton Beasley (succeeded in 1917 by William Hardwick), in collaboration with the Commonwealth Architect J. S. Murdoch.

Construction started in 1914 and, due to delays occasioned by the First World War and other causes, completion was only achieved in 1923, when the new Perth General Post Office became the city's biggest building.

6.15 THE GENERAL POST OFFICE

The opulent and grandiose Beaux Arts design was intended to display to the community the new Commonwealth's prestige and importance. The east elevation is impressive with its monumental stone facade and neo-classical features, like the three-storey ionic columns.

The GPO is a key element of Perth's townscape. As the central building of Forrest Place, it combines well with the Commonwealth Bank and Perth railway station to create the Forrest Place precinct, which was intended to be Perth's major civic space. The architecture of later buildings in Forrest Place doesn't harmonise as successfully with the old.

COUNCIL HOUSE

The building was designed by Howlett and Bailey and opened in 1963. It's the finest exaple of the international modernist style in Perth; there aren't many others still intact. Its detailed features display Jeffrey Howlett's originality and creative flair. The prominent T-shaped white sunbreakers are superimposed in an alternating pattern across the building and coated with fine mosaic tiles.

6.16 COUNCIL HOUSE

The heritage value of Council House took a long time to be recognised. In the 1990s the Minister for Heritage refused to allow the place to be included in the State Heritage register. Indeed, the premier wanted to have it demolished – he thought it was an intrusion in the city's so-called Heritage Precinct. A great campaign to save the place was waged by the architectural profession, the National Trust, CityVision and many others, which led to the eventual refurbishment and heritage listing of Council House in 2006. It remains the headquarters of the City of Perth.

DUMAS HOUSE

Dumas House is a fourteen-storey office building constructed during the 1960s. The building overlooks Kings Park and is close to Parliament House.

Dumas House was part of the 1955 plan to centralise all WA Government departments. Public Works Department architects G. Finn, E. Van Mens and P. Maidment won a national competition to design the five office buildings that would house State Government departments. Only one, Dumas House, was ever built, in 1965.

6.17 DUMAS HOUSE

Dumas House is a good example of the postwar international style, with a modular grid building plan, glazed panelling and an open piazza. The building was adapted for Australian conditions by adding horizontal slabs that project from the sides of the building and provide shade.

PERTH CONCERT HALL

Perth's first purpose-built concert hall was designed by Howlett and Bailey in what is known as the Brutalist style, using white, heavy, off-form concrete construction. It was the first concert hall built in Australia after World War II. The official opening

6.18 Perth Concert Hall

took place in January 1973 with a great ball that went on till dawn. It was a great celebration of the coming of age of music in Perth – at last we had a world-class concert hall, and enthusiasm for classical music was firmly established in Western Australia.

The Concert Hall has some of the best acoustics in Australia; it has been the performance home of the West Australian Symphony Orchestra since 1973.

ALLENDALE SQUARE

This office tower, designed by Cameron Chisholm and Nicol, was completed in 1976. The building is rotated at 45 degrees to St George's Terrace, which makes an admirable interruption to the other St George's Terrace facades, which are all square on to the street.

6.19 Allendale Square

The tower is clad with aluminium panels made from locally mined and refined bauxite. When it was completed, the building was the largest fully aluminium-clad, freestanding tower in Australia, and one of the largest in the world. It's the first and only such building in Perth and, by virtue of its originality and sophistication of design, it stands out among the bland office towers of the Central Business District.

THE FUTURE

Writing this in 2015, one of Western Australia's biggest mining booms appears to have ended. The nineteenth-century gold boom gave us such fine public buildings as the old Lands Department and His Majesty's Theatre (see previous images). These buildings had style and self-confidence, sometimes with an exuberance quite lacking in the twenty-first century.

ST GEORGE'S TERRACE

So far most developments in Perth since the 1980s have been apartment buildings and high-rise office blocks, like these along St George's Terrace; most have no more style than the grey-suited men who occupy them – some are just a bit better dressed than others. In contrast to the surviving buildings from the past, today's major buildings are mostly built for private use by corporations or apartment residents. You need a pass to enter them. The major new waterfront development at Elizabeth Quay will be more of the same: commercial high-rise offices and apartments, with public access only to ground-level cafes and shops. Will this be the legacy of the twenty-first century mining boom? Not many public buildings have been built since the Perth Convention and Exhibition Centre, of which the less said the better (see image 5.1).

STATE THEATRE CENTRE

6.20 STATE THEATRE CENTRE

One new public building of note is the State Theatre Centre in Roe Street by Kerry Hill Architects. Its exterior is elegant and so restrained as to be a bit self-effacing; the golden-coloured interior is more opulent. In isolation it's a beautiful building, but the hope was that it would give rather more uplift to its drab surroundings in Northbridge.

PERTH ARENA

An entirely different style was adopted for the Perth Arena in

6.21 PERTH ARENA

Wellington Street by Ashton Raggatt McDougall with local architects Cameron Chisholm Nicol. It's a big landmark building, visible for miles around, with an aesthetic which matches the music that is performed in it.

LOOKING FORWARD

Looking to the future, Perth should gain a new museum on the site of the old WA Museum. However, there seems little chance of a new museum of Indigenous art being built on the waterfront, as had been hoped. The railway line that cuts Northbridge off from the CBD is being partly sunk and this will open up opportunities for good development there. My dream is that money will be found to sink Mitchell Freeway where it cuts off Parliament House from the Barracks Arch and St George's Terrace to provide good public open space at the west end of town.

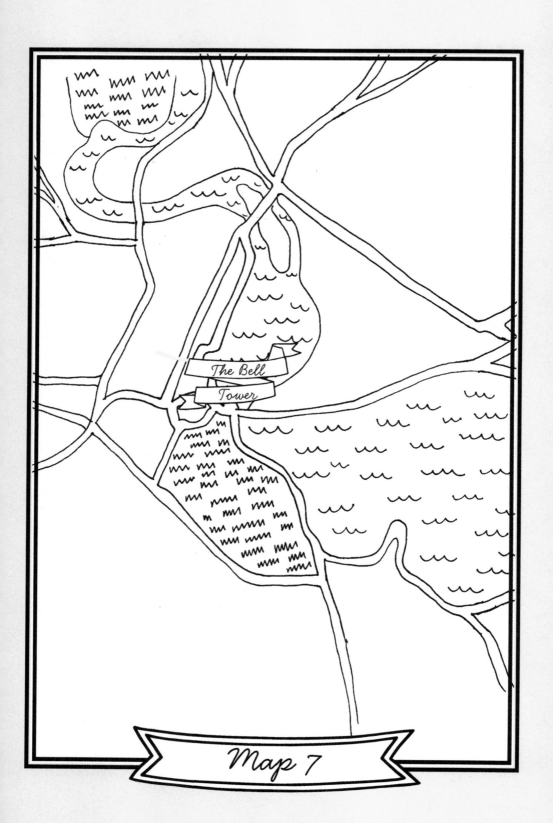

The Bell
Tower

Map 7

7

ALTERNATIVE FUTURES ON THE FORESHORE

Julian Bolleter

In science fiction stories concerning time travel, an alternative future is a possible future that never transpires. Our cities are also littered with alternative futures that, for one reason or another, never materialised. This is particularly the case on Perth's foreshore. Perth has been hatching plans for its foreshore since 1833 when the 'Arrowsmith plan' showed a generous park on the water's edge. Since then, shoals of schemes have washed up and breathed their last on the foreshore's banks. In recent times these include 153 schemes from an international urban design competition conducted in 1991; proposals by local advocacy group CityVision in 1988 and 2010; schemes devised as part of a state government tender process in 2007; proposals from a City of Perth urban design competition in 2010; and fifty plus schemes produced by Ashton Raggatt McDougall (architects for Elizabeth Quay). In this period the foreshore has become literally choked with alternative futures, yet you would not know it from being there: the barren, windswept expanse of Langley Park gives little indication of the plethora of failed proposals for its redesign (Figure 1).

7.1 THE BROAD, WINDSWEPT EXPANSE OF LANGLEY PARK, 2013

The tragedy of Perth Water, the lake-like section of river adjacent to the city centre, is that planners have resolutely wrestled into being the most destructive proposals: including the tragic infilling of Mounts Bay for a freeway interchange, and the monomaniacal reclamation of the river for ambiguous recreational purposes. On the flipside, when entrusted with worthy proposals our leaders have lost their nerve. This chapter will explore three alternative futures that never came to fruition: a 1931 proposal for an artificial island in Perth Water, a 1991 competition-winning proposal for a waterside park, and an urbane 2008 scheme for the development of the Esplanade. It is my intention to momentarily breathe life into these three alternative futures, to see what is and what could have been.

PERTH ISLAND: AN ALTERNATIVE FUTURE FOR PERTH WATER (PROPOSED 1931)

Between the 1880s and the 1970s Perth's leaders and planners orchestrated the infilling of vast areas of Perth Water's marshy edges.[1] On a pragmatic level, this exercise was carried out to provide Perth with recreational spaces necessitated by the absence of any substantial central parkland in Perth, and later to provide land area for the freeway interchange. On a symbolic level this exercise can be explained as an attempt to recreate an English idea of a proper river characterised by "picturesque banks, broad waters and gentle currents" and also an impulse by which "native rivers had to be properly trained as instances of national enterprise".[2] Initial reclamation efforts saw the creation of the Esplanade in the 1880s and continued with the South Perth foreshore and Langley Park

---

1   In total, reclamation has claimed 607 hectares of wetland along the shores of the Swan and Canning estuaries alone, equivalent to the size of 300 MCG ovals. G. Seddon, *Sense of Place*, Perth: The University of Western Australia Press, 1972.

2   W. Taylor, 'Rivers Too Cross: River Beautification and Settlement in Perth, Western Australia', *National Identities*, no. 5 (1), 2003, p. 25.

in the 1930s. The reclamation of Heirisson Island and the Victoria Park and South Perth foreshores was subsequently completed in the 1950s.

The apotheosis of the reclamation exercise was reached during the depths of the Great Depression. In 1931 local engineer Frank Vincent proposed the creation of a 120-hectare island by dredging the shallow riverbed of the surrounding areas of Perth Water to a depth of 4.5 meters. The island was conceived both as a way of reviving confidence in Western Australia, as well as providing valuable land close to the city. However the actual program of the island was vague, Vincent indicating that it may contain private dwellings, up-to-date golf links (readily accessible to the busy city worker), an aerodrome, and a shopping centre. While impressive from the air, the visual impact of the island from eye level would have been abhorrent. P. Egan, in a letter to the *West Australian*, described a likely exchange between a visitor to Perth and his host, upon arriving at the riverfront:

> 'This,' says the Perthite, 'is Perth Water.' 'Don't think much of it,' comments the visitor; 'what's the idea of having your jail over there?' and he nods toward the dump (Perth Island). 'That's not a jail, it's an island; one of our beauty spots,' says the friend. 'Well, why don't you blow it up and dredge it out of the way?' inquires the puzzled visitor. 'Take it away?' says our representative in shocked tones. 'Why, we put it there on purpose; used to be nothing but water between here and South Perth a long time back, and now see what we've done; cost us five million, and we're still paying for it – that's why our rates are so high; look at it, man!' 'No,' says, the visitor, 'it makes me sick.'

While stymied by political and public hostility, the plan to build a residential island could have produced, in time, a city on the water. Buildings on the island would have required deep piling due to reclaimed earth's tendency to shift and settle over time. The significant cost of these structural works would have entailed the construction of tall buildings so as to recoup costs. The urban character incubated by Perth Island may well have been extreme (Figure 2). Islands are often perceived to be 'outside the law' and there is the expectation of some release from the restraints of the mainland.[3] In this respect Perth Island would have been the logical location for Perth's Crown casino in the 1980s, for casinos flourish in the 'easing of restraints' frequently offered by Islands (Macau being one such example). Despite hostility towards the

7.2 A VISION OF WHAT FRANK VINCENT'S PROPOSED 120-HECTARE ISLAND FOR PERTH WATER MAY HAVE LOOKED LIKE TODAY

Perth Island scheme, reclamation of Perth Water continued, albeit in a slightly less dramatic form. In the 1970s Perth's 'reflection pool,' Mounts Bay, was reclaimed for the freeway interchange. At this point public opinion turned definitively against further reclamation. It was too late, however, for by this point Perth Water was enclosed on all sides by a barren and windswept expanse that severed the river from the city.

---

3   G. Seddon, *Swan Song: Reflections on Perth and Western Australia 1956–1995*. Perth: The Centre for Studies in Australian Literature, 1995, p. 133.

WATERSIDE PERTH: AN ALTERNATIVE FUTURE FOR LANGLEY PARK (PROPOSED 1991)

In 1991 the State government convened an international design competition for the entirety of Perth's city foreshore. The aim of the competition was to solicit solutions to the problem of a city severed from its river by the green belt of Langley Park and the Esplanade. The competition brief encouraged a landscape response to this issue. Surveys conducted by the City of Perth in 1986 established that the public favoured options for the foreshore that included "open grassed fields, informal parkland and naturalistic river edges," and that they strongly disapproved of the intrusion of the 'city' into the reclaimed green belt. This sentiment reflected an enduring idea of the city of Perth as a city within a garden setting, the 'garden' comprising Kings Park and the foreshore green belt.[4] This enduring image of Perth as a garden can be traced back to evocative accounts of the Swan River landscape penned by British explorers and settlers:[5]

> The warmth of spring (in 1829) enabled the pioneers to more closely explore the woods. In September a multitude of wild flowers of every imaginable colour adorned the banks of the Swan, and afforded unspeakable delight to the people…They nestled on the banks, covered the hills, dotted the plains and vistas, and lent such a lovely air to

---

4 W. Taylor, 'Rivers Too Cross: River Beautification and Settlement in Perth, Western Australia', *National Identities*, no. 5 (1), 2003, p. 34.

5 This reading of the Swan River landscape as some kind of new Eden was not shared by all, and indeed the Swan River colony struggled with the wretchedly unproductive soils. As the *Morning Journal* newspaper reported in 1830: "instead of the land about the coast being a sort of Paradise, it is, for the most part, little better than a barren waste. It seems indeed that the Paradise is yet to be discovered beyond the hills." I. Berryman, *Swan River Letters, vol. 1,* Perth: Swan River Press, 2002, p. 22.

the scene that the imaginative among them might well consider the Swan River country a huge garden.[6]

In accordance with an Arcadian image of Perth, entrants to the 1991 competition typically proposed broad swathes of planting and the scraping back of land reclaimed in the late nineteenth and early twentieth century so as to trace the original, meandering shorelines. Characteristic of these tendencies was the winning submission produced by the Massachusetts firm Carr, Lynch, Hack and Sandell (Figure 3). In addressing the perceived disconnection between the city and river, the design team proposed to excavate a significant section of Langley Park to create the 'Old Shore Creek,' in order to draw the river back to the existing city edge. The island created by this excavation was to be planted so as to celebrate the 'beauty of Western Australia' and to contain an assortment of tea houses, mosaics, sculpture gardens, amphitheatres and natural grasslands.

Central Perth had an insignificant number of residents in 1991 and as such this expansive and expensive waterside park would have been initially superfluous to requirements. However, the park would have served central Perth's rapidly growing residential population well; particularly given that the significant tree planting in

7.3 WATERSIDE PERTH', THE COMPETITION-WINNING PROPOSAL FOR A GENEROUS FORESHORE PARK

6 W. Kimberly, *History of Western Australia*. Melbourne: P. F. W. Niven & Co, 1897.

this park would now be mature. While ostensibly a landscape composition, Waterside Perth would have had a transformative effect on the adjacent city as increased real estate values would have precipitated high density redevelopment along Terrace Road.

Despite the popularity of the scheme with the public, the project ultimately became unachievable because of restricted City of Perth and state government funds. The scheme foundered and the vast lifeless plain of Langley Park shrugged off yet another plan for its redesign.

THE CIRCLE SCHEME: AN ALTERNATIVE FUTURE FOR THE ESPLANADE (PROPOSED 2008)

While previous designs for Perth's foreshore had reflected the public's opposition to high density development and its appreciation of expansive landscapes, a 2008 scheme by architects Ashton Raggat McDougall proposed the development of the Esplanade to form a new urban district of the city (Figures 4, 5). The dense urbanism of this district was to frame an excavated circular inlet, the 'River Circle,' which would entwine the river and the city. A 'Swan Island' – an island literally shaped like a black swan, the symbol of Western Australia – was to be set within the River Circle inlet (Figure 6). An iconic Indigenous Cultural Centre also jutted out into the Swan River on the southern edge of the inlet, thus forming a cultural anchor for the proposal.

While the urbanity of the scheme represented a departure from earlier Arcadian visions such as Waterside Perth, it also reflected a growing desire for Perth to become more activated, vibrant and diverse; to become less a suburb and more a 'real city.' Perth had become 'exceptionally self-conscious,'about its image, about its global liveability ranking, about why bright young things tend to leave and, most notoriously, about how to shake off the 'Dullsville' tag that its citizens regrettably assigned [to] it in a pique of self-flagellation.[7]

7.4 THE 'CIRCLE SCHEME', 2008

This tag was cheerily confirmed by ex-Victorian Premier Jeff Kennett on a visit in 2007, when he characterised Perth as being 'so open and pristine it is almost antiseptic.' Perhaps in response to such damming assessments this scheme attempted to forge a new image of Perth in which a dense, urbane and activated district broke through the isolating open green belt of the Esplanade and finally embraced the Swan River.

7.5 THE 'CIRCLE SCHEME' AS IT WOULD HAVE APPEARED FROM MT ELIZA

Despite public approval for the scheme, segments of the local media played havoc with it, labelling it 'Dubai on the Swan'. This stereotype centred on 'Swan Island', which was designed to be read from Google Earth, similar

7   R. Weller, *Boomtown 2050 : Scenarios for a Rapidly Growing City*, Crawley: UWAP, 2009, p. 38.

7.6 The 'River Circle' inlet and 'Swan Island'

to urban logos of Dubai's offshore island developments ('The Palms' and 'The World'). The tall iconic tower to the south of the inlet also served to further confirm the association with Dubai, at least in the minds of those opposed to the scheme. This occurred at a time when Perth was particularly sensitive to comparisons with Dubai, given Dubai's bankruptcy and Perth's similar reliance on mining wealth. Unfortunately this reading of the scheme, which centred mostly on issues of style, tended to obscure the public gestures that were at the core of the scheme.

With a change of state government in 2008 from Labor to Liberal the scheme was abandoned and the new Premier Colin Barnett announced that an alternative proposal would be sought around a rectangular inlet. This new proposal is now Elizabeth Quay, the public domain component which is due for completion in late 2015. This scheme extends Perth's colonial city grid to the water in a sensible fashion. While this provides a rational structure, it precludes the rich associations of the 'River Circle' which alluded to forms such as the WACA oval, the Aboriginal flag, and perhaps a Waakal egg. There are many who mourn the premature demise of the original circle scheme, an idiosyncratic and evocative proposal, which through vociferous opposition and the vagaries of the electoral cycle, got 'Perthed'.

EPILOGUE

The failure of Perth to realise proposals for the foreshore can on one hand be viewed as an indictment of Perth's leaders. Indeed in the period between the Voyager 1 spacecraft being launched (1977) and it leaving the solar system for the mysterious realm of interstellar space (2013), Perth's vacuous foreshore remained in a dormant state, despite numerous plans for its redesign.[8] On the other hand, commentators have speculated that the foreshore's role during this period may best function as a "tremendous generator of ideas".[9] Of course the necessary fuel for this 'ideas machine' is the belief that one day something will happen.

The legacy of all the alternative futures proposed for Perth Water is that they provide a record of shifting perceptions of how Perth, in spatial and cultural terms, relates to the ancient Swan River. From the early twentieth-century notion of the river as a blank space awaiting beautification and development, to the late twentieth-century idea of the city immersed in a riverine garden setting, to finally the early twenty-first-century vision of an urban embrace between the city and river. While these alternative futures reflect our attempts to reshape the river in accordance with our symbolic, pragmatic or economic agendas, in this century the river will reassert its ability to shape the city. Mapping of the 1.1 metre sea level rise predicted to have occurred by 2100 shows Langley Park, Heirisson Island and the South Perth foreshores almost completely underwater (Figure 7). The combination of this predicted sea level rise

8   Construction began on Elizabeth Quay, a small section of Perth's foreshore, only in 2012.
9   University of Western Australia academic Beth George made this observation in a proposal for the Australian Pavilion at the Venice Architecture Biennale.

with flooding from increasingly dramatic storm events could be catastrophic. Unless it can be barricaded, the majority of Perth's foreshore will be 'reclaimed' by the river, possibly reverting back to a pre-settlement landscape of rush beds and salt marshes. This would be a fitting affront for a city that has resolutely drained thousands of hectares of wetlands and river edges in order to create a tabula rasa for development and civic beautification. It is within this chastening context that a new generation of futures for Perth Water will need to be considered.

7.7 THE PREDICTED EFFECTS OF SEA-LEVEL RISE
ON PERTH, 2100

The Bell
Tower

Elizabeth
Quay

Map 8

WHITE CITY

Marcus Canning

Back in 2013 when we were developing the Fringe World Festival graphic identity for the year ahead, the team discussed what an authentic brand for Perth summer might feel like. The 'Lost Perth' Facebook page had recently appeared and become an overnight social media sensation, achieving over 40,000 likes in less than three weeks. We were duly impressed, and it became a rather kooky source of inspiration for the custom illustrations that then featured in the 2014 Fringe campaign. Two years later Lost Perth has passed 100,000 likes, has spawned two printed anthologies and a number of Channel 9 spin-off micro-documentaries, and Fringe World is now the third-largest Fringe festival on the planet and one of the fastest growing festivals in the world.

Both of these phenomena owe some of their success to the personality of Perth, which can at times be proudly parochial. Both have strong aspects of popular participatory theatre in their DNA. Of the two, it's Lost Perth that is the most nostalgic and sentimental, built from a collective social memory that is filled with the personal, the particular and swag loads of the peculiar. A trawl through its contents is a light shined bright on what Perth people think an authentic Perthonality is all about…and it's hardly the Grand Narratives of history. The weird UFO thing that perched on Leach Hwy in the 1970s features more than Government House; Fat Cat makes more appearances than any Governor. The Big Important Places named after Big Important People don't get much of a guernsey, but Perth's lost theme parks and other long-gone zones of ludic pleasure and leisure do…big time.

Remember Atlantis Marine Park? There's a dancing dolphin pod worth of mini-Mount Rushmoresque King Neptune photos. The drive-through Lion Park with the sign at the entrance, "Poms on push-bikes admitted Free"? The cable-car across scorched paddocks at El Caballo Blanco? Mandurah's mind-boggling mini-golf Neuschwanstein-inspired Castle Park folly? Dizzy Lamb Park with its petite Statue of Liberty in paddle-boat pond setting? Pioneer World with its Performing Pioneers? What about Pizza Showtime Theatre with its deranged bushwhacker piano-whacking animatronic singing kangaroo? For your sake, I hope not. That singing robot-roo with its animatronic eyebrows was sent from hell to traumatise young minds and bestow life-long hang-ups involving pizza and bush-dancing.

If you're a visitor to Perth and/or under the age of thirty, then none of these references will be ringing any bells for you. If you're a visitor to Perth and actually looking to ring some bells, like, literally, then head on down to the river's edge and visit The Bell Tower, Home of the Swan Bells, but don't expect an architectural marvel. The design of the tower has been likened to a cockroach humping a hypodermic, which could be cool in a Venturi's Duck kind of way if it were intentional, but it's not. Anyway, whilst we're down at the Esplanade, and thinking about the whole 'Less is More' vs. 'Less is a Bore' thing, let's talk about the surrounding Elizabeth Quay precinct and what came before.

The history of post-white invasion Perth has been played out along this strip of city frontage since the city was officially founded in 1829 just a little way up the hill near the Perth Town Hall. The river's edge has been a kind of historical litmus paper, registering the highs and lows of the social, cultural and economic fortunes and fabric of city and state. First thing to know, the shore is a total fabrication. The aptly named Old Court House near Council House is Perth's oldest surviving public building. Back in the day it had river waters lapping at its back steps and the Water Police boatshed as a neighbour. Reclamation of a scale that would make our Dutch as well as British forefathers ruddy with pride has occurred all along the riverbank since foundation, eventually followed by reclamation of the reclamation.

In 2012 Premier Colin Barnett and Minister John Day turned the first sod on a rather large excavation of colonial infill that would take the next three years to complete. Imagine if you will, the combined mass of 83,333 adult female Asian elephants. The equivalent in soil was removed from the Esplanade Reserve following the sod turning to create the Elizabeth Quay inlet that we enjoy today. On the city side, the edge of the quay is pretty close to where a rag-tag river-boat market ran in the infant decades of the city up until 1860s – Perth's first shopping mall – not that much shopping was going on back then. The utopic ideal of Australia's first convict-free/free white-settler colony had met the harsh reality-check of too few people trying to make ends meet in the most isolated backwater outpost in the Empire. The Swan River Colony was on the verge of financial dead duck.

Karl Marx refers to the fledgling failings of the Swan River Colony in his critique of colonisation contained in *Das Kapital*, published around the same time British penal transportation was wrapping up in the late 1860s, with Perth the last remaining Australian colony still an active participant. Governor Stirling had reached out the hand of desperation and grasped a convict lifeline at the start of the 1850s at the same time Queen Victoria was staging her Great Exhibition of the Works of All Nations in London's Crystal Place. All extant colonies, including the ugly duckling WA, had shown up and put on a display.

The Crystal Palace kick-started half a century of international expo fever and even Perth got its own poor man's version with the Perth International Exhibition of 1881, staged in a tin shed version of the Crystal Palace on the newly completed riverside Recreation Ground. This was the Esplanade's first major use and it saw more than 20,000 citizens pass through its doors from a scattered Perth population of under 31,000, with "the crowds of well-dressed sightseers upon the green slopes of the ground, and the blue waters of the river as a background beyond, forming, as a whole, a spectacle such as has never been witnessed in the colony before."[1] On the same spot in 2011 over 100,000 gathered from a population pushing 1.9 million to eat sausages, wave flags and try to catch a glimpse of Her Majesty Queen Elizabeth II and her cantankerous consort at the 'Big Aussie BBQ', a civic celebration similar to the Esplanade's Proclamation Day event of 1890. The latter was an enormous morning tea party where some of the crowd participated in a game fitting for the attaining of self-government – running after a greased-up pig and attempting to tackle it to the ground.

Self-government may have been bestowed, but WA's fortune was still entrenched in a squatocratic farming and frontier economy. From a prosperity point of view, the bacon wasn't properly brought home until 1893 when Paddy Hannan discovered gold near Kalgoorlie and sparked the rush that led to the state's population quadrupling over the next decade.

---

1   "International Exhibition," *The West Australian*, Tuesday 22 November 1881, p. 4.

This was the same year Chicago's gargantuan World's Columbian Exposition was held, popularly known as White City, a moniker that was then picked up and used to name thirty-one other semi-permanent fairgrounds across the globe over the ensuing decades. Twenty-seven of them were in the US, two were in the UK and two in Australia. One was in Sydney, but the one we're really interested in ran from 1922–1929 on the spot on the edge of Elizabeth Quay where the underground train station now disgorges commuters into the precinct.

Chicago's 1893 White City didn't derive its name from celebrating 400 years since Columbus discovered the 'New World' on behalf of the white hordes to follow, but rather due to its central architectural conceit. The Court of Honour at the exposition's heart was lined with monumental temporary buildings whose plaster of paris white stucco and design exuded an American Renaissance Neoclassical grandeur under the illumination of more light bulbs in a public space than ever previously used. The effect was blindingly white, thus the moniker White City. It was also unbelievably popular, with over 27 million visitors during its six months of operation. This popularity was fuelled largely by new inventions from the left field of the leisure industries on show at the fringe of the exposition.

Clustered along the mile-long Midway Plaisance park an assemblage of ticketed carnival entertainments, sideshow amusements and other somewhat illicit attractions had been put together by a twenty-three-year-old music entrepreneur called Sol Bloom. New and franchisable leisure pursuits that premiered on Chicago's White City Midway included hamburgers, juicy fruit chewing gum, a ticketed movie theatre in the form of Eadweard Muybridge's Zoopraxographical Hall and the world's first ferris wheel.

When Perth's White City was built some twenty years later, its organisers looked to the Midway rather than the Court of Honour for inspiration. They were the Ugly Men's Voluntary Workers Association, commonly known as the Ugly Men, and if they were around today, it's highly probable they'd be Lost Perth fans. They first formed in 1917 to help build houses for WWI war widows and as demands on their charitable efforts grew and diversified, so too did their entrepreneurial zeal.

Their first fairground was built in the gardens behind the Supreme Court, but due to the disturbance it wreaked on proceedings therein, a more permanent site was provided in 1922 down at the river's-edge end of William Street. Perth's White City was born, also known as Cooee City as well as Uglieland over its brief but significant history. During this time the Ugly Men also built and ran fairgrounds in Fremantle and the Goldfields. When it came to popular working-class nightlife action in 1920s Western Australia, the Ugly Men reigned supreme, not that they were a precursor for the mafias, mobs, MCs and Beer Barons that would come to control Perth entertainment precincts over the decades to follow. The Ugly Men shared the love, as well as the coin, with their efforts generating what would be valued today as close to $4 million dollars each year for underprivileged children and other social groups in need. The largesse of this charitable enterprise made the concerted and escalating attack against it by various Christian groups that followed inherently ironic, including the call by Chief Protector of Aborigines A. O. Neville to make White City…white.

Since opening, the fairground had been an 'open door' kind

of space where all were welcome. It was as popular with young Noongars as it was with the rest of the working-class populace. Neville found this egalitarianism to be highly unsavoury, and had even graver aspersions regarding young Noongar women, writing to the Police Commissioner that,

> There are a certain number of them who go there mainly for the purpose of inveigling some white man to accompany them somewhere else… It is my desire that neither half-castes nor aboriginals be permitted to frequent the White City on any pretext what so ever. It is simply debasing the natives, and the contests lower the status of whites in their eyes.[2]

His concerns fuelled the 1927 Prohibited Area declaration, which gave police the power to force Indigenous people not on 'lawful business' to leave the city, and it stayed in place till 1948.

A VISION OF WHAT FRANK VINCENT'S PROPOSED 120-HECTARE ISLAND FOR PERTH WATER MAY HAVE LOOKED LIKE TODAY

Excerpts from a vitriolic rant in the popular press of the day captures the varied concerns and sentiments about Perth's White City:

There still flourishes in the city a place which, at best is an architectural eyesore and a moral disgrace…[it] undoubtedly has a demoralizing

2 Quoted in S. Kinnane, *Shadow Lines*, Fremantle Arts Centre Press, 2003, p. 215; cited in State Library of Western Australia, *Swan River Stories*. http://www.slwa.wa.gov.au/swan_river/living_with_the_land/white_city.

influence over the younger of Perth's citizens…there is a relaxation of the proprieties which proves an irresistible lure…[It] contains a large open air dance floor on which youths, with their hats on their heads, perform intricate and sometimes immodest steps with young women whom probably they have never seen before…White City has proved to be a magnet for larrikins and loafers… Architecturally, it is an abomination…[It is] one of the few blots on the picturesque riverfront of Perth.[3]

By the time a deputation to the Premier demanding the permanent closure of White City was organised in 1927, groups rallying behind the cause included The Council of Churches, the Women's Guilds of WA Inc., the National Council of Women of WA, the Women's Christian Temperance Union of WA, the Young Women's Christian Association of WA, the Chamber of Manufacturers, the Y.M.C.A. the Argonauts, the Town Planning Association and the Institute of Architects.

Proceeds from White City in the week of this deputation were going to the Maimed and Limbless Men, referred to by the Ugly Men as the 'Wingies and Stumpies'. It was a war of social mores fought on the battle ground of political correctness and in the lead-up to WA's Centenary Celebrations of 1929, the morally high, if not mighty, won the day. White City hosted its last goat race and was torn down.

Fast-forward to 2016 and The Perth International Arts Festival has held the first of its series of 'festival garden' programs overlooking Elizabeth Quay, located just across the road from what was once the White City site. The public promenade

---

3   "WHITE CITY. Why It Must Go," *The West Australian*, Tuesday 29 November 1927, p. 14.

is open and surrounding private developments are underway, including the new Asia-Pacific headquarters for Chevron and Australia's first purpose-built luxury Ritz-Carlton Hotel. It could well be another decade before the entire scheme is wrapped and there will always be those who think it should have gone another way. As pointed out in a recently published history of the site, "the foreshore has been contentious since the first plan for Perth was drawn up. Indeed we estimate that well over two hundred proposals have been made for the Perth foreshore since the first identified plan in 1833."[4]

Elizabeth Quay is the scheme that finally made it to the table and it will continue to redefine Perth's relationship to its waterfront for years to come. As a nod to Perth's forgotten theme parks, I hope the planned cable-car to Kings Park eventuates. As a cultural back-turn to the shame legacy of the AO Neville administration, we can also hope that the landmark Indigenous cultural centre also proceeds. I'm pretty sure the Ugly Men would wholeheartedly agree.

---

4   J. Bolleter, *Take Me to the River: The Story of Perth's Foreshore*, Crawley: UWA Publishing, 2015.

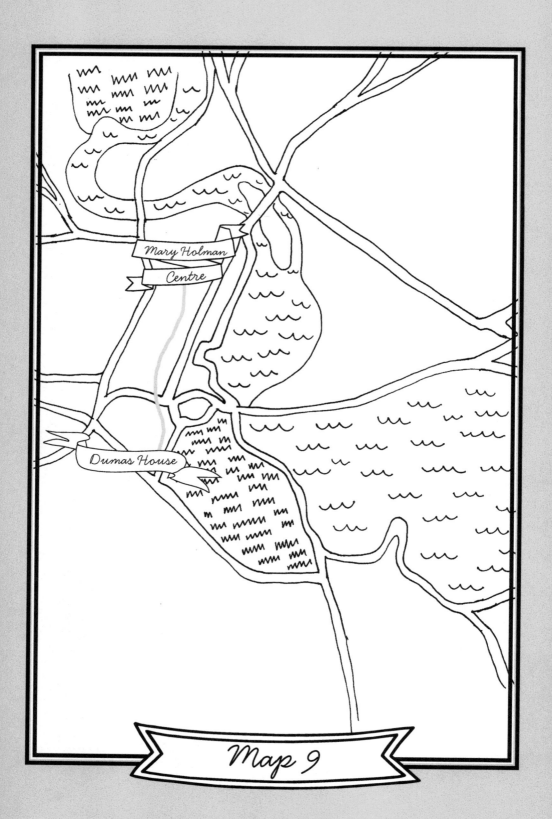

Mary Holman
Centre

Dumas House

Map 9

9

PERTH VISION

Peter Kennedy

On a quiet news day in the late 1980s, when *The West Australian* newspaper was temporarily housed in the Forrest Centre at 219 St Georges Terrace, a rather naive young reporter complained to the editor-in-chief, Bob Cronin, that "nothing is happening". Cronin's immediate response? "Get out on to the Terrace, and if you don't come back with three stories then you're not trying." And he was right. Perth was that sort of city where many of the newsmakers – business, financial, industrial and political – worked virtually cheek by jowl in the central business district. And most of them were striding the footpaths at some stage during the day, especially at lunchtime.

The West Australian's long-term home had been Newspaper House at 125 (now 129) St Georges Terrace and, when the afternoon *Daily News* was also being published there, it was media action central. *The West's* driving force for many years was managing director Jim Macartney – "JM" to his staff – who liked to make people jump. Coincidentally the accounting firm Hendry Rae and Court, leased offices at the front of Newspaper House. It might have been reasonable to assume that when one of the firm's partners, Charles Court, entered Parliament in 1953 as the Liberal MP for Nedlands, the geographic proximity of their offices would be to Court's advantage when it came to media coverage. Not so, at least early on. Macartney thought that the hard-driving Court was a "bit of an upstart" who had to be put in his place. Court found it hard to get a good run in *The West*. In fact in the early '60s when Court was the energetic Minister for Industrial Development and gave a strong story to the rival *Sunday Times*, Macartney fired off a letter telling him in no uncertain terms that *The West* was the paper of record, and all such stories had to be published first in his paper. They eventually came to an understanding, and by the 1970s – after Macartney had gone – Court enjoyed a good run in "the paper of record".

By way of contrast, *The Sunday Times* was "north of the line" in Stirling Street in the heart of union territory – Trades Hall was in nearby Beaufort Street, and was a hive of union activity. In the 1920s another newspaper, the *Westralian Worker,* which was owned by the Australian Workers' Union and edited by John Curtin, later Australia's wartime prime minister and a Labor hero, was also in Stirling Street. Before entering politics, Curtin had been state president (1920–25) of the Australian Journalists Association and got to know his members, including Frank Davidson from the very racy *Mirror*, who later edited *The Sunday Times*. At one stage the cadet journalists' represent-ative on the AJA's district committee was Paul Hasluck from *The West*. Curtin was impressed by Hasluck, and helped the ambitious journalist transfer to the Department of External Affairs (now Foreign Affairs) in Canberra. Hasluck eventually entered politics, coincidentally as the member for the new seat of Curtin (1949), became a long-term Menzies government minister and later governor-general.

Soon after I joined *The West* in 1970, I was assigned to the industrial round. I was advised to "get out of the office", which meant wearing out lots of shoe leather "on the beat". The unions in particular had a healthy suspicion of "the capitalist press", and it was considered that it would be to my advan-tage to meet their officials face to face. And it was. Covering fortnightly ALP executive meetings in the bowels of Trades Hall, I got to know the much feared party strong man, "Joe" Chamberlain, who had been a key figure in the acrimonious national Labor Party split in the mid-1950s. In fact, reporters waited outside the meetings to speak to delegates because, although Chamberlain said we were welcome, he wanted to vet our copy before we phoned our stories back to the office. That wasn't on, of course, and eventually he caved in.

Most days on the industrial round would start at the WA Industrial Commission, then housed at Vapech House at the western end of Murray Street. It was a hive of activity, and a great place to meet and talk with senior advocates from the unions – usually the secretaries – employers and the government. The commissioners also wielded a fair bit of power, with Bernie O'Sullivan – who mid-week doubled as the controversial football tribunal chairman – Eric Kelly and Bruce Collier becoming well known. Several of the advocates later became commissioners in the federal as well as the state tribunals, doubling as useful sounding boards for an industrial reporter.

One promotion was especially controversial. Jim Coleman had been the long-term secretary of the Trades and Labor Council, and was elevated to the post of Western Australia's first resident member of the Australian Conciliation and Arbitration Commission in the dying months of the Whitlam federal Labor government in 1975. Earlier that year, Coleman had disrupted a full bench hearing of the WA commission by reading a statement from the public gallery. This enraged O'Sullivan, who immediately adjourned proceedings and left the court. The incident didn't help achieve the desired smooth relations when Coleman joined the Commonwealth tribunal. In fact relations were downright frosty and, far from being housed in the same building as the state tribunal – as was considered desirable – quarters were found for Coleman at Lombard House, on the other side of the city in Adelaide Terrace. That was not only inconvenient for all the advocates but also industrial reporters. Today the two tribunals are, seemingly, happily ensconced at 111 St Georges Terrace, the site of the sensational WA Inc royal commission in 1991–92, which resulted in the jailing of two former premiers – one Labor, one Liberal – and a former deputy premier (Labor).

Vapech House is now owned by Liberal Party benefactor Terry Jackson, and became the home of the WA Liberal Party for many years, being rebadged as Menzies House.

(has become the home of the WA Liberal Party. The building has been rebadged, appropriately, as Menzies House.)

After leaving the hearings at Vapech House, I would head to the Trades Hall. Remember, these were the days before super unions, which led to many amalgamations in the early 1990s. Almost twenty unions were housed in the grand old building in Beaufort Street. The unions were right wing, left wing, and middle of the road. The union secretaries liked to test the wet-behind-the-ears industrial reporter from *The West*. One, from a public sector union, warned that if I reported him incorrectly, I needn't bother knocking on his door again. We established a good working relationship.

It's fair to say that industrial relations in the Pilbara's fledgling iron ore industry were out of control in the 1970s. It also became apparent that union officials based in Perth had little influence on events. Even avowed communists such as Jack Marks of the Amalgamated Engineering Union (he later mellowed and joined the Labor Party), who liked a bit of disruption, would sometimes throw their hands up in despair. The "pommy shop steward" tag gained popularity as many of the on-site officials linked with the disputes spoke with broad English accents.

In the mid-70s a group of businessmen decided enough was enough. They organised a well-supported anti-union lunch-time rally and marched to Trades Hall to denounce union disruption. Some of the marchers were my relations. I knew my resulting story would be carefully scrutinised. Balance was more important than ever!

At that stage the Labor Party was a significant landlord in Beaufort Street, owning the properties from the Trades Hall south to the Court Hotel. Construction of the multi-storey Curtin House was started during Labor premier John Tonkin's term (1971–74) and the building was jointly opened by Tonkin – by then back in opposition – and Gough Whitlam as prime minister, in April 1975. While in government, Tonkin had cunningly negotiated a deal for the Health Department to be a major tenant. This outraged Charles Court, by then Liberal leader, who said no Liberal MP would ever occupy the ministerial office in the building while it was owned by Labor. He was true to his word.

How times change. The Labor Party eventually sold these prized properties to service election, legal and other expenses. And the Court Hotel, far from being the pub for hard-nosed union officials to plan their next industrial campaign, is now a meeting place for the gay community. Ironically, Trades Hall, after several changes of ownership, is now back in union hands. It is owned by the very well-resourced CFMEU, which grew out of the merging of several bodies, including the Builders Labourers Federation, which had very modest facilities in Beaufort Street in the '70s.

Another change has been the demise of Forrest Place as the traditional lunchtime forum for election rallies. Robert Menzies, Bert Evatt, Arthur Calwell, John Gorton, William McMahon, Gough Whitlam, Bob Hawke, Bill Snedden and John Hewson all spoke at rowdy rallies. Post-war state leaders such as Ross McLarty, Bert Hawke, David Brand, John Tonkin and Charles Court did likewise. But things changed significantly in March 1974. Labor's state election rally in Forrest Place, with then PM Whitlam as the main speaker, attracted a massive crowd. But many were farmers, hostile at Whitlam's decision to phase out the superphosphate bounty. And they threw everything at him, including eggs, tomatoes, drink cans and pies. He was undaunted but police were relieved when his car drove off after the rally. They had feared for the PM's safety. The authorities then decided the Esplanade would be a safer venue for such rallies, and it was the beginning of the end for Forrest Place.

My last port of call in the daily round was often the WA Employers' Federation office in Adelaide Terrace, opposite the ABC (now in Fielder Street, East Perth). The employers, whose staff at one stage included premier Colin Barnett, have always favoured the eastern end of the city, and are now housed in a custom-built head office in Hay Street, near Queens Gardens. The opening of the building in February 2000 by prime minister John Howard gained more publicity than expected. Hundreds of construction workers from nearby projects downed tools to boo and hiss guests as they arrived. There was some uncertainty as to the response when Howard appeared. The protesters stayed in their area for the PM's arrival, but a police tactical response group with batons, helmets and shields appeared from nowhere and descended on, and harassed, the waiting media, me included. I won an award for my live description of these dramatic events on ABC Radio.

Naturally the dynamics of the central business district have changed. As works minister in the 1950s, John Tonkin's office was in the Old Barracks building at the top of the Terrace. Only the Arch remains. While Charles Court used to stride along the Terrace on Saturday mornings in the early 1960s from his old firm's accountancy office in Newspaper House to his ministerial office in the old Treasury building on the corner of the Terrace and Barrack Street, the ministers – and premier – later in the decade moved to the new Superannuation building (later May Holman Centre) at nearby 32 St Georges Terrace.

There was more change in 1984. Brian Burke as premier – and several ministers – shifted west to the new Capita building at 197 St Georges Terrace, closer to Parliament House. That was very convenient for *The West*'s reporters during the paper's brief shift to the Forrest Centre next door, before heading to their new home at Herdsman.

The Premier's office has stayed on the move too. Under Colin Barnett it shifted to a refurbished Hale House – widely known as the Emperor's Palace – in Parliament Place in 2012. And more ministers are now based in the revamped Dumas House in Kings Park Road.

Ministers can still be found in the CBD, although less frequently. I once ran into planning minister John Day on the Horseshoe Bridge. He was on his way to the museum in his capacity as arts minister. Looking west over the evolving Perth City Link project, he remarked at the rapid pace of change around the city, which now included multiple transport and pedestrian tunnels.

I thought that if the planning minister is finding the pace rapid, imagine what it's like for ordinary citizens. Regardless, reporters will continue to seek out the decision makers. That's one thing in the city that won't change.

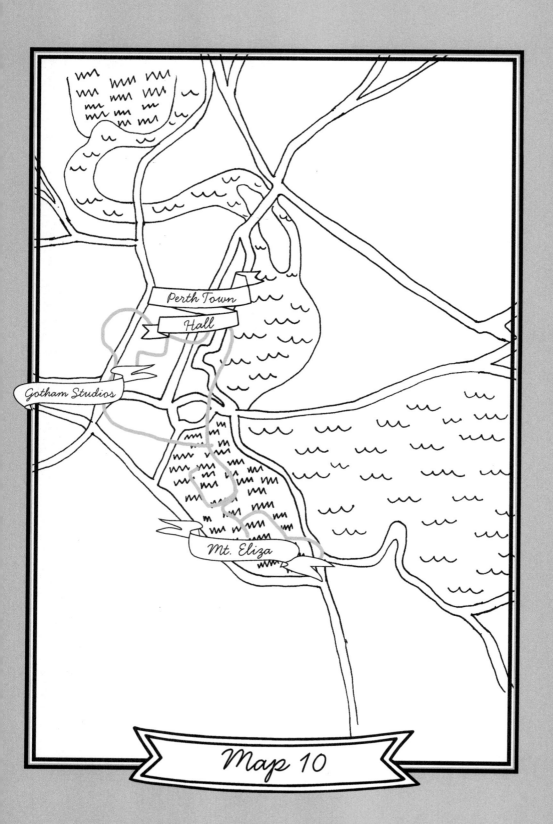

Perth Town Hall

Gotham Studios

Mt. Eliza

Map 10

10

PICTURING A CITY: THE EXPERIENCE OF PERTH

Clarissa Ball

Some time in 1935, Portia Bennett set up her easel in the heart of the city of Perth to work on her painting *Perth Town Hall* (Figure 9.1). Bennett's painting reveals that in the mid-1930s, the intersection of Hay and Barrack Streets was a commercial hub and the site of myriad incidents of daily life, much as it is today in 2015. Although Bennett's painting is of a modern city, the focus of her painting is the Perth Town Hall, the only town hall in Australia that was built by convicts. In 1935, Perth was still a young city but the inclusion of the Perth Town Hall in Bennett's cityscape immediately inscribes her work with a sense of history, albeit a history that is based in part on Western Australia's brutal penal background. Although the Perth Town Hall had been completed in 1870, only sixty-five years before Bennett captured this view, its central position in her image provides a 'then' and 'now' framework that speaks of the progress that had occurred between 1870 and 1935. With crisscrossing power and tram lines that frame the view of Town Hall, a tram travelling along Barrack Street near a stationary car, and an electric streetlight that sits above a shop front, Bennett's painting uses Perth Town Hall as a backdrop against which modern forms of transport, communication and energy provide compositional dynamism while animating the life of city dwellers. As a painting of contrasts between old and new, between nineteenth-century urban structures and twentieth-century modes of existence, Bennett articulates the transformative effects of modernity. Moreover, the implicit passage of time is emphasised by the conspicuousness of two of the Town Hall's four clocks, which clearly read 9.30.

Harald Vike's *Perth Nocturne* (Figure 9.2) of 1934 provides an illuminating contrast to Portia Bennett's *Perth Town Hall* and offers a very different insight into life in 1930s Perth. Although both works were painted within twelve months of each other, and both were painted from a slightly elevated point of view above an intersection in the centre of the city, these works are radically different in their facture and modernist sensibility. Bennett's painting shows the city at 9.30 in the morning, whereas Vike's painting portrays the city by

9.1 *PERTH TOWN HALL*, PORTIA BENNETT, 1935.

night. Bennett uses a relatively flat and restrained palette that gives her cityscape an air of uniformity, while Vike chooses a vibrant palette that creates an incandescent rhythm on this dark, moonless night. Bennett structures her painting so as to foreclose on an expansive view of the intersecting streets, while Vike extends his wide street deep into the picture plane in a manner reminiscent of nineteenth-century French paintings of Baron Haussmann's boulevards lined with shops and apartments. And, whereas Bennett foregrounds the power and tram lines to give structure to her painting, they are barely discernible in Vike's.

Like Bennett's *Perth Town Hall*, Vike's *Perth Nocturne* shows a major intersection in the city of Perth, the crossing of Barrack and Murray Streets, a site that is only one block to the north of Bennett's Barrack and Hay Streets. Although close in proximity,

9.2 *PERTH NOCTURNE*, HARALD VIKE, 1934.

perhaps only a two- or three-minute walk from each other, these two intersections could not be more different in their painted form. Similarly, there is little in these paintings to indicate that they were painted only a year apart from each other. One clue to the startling differences in these works, and in turn to the artists' different interests and engagements with urbanism and modernity, lies in the titles of the paintings. *Perth Town Hall* is, as its title suggests, an image of the Perth Town Hall and the accurate rendering of this building is Bennett's primary concern. The musically titled *Perth Nocturne*, on the other hand, not only draws an analogy with music but also recalls James McNeill Whistler's nocturne paintings of London, which are atmospheric, moody visions of a modern city at night when details and form lose precision and legibility.

Perth Nocturne is a strikingly modern painting in which Vike is pursuing entirely different goals to Bennett. The magical luminosity of the street lighting and the vivid glow that radiates out of the illuminated shop windows and from the lights of the car, create patches of brightness that animate the city streets. Here, modern technology is the source of light and it is technological, rather than natural forms of illumination that allow the groups of people who populate Vike's Perth by night to successfully navigate their way through the city. But it is not simply that lighting technologies transform the appearance of the urban landscape, nor is the passage of time of primary interest to Vike. Rather, it is the very experience of modernity, the unexpected sensations, encounters and possibilities that are inherent in modern urban spaces. Vike captures and articulates the marvel of these experiences with thick brushstrokes of rapidly applied oil paint that give form to the light as it reflects off the wet streets. In spite of *Perth Nocturne* portraying a very dark and wet night, it is a luminous painting that is activated and animated not so much by its narrative subject, as is the case with *Perth Town Hall*, but rather by its painterly incandescence and articulation of urban experience.

The Barrack and Murray Street intersection that Vike painted in 1934 is now unrecognisable but the Town Hall that forms the centerpiece of *Perth Town Hall* is still standing, thus rendering the location in Bennett's painting readily identifiable. As with all modern cities, Perth has been, and continues to be, in a constant state of change. Urban and spatial structures are endlessly renewed and reconfigured in response to changing needs, population growth and new technologies. The city skyline now bears no resemblance to that which would have confronted Bennett and Vike in the mid-1930s, a decade that saw the beginning of Perth's vertical expansion with the construction of its first skyscrapers and inner-city multi-storey apartment blocks. While Bennett and Vike might struggle to recognise vast sections of Perth were they to stroll its streets in the opening years of the twenty-first century, they would have little difficulty recognising Perth's natural landmarks if they looked to the south and west of their painted locations, towards the Swan River and Mount Eliza (Kings Park).

The Swan River and Mount Eliza have always proved popular subjects for artists, and views from Mount Eliza have been especially appealing since the elevated vantage point affords sweeping, uninterrupted views of the city and river below. Since the earliest days of the colony, artists such as Frederick Garling and Horace Samson have taken advantage of the outlook from Mount Eliza to show the expansion and transformation of the city and its immediate environs. Amongst the many images of Perth that have been painted from atop Mount Eliza, the work of Guy Grey-Smith stands out as unique precisely because his paintings *Perth City from Kings Park* (1948), *Perth from Kings Park* (1949), and *View from Kings Park* (c. 1949) (Figure 9.3) are not readily identifiable as scenes of Perth. Were it not for the titles, these paintings could easily be views of the south of France or northern Italy.

In his paintings of the city from Kings Park, Grey-Smith achieves a balance between abstraction and representation that belies topographical precision. The microscopic fidelity

9.3 *View from Kings Park*, Guy Grey-Smith, c. 1949-1954.

to the details of botanical and geographical forms that is so often a feature of landscape painting is discarded by Grey-Smith and gives way to more generalised effects and to suggestion rather than definition. The trees are not recognisable as eucalypts, the buildings are simplified into unidentifiable blocks of squares and rectangles, and the Swan River is rendered schematically. Grey-Smith's only concession to traditional ways of depicting landscape is the trees that are positioned in the foreground, on either side of each painting.

This device has many antecedents in depictions of distant views and can be seen in Garling's *View from Mount Eliza* (1827), Samson's lithograph *Perth, Western Australia, from Mount Eliza* (1852), Edith Trethowan's wood engraving *Mounts Bay Road Towards Perth* (c. 1931), and Irene Carter's *Perth from Kings Park, Western Australia* (c. 1945). The trees that stand to the left and right in each of these images frame the view, rather like a window frame, and give direction and focus to the distant prospect. This feature is put to dramatic effect in Grey-Smith's *View from Kings Park*: the vibrant red and orange tree trunk at the right of the painting forms an arc that echoes the curvilinear expanse of blue to the left and embraces the view beyond so that the deep recession that normally constitutes distant views is flattened. This spatial ambiguity is more pronounced at the left of the canvas where the trunks of two trees move in and out of the passage of modulated blue paint that represents the Swan River.

Grey-Smith's playful manipulation of perspectival space is equally apparent in *Perth City from Kings Park*, a painting that he undertook in the year of his return to Perth in 1948, after spending three years studying at the Chelsea School of Art in London. In this painting, the sequence of receding planes that lead the eye into the distance is abruptly disrupted by the cluster of buildings that are nestled beneath the fork of the tree at the right of the painting. These pale pink and light blue buildings are painted out of scale when considered in relation to the Darling Ranges that stretch along the horizon line and yet, within the overall compositional structure of the painting, the ratios and spatial relationships of the buildings do not strike as awkward.

In the broader historical context of images of Perth that have been painted from the vantage point of Mount Eliza, the work of Guy Grey-Smith attests to his determination to see things anew. His highly personal and experimental method departs from the mimetic function of earlier scenes of the city where the imposition of order on appearances is paramount. Grey-Smith's paintings make tangible the delight that he takes in the materiality and properties of paint, and his modern evocations of space, light, and the city reveal very different attitudes to those that underpinned the work of Garling, Samson, Trethowan and Carter. Their images function as an historical timeline, revealing the gradual growth of the city, its changing relationship to the Swan River, its evolving skyline, its developing urban infrastructure and its incorporation of new technologies. Their images provide a glimpse into the urban and social history of Perth from the early days of the colony through to the mid-twentieth century by which time the impulse to depict Perth as a site of civilisation and as an appealing destination for migrants was no longer a driving force of its visual representation. Such concerns are secondary to Grey-Smith, whose bold facture conveys a confidence not just in his exuberant manipulation of paint but perhaps too in his belief that, by mid-century, the city of Perth is becoming increasingly self-assured so that it no longer needs the visual self-confirmation that underpins the topographical accuracy and detailed precision of earlier images.

The shift of sensibility evident in Grey-Smith's paintings was a departure from an artistic tradition that portrayed the city as a site that was continually domesticating and civilising its surrounding landscape, features that are crucial to the idea of progress within an urban setting. Throughout history, cities have been literally and imaginatively constructed as spaces of progress, improvement and advancement. When Governor Weld officially opened the Perth Town Hall on 1 June 1870, the word 'PROGRESS' was written on an arch that stretched over Barrack Street near the Town Hall.[1] The potency of this gesture could not have been more explicit in its articulation of the link between the construction of new buildings and notions of progress.

For much of the twentieth century, visual representations of the city of Perth have tended to provide a celebratory confirmation of the belief that its urban structures are signs of progress. The idea of progress resides not just in newly constructed buildings or urban renewal projects, but also in those buildings that have been deemed worthy of preservation and thus exempted from demolition. The decision to retain certain buildings is a means of ordering and systemising history but is more frequently understood as evidence of a civil, progressive society. In the 1980s, a group of young artists produced a body of work in which buildings that have since been demolished figured prominently. But the paintings of Tom Alberts, Richard Gunning, Thomas Hoareau and André Lipscombe do so much more than depict mere reflections of what Perth looked like in the 1980s. In their paintings, urban structures resonate as sites of profound personal significance, as places that house memories and layers of experience.

---

1   T. Stannage, *The People of Perth: A Social History of Western Australia's Capital City*, Perth City Council, Perth, 1979, p. 195.

Earlier artists had tended to paint the city from a detached elevated position, like Mount Eliza or from a location slightly above streets such as St George's Terrace or Murray Street. From these remote positions, artists were able to provide panoramic views of the city, or long, distant views of its streets. In the 1980s, Alberts, Gunning, Hoareau and Lipscomb adopted a very different perspective and zoomed in on the inner city from where they painted intimate, close-up scenes that featured all sorts of incidental events that constitute the fleeting and ephemeral nature of urban experience. The telescopic perspective of their paintings is not surprising given that many of these artists established studio and living spaces in the heart of the city from where they witnessed on a daily basis, and at a minute level, the rapid and widespread transformations taking place around them.

The 1980s was a decade of extraordinary change and innovation that facilitated greater patronage of local artists and saw increased, better-informed critical discussion of Western Australian art. The moribund WA Arts Council was replaced by the Western Australian Department of the Arts; the Perth Institute of Contemporary Art was provided with start-up funds and a building in the Perth Cultural Centre; artists were provided with subsidised studio spaces such as Gotham Studios; state funding for the visual arts increased and new funding schemes enabled more artists to take-up fellowships, grants and scholarships. Also, in 1983, the University of Western Australia established the Centre for Fine Arts which, under the inaugural Head of Department, David Bromfield, soon began to publish new research in Western Australian art history. Betty Churcher was appointed as the new director and John Stringer the new senior curator at the Art Gallery of Western Australia, and local businessman and art collector Robert Holmes à Court was appointed to the Chair of the Gallery Board of Trustees.[2] Under their leadership, the support of local artists became a key priority and with new funding initiatives and a strong interest in Western Australian art history, Perth-based artists found themselves working in a far more supportive and vibrant cultural context than ever before.

It was also a decade that witnessed another economic boom and, as is often the case during times of economic prosperity, a number of older buildings were demolished to make way for high-rise towers. The 1980s opened with the demolition on St George's Terrace of the Colonial Mutual Life building which, at fourteen storeys, is regarded as Perth's first skyscraper. At the western end of St George's Terrace the Oddfellows and Arbordale Flats were demolished, as were two other residential complexes, Bishop's Grove and St George's Mansions. Between Murray and Wellington Streets, Forrest Place was extensively redeveloped and, to make way for the Forrest Chase retail complex, the Padbury Buildings, the Angus and Robertson bookshop and Boans department store were just some of the buildings demolished. In the same vicinity, a little further to the east on Wellington Street, the Imperial Hotel was demolished. In the 1980s, all of these sites made their appearance in the paintings of Alberts, Gunning, Hoareau and Lipscombe. The Oddfellows Flats, where both Gunning and Hoareau lived and worked from late 1982, appears in Gunning's *My Studio*

---

2   A. Archer, *After "The Time of Dark Swirling in Flatland": The Emergence of a New Generation of Perth Artists 1980–1993*, Unpublished MA Thesis, School of Architecture and Fine Arts, University of Western Australia, 1996, pp. 7–23 *passim*.

(c. 1984) and *Studio No. 3* (1984). Across the road from the Oddfellows Flats was Bishop's Grove, where Hoareau relocated and whose flat was later occupied by Lipscombe when Hoareau moved in 1985. Bishop's Grove can be seen in Hoareau's *Where Does The Bishop Live?* (1984) and *Big Head Overlooking City* (1986), and in three works by Gunning, *Bishop's Grove, Bishop's Grove Study* and *Bishop's Grove in Spring Time*, each painted in 1984. Lipscombe portrays the construction of Forrest Chase in *Forrest Centre Construction Site* (c. 1986) and a short walk from this location was the Imperial Hotel, which Hoareau painted in *The Land that Time Forgot* (1989).

These paintings, along with many others produced during this decade of economic, urban and cultural transformation, represent the city as something more than a series of descriptive streetscapes. For these artists, the city is a site of personal mythologies, a space where shared metropolitan experience co-exists with the brief, fleeting encounters that constitute urban existence. In works such as Hoareau's *Lovers Business as Usual* (1988) (Figure 9.4) and Alberts's *As the Crow Flies* (1989), (Figure 9.5) the emphasis is as much on urban experience as it is urban appearance, and this attempt to convey the fabric of human relations within the urban milieu gives these works a density of meaning that is so often absent from images of Perth. These paintings, along with Lipscombe's *Perth Figure* and *City and Figure*, Hoareau's *Man on Fire*, and *Goin Home*, all of 1986, and Alberts's *Untitled* (1989), speak of the spontaneous and disjointed nature of urban experience and the often bizarre, dream-like encounters that make up urban existence. The mixture of immediacy and distancing, the stable and the fleeting that pervades the work of this group of artists is set against a built environment that itself speaks notions of permanence and impermanence. With buildings in various stages of construction and destruction, with skylines and horizons punctuated by cranes and scaffolding, and with fully intact buildings standing alongside fragments

9.4 *Lovers (Business As Usual)*, Thomas Hoareau, 1988.

or discarded remnants of structures, these artists forego the quaintly picturesque stability that marked earlier representations of Perth to focus on the transient and ephemeral qualities of twentieth-century urban existence.

A twenty-first century viewer might consider the urban images by Alberts, Gunning, Hoareau and Lipscombe in much the same way that historians now approach the work of Portia Bennett,

Amy Heap or Irene Carter, to ascertain the changing face of Perth and to rediscover those buildings lost in the processes of urban transformation. While it is true that all of these artists provide visual evidence of the cycle of destruction and construction that has always been a defining feature of cities, the work of Alberts, Gunning, Hoareau and Lipscombe

9.5 *As the Crow Flies*, Thomas Alberts, 1989.

does something more than nostalgically bear witness to 'days gone by'. Their images of Perth in the 1980s resonate with a familiarity that goes beyond the built environment to speak to the ways in which personal memories are forged out of urban experiences. For these artists Perth forms a backdrop, and sometimes a very theatrical backdrop, as is the case in Alberts's *As the Crow Flies* or Hoareau's *Lovers Business as Usual*, which is rich with allusions that relate to personal experience. These personal experiences, memories and mythologies emerge not just from one's relationship to particular buildings but equally, and perhaps more so, out of the sensations, feelings and perceptions that accrue as one navigates the city streets. The advertising hoardings and discarded shop signs, the man who sleeps on the footpath in *As the Crow Flies*, the snippets of conversation that one overhears as seen in Hoareau's paintings, the poignancy of lovers who passionately kiss in front of the railway station, the discomfort that attaches to a man eagerly staring at a female nude encased in a window vitrine, the wistful stare of a young woman standing in isolation, the jarring collisions of scale that see an enormous naked man loom large against and beyond the city skyline – this is metropolitan life, memory and personal mythology.

In the opening decades of the twenty-first century, when Perth is again undergoing massive urban transformation with the building of Elizabeth Quay on the riverfront and the sinking of the railway line that will connect the centre of the city with Northbridge, all of the paintings discussed in this essay reveal what Perth was once like. Each painting reveals something of historical value in the record they provide about Perth's urban formation and transformation. However, with occasional exceptions, such as the work of Harald Vike, it is not until the 1980s that representations of Perth go beyond mere appearances to convey the experience of walking its streets. This is not to suggest that earlier representations of the city have no value, for clearly they do. They chart population growth, shifts in urban design, changes in technology and urban infrastructure, evolving gender relations and shifts in spatial politics, and even often overlooked aspects such as changes in fashion and car design. The urban images of the 1980s artists, however, go beyond the facades of the built environment to explore the nature of metropolitan experience, to uncover the complexity of human relations in an urban setting and to convey modes of sensory existence in the urban milieu. On the one hand, the images by Alberts, Gunning, Hoareau and Lipscombe represent a city that is now as unrecognisable as that painted by Bennett, Carter and Heap. On the other hand, the city represented by the 1980s artists continues to be entirely recognisable precisely because the ephemeral nature of urban existence, with its fleeting, spontaneous and disjointed encounters, remains as familiar in the twenty-first century as it was in the closing decades of the twentieth century. Even though Perth no longer looks as it did in the 1980s, strolling through its streets is an experience that, in many ways, replicates the perceptual and sensory experiences of Alberts, Gunning, Hoareau and Lipscombe. It is this aspect of their work that renders the city of bygone days so familiar.

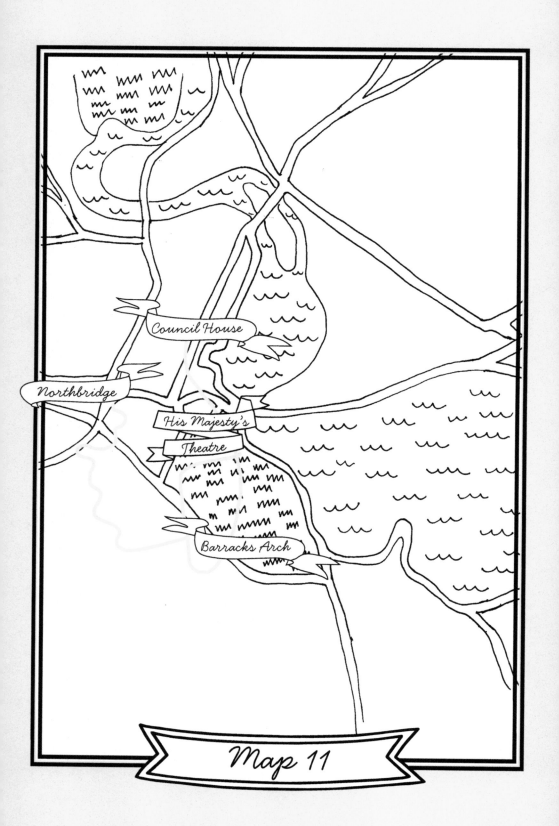

Council House

Northbridge

His Majesty's

Theatre

Barracks Arch

Map 11

11

BRIGHT LIGHTS: LIVING IN PERTH

Diana Warnock

It's no surprise that as a kid from the country (Kookynie, between Menzies and Leonora on the goldfields) I should have found Perth my own personal Aladdin's cave in the 1950s. It's more difficult to explain why, more than fifty years later, I still find the city my own special place.

It is, after all, an immense, underpopulated flat suburban sprawl: from north to south, Perth is almost the size of London or Paris, with only a fraction of the population of those great European cities. What, then, is the secret of my continuing enthusiasm?

A confession: I am a complete city addict. From the time I arrived at the door of my inner-city flat – "Suit professional lady, 8 pounds a week" – I was smitten. With the desert's red dirt still in my veins, I loved feeling the pavement under my feet and the buildings close beside me; I even loved the distant sound of the traffic at night and the sense of life all around. I was a young journalist, on the 'main drag'. It was the bohemian life!

Unusually, then, I am a long-time inner-city resident, fifteen minutes on foot from the old General Post Office in Forrest Place. For almost all of my adult life I've lived where most Perth people don't, and I'm still totally in love with the experience.

For most of that time I lived there with another passionate city dweller, the late Bill Warnock. Born in Glasgow's legendary Gorbals, an area plagued by poverty and gang crime, Bill arrived in Perth in 1948 and was an Australian by conviction (I used to say he was fifty per cent Irish, fifty per cent Scottish and one hundred per cent Australian). He often quoted his father John McKay Warnock, who said on arrival in Perth: "Don't tell anybody, son, but I think we've arrived in Paradise".

It is true that Perth is a tiny human hub very far away from the rest of the world. But it is hard to ignore its startling physical beauty, its superb climate and its laid-back, almost too-relaxed, way of life.

Consider the Swan River, mirror-still and misty on a winter's morning, its waterside buildings catching the blaze of the setting sun in summer. Consider King's Park, that magnificent patch of green on top of Mount Eliza, full of runners, walkers or wandering tourists, the 'dress circle' of this small New World capital. Think of the buffeting sea breezes in summer and cold easterlies from the vast inland desert in winter.

Where else in the world can you surf and swim in a clean, clear blue-green ocean twenty minutes from the central business district of a capital city?

Sometimes, walking into this small city from its western edge on a still-warm summer Friday evening, you can hear laughter from young office workers in street cafes and bars, pavements pulsing with bright talk and exhilaration at the week's end.

And sometimes, swinging through Northbridge (the Soho or Pigalle of Perth) in the early evening, before the late-night drinkers move in, it can seem like a much larger city, with a buzz of activity from the State's art gallery, cafes and pubs, the museum, the Chinese, Greek and Italian restaurants, the library and the central train station, each drawing its own particular crowd.

For an arts lover, though, the city comes especially alive during the summer arts festival, the longest-established in Australia. Eagerly awaited each year, the Perth International Arts Festival fills both city streets and theatres with acrobats, dancers, musicians and performers from around the world, with sights and sounds to lift the heart and dazzle the mind. Total magic!

For a long time Perth's story was one of constantly vanishing heritage, buildings both distinguished and merely familiar disappearing in a cloud of demolition dust, usually following a mining boom. The old Esplanade Hotel, the old colonial barracks at the top of St George's Terrace, the old Emu Brewery in Spring Street...these and countless others suffered a similar fate.

Now, however, something has changed for the better. Look at His Majesty's Theatre, its creamy Edwardian elegance standing out at the corner of King Street, the street itself now a historic precinct, filled with beautifully restored nineteenth-century buildings. Those buildings are now home to high-end boutiques with famous European names and to very smart apartments. Now, like many Perth streets, King Street is alive with Saturday morning cyclists, heading for their favourite coffee shops.

There is a great bustle now, too, created by inner-city developments on St George's Terrace, which include restaurants, cafes, bars and art galleries in and around the former Technical College and Newspaper House. There, a long-time building site has turned into an exciting, pedestrian-friendly area. And look at the former Cardigan Boarding House at the top end of the Terrace: it's undergone a fabulous metamorphosis into the glamorous Terrace Boutique Hotel. Bishop's House in Spring Street, with its large garden, now houses a high quality restaurant. Perth's guardians, it seems, are getting smarter.

Among those guardians was Bill Warnock, co-founder of the urban think-tank CityVision, a group of enthusiastic volunteers (architects, planners, designers) who simply wanted to see a more exciting, inclusive and significant capital for Western Australia. CityVision wanted to see thousands more people living in the city centre; they wanted to see better heritage preservation, better streetscapes and more street art, better public transport, more flexible trading hours, more small bars and cultural facilities, and much more vibrant street life.

The dialogue about Perth's future has been taken up by politicians, citizens, newspapers and numerous groups devoted to the city centre. Many owe their origin to the visiting Danish planner Jan Gehl. This shared adventure has made Perth a much more vibrant city in the twenty-first century.

CityVision is especially proud of the successful popular campaign it led for the preservation of the award-winning 1960s building, Council House, home of the Perth City Council. Now handsomely restored, it continues to stand boldly in the 'colonial precinct', that area housing Government House, the old Supreme Court, the Anglican Cathedral of St George, the old Treasury building and the historic convict-built Town Hall.

Now let me take you for a walk down my street. It is summer and the jacaranda trees – beautiful replacements for the much-maligned Queensland box trees – are like a low cloud of purple. The street furniture is jarrah and Federation green…this is a tourist precinct now! The quickly warming summer morning has flushed out a screaming mass of cicadas and the bird life is remarkable for the inner city. Apart from the ubiquitous ravens and doves, there are parrots, honeyeaters, willy-wagtails and plovers. These seem to remain safe from the street's over-fed cats.

Hitting the Terrace at a vigorous pace, I am surrounded by both the present life of the city and my own 'remembrance of things past'. I see the low-rise flats where my grandparents lived in retirement; the old hotel that was the scene of a memorable romantic assignation; the grand old Adelphi where fashionable country wedding receptions were held. All gone now, but replaced by elegantly cool canyons of glass and steel.

Walk a little further and you pass the sadly truncated Palace Hotel (now a bank), the place where the Rep coffee shop once stood, with its exotic fruit sundaes, and Howard Street which was the site of the Shiralee, the 1960s music-and-coffee-hangout. Happily, this tiny street is once again a hive of small bars and places to meet.

Walk across town via Barrack Street and you pass the spot where the Liberty Cinema used to be, venue for "Continental films" before the art-house movie houses opened; walk a little further on and you find the former site of the famous Coffee Pot, late-night meeting place of the young and trendy (before the latter word was invented).

These and many others are for me haunted by the friendliest of ghosts, and so many have been replaced by things that add richness and interest to Perth, such as the newly splendid Treasury Hotel and the refurbished Cathedral Square, that they must be celebrated.

And what of Perth's future? What will a future young city enthusiast find to like or even love about our west coast capital? What will be his or her pleasures and delights?

I predict an ever-increasing population will share the city's pleasures and delights; the restaurants, bars and cafes will offer a bewildering range of choice for business or romantic meetings, and new hotels will display the utmost service and sophistication. The arts, as always, will greatly enrich the lives

of both residents and visitors, with festivals, famous entertainers and home-grown creative activity.
Cities. The greatest human invention after language!

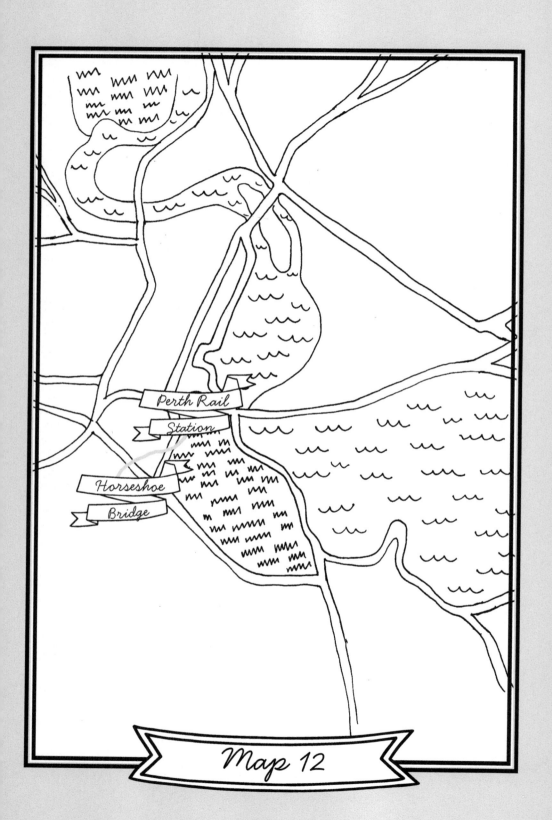

Perth Rail
Station

Horseshoe
Bridge

Map 12

12

SIDINGS

Paul Carter

A city like Perth might be traversed in many ways. A mobile view of the city obtained from almost any form of mechanised transport creates a fishbowl illusion. Streetscapes either side tend to wrap round the vehicle, swelling up left and right and ebbing away behind. A comparable sense of curvature nested inside the city's rectilinear scaffolding can be experienced simply by standing before a wall and keeping one's head motionless while swivelling the gaze alternately left and right: the width of the wall looks bent like an incipient rainbow. Within different modalities of apprehending our built surroundings, the body asserts its spherical consciousness. Letting the projective constructions of the eye guide our perception of our surroundings, we enter a world of hollows. Concavities begin to dimple street endings, while previously funnelling perspectives drawing to a vanishing point suddenly swell, their billowing convexities nearly shutting off passage. Once the threshold of contemplating oneself in the picture has been crossed, the city is seen to host plural perspectives. It becomes difficult to have patience with paintings still painted as if walls were flat or depths boxlike

"It seems inevitable that curves must eventually constitute the basic language for picturing our rectangular world of boulevards and buildings and boxes," writes painter Robert Hansen.[1] But the same thought might be applied to the historical construction of place. Perth, for example, is predominantly a grid formation laid over and across a curvilinear system of seasonally flooding creeks, billabongs and associated lake systems. The historical rationale of Perth – the notion of beginnings, growth, renewal

---

1   Robert Hansen, 'Translator's Foreword', Albert Flocon & André Barre, *Curvilinear Perspective: From Visual Space to Constructed Image*, Berkeley: University of California Press, 1987, p. xxii.

that provides the mythos of public planning – is the temporal expression of the grid: one thing leads to another logically, one exposure or section of the city very much like another. The Marxist philosopher Ernst Bloch complained that "Conventional history does not recognise the problem of variable dimensions of time, let alone that a nonrigid concept of time itself might be called-for on the basis of the variant distribution of the historical matter." The city is warped temporally as well as spatially: just as it has a perceptual topography, so it has an emotional history. Whitefella history in Perth very often walks over the dips and hollows of Aboriginal spacetime without even noticing it.

A case in point is the continuing custom of marking passage along the walls that adjoin the railway track east of Perth's Central Railway Station. I am led to believe that the custom of leaving a signature, monogram, tag or other flourish goes back to the period of Nyoongar exclusion from the city centre. The policing of a Prohibited Area (1927–1954) disrupted ordinary social routine and circulation. The new margins created in this way became meeting places that were inevitably also sites of protest. Rectilinear and curvilinear world views clashed: a statement that applies with particular force in Perth where the exertion of control over the movements and interactions of Aboriginal peoples had its notorious precedent in the efforts of the government to stop [Fanny] Balbuk from visiting her traditional hunting ground (a swamp located where Perth's Central Railway Station now stands). Ignoring the consolidation of the grid, Balbuk persisted in walking direct, steering a straight course from Heirisson Island to the place where the jilgies or crayfish were to be found: Through fences and over them, Balbuk took the straight track to the end. When a house was built in the way, she broke its fence palings with her digging stick and charged up the steps and through the rooms. Time and again she was arrested....'[2]

An essay about Perth's street art could make the case that these (usually dated) signatures represent an unusual variation (or reversion) in urban graffiti practice. The authorship of the elaborate wall art north and south of the railway sidings is unclear. In any case, the signatures (sometimes in texta, sometimes scratched through the paint to the white underlay) sit amid the jungle of near phosphorescent arabesques like tiny canoes amid the billows of a stormy sea. They are tiny, easily overlooked – but located against the brightest backgrounds where they will be most easily seen. The aim is not to overlay the wall designs but to *colonise* them; the wall becomes an open diary of comings and goings – prominent Nyoongar families are represented here, through names that are supplemented or deleted on a day-to-day basis. A kind of invisibility in full view is cultivated, rather like the stratagem described in Edgar Allan Poe's short story, *The Purloined Letter*, where the treasure or valuable information is, as it were, concealed by not being concealing. In Poe's famous detective story, the letter in question is over-written and refolded to suggest its worthlessness. The detective narrator of the story sees through this disguise, however, correctly perceiving that the 'hyperobtusive situation of the object' is a double feint – a document of invaluable political significance being disguised as unobtrusively valueless.[3] Some of the tags express this paradox stylistically. For instance, a

---

2 Daisy Bates, *Passing of the Aborigines*, London: John Murray, 1957, 70.

3 Edgar Allan Poe, "The Purloined Letter," in *Tales of Mystery and Imagination*, Herotfordshire: Wordsworth Editions Limited, 1993, pp. 133–143.

relatively flamboyant piece of calligraphy will select a colour that blends into the background. It is frequently the case that signatures are grouped within panels of colour, presumably on the flock principle that there is safety in numbers: if you know where to look, the name of interest will soon appear; to the outsider, a swarm of signatures is confusing.

The double perspective evidenced here has its urban counterpart. The broad contrast between the city of straight lines and the city of hollows finds expression in the contradictory nature of the current commercial advertising hoardings, examples of which are also conspicuous along the narrowing edges of Roe Street and Wellington Street due east of Perth Central Station. Hoardings, in the traditional sense, are things that are hoarded. Treasure is hoarded, and because of its value, hidden out of sight. In a curvilinear society, as it were, the hoard belongs in the uttermost hollow. By contrast, our contemporary sense of hoarding associates the term with maximum exposure. How was the meaning of the word turned inside out? Perhaps different words are involved. Alternatively, the materialisation of the hollow – as the wall, scaffolding, fence or boarding that encloses, protects and secures the treasure – inevitably creates a wall or side with two faces. One encloses, the other exposes. I suppose the function of the advertising hoarding is to draw attention to a treasure, a commodity that might otherwise go unnoticed. There is a peculiar pathos about the freestanding billboard, proof against cyclone but essentially empty, its elaboration of struts, braces and lighting supporting a structure that shelters or otherwise possesses nothing.

An alternative navigation of Perth begins with a recognition that the wall is a side. To the immediate east of the Perth

Central Station, walls amplify or multiply the sidings within the railway precinct. In this other experience of inner Perth these surfaces are not the fortification of property interests; they can be compared to the frictional coefficient of two surfaces rubbing against each other. They are edges – a term that carries with it the counter association of 'edging along'. Together with sharpness, there is the sideways manoeuvre of balancing one's way across a cliff. In the eye of prejudice the city can feel like this. How did Balbuk take the straight track to the end? Not by a wholesale demolition of fences but, I imagine, by the removal of the weakest paling, and slipping sideways through the gap. Exposure of the side of the person was critical to this transgressive subterfuge. A certain roundness of hip threaded the palings, set like prison bars in her path. Balbuk faced the grid with strategic directness, cultivating a straightness foreign to her walking style – in general, Daisy Bates relates, Balbuk followed the curving track responsive to the lie of the land. Her direct path was not scored across the grid: it remained seasonal, rhythmically aligned to the turning of the year, sidereally accomplished as well as tactically astute.

The other Perth of hips and hollows, of serpentine surfaces, does not accept the category of vacancy. Its embodied perception of place is all humming, the air dense with emotional fibres, the signatures quickly inscribed in passing, critical to retaining the tradition of the trace. Without the impressionable surface, the wall that in the mobile eye of the passenger swells and contracts, no evidence of the passion would be available to outsiders – passion, passing but also suffering. The tags written and rewritten into the walls notate the secret traffic of families whose historical trauma remains unwritten in the official record. These are sidings in an active sense: no empty passenger carriages await their appointed hour along the paths in and out of Perth. Writing accompanies the passage, not conforming to a timetable but writing it. Traffic is said to be derived from a Latin compound (*trans* + *fricare*) meaning cross friction, as if crossing the road were a source of conflict. The permanent way of the railway track preserves no sign of this crossing or the emotion associated with it; its welded ribbon rails could go on forever. But something nevertheless crosses them, a different way of sliding through invisible spaces (for in the eye of the Aboriginal beholder, the city might not exist).

A late Latin word exists, *frictiare*, meaning "walking and leaving footprints (just like animals do)." It has a strange counterpart in a Nyoongar word: *bidi*, meaning "A vein; the main path, or track, pursued by the natives in passing from one part of the country to the other, and which leads by the best watering places; also a sinew."[4] The tags along the paths east of the station belong to a different culture, one that counts the cost of passing. What possible truck can it have with vanishing points and vanishing lines? A different perspective has remained essential, observable whenever we dare to register what we see with our bodies. The pioneer of curvilinear perspective as an artistic technique, Albert Flocon, recalled his escape from "the thunderclap of the thousand-year Reich" and his absorption into Paris: Thus the life of the refugee, the exile (from the Latin *exsilire*, to jump out, to be shut out). And suddenly one sees everything inside from the outside. So, in

---

4   George Fletcher Moore, *A Descriptive Vocabulary of the Language in Common Use amongst the Aborigines of Western Australia,* published with *Diary,* Part 1, 8, under letter B, London: Wm. S. Orr & Co., 1892.

Perth, down by the railway tracks, exiles in their own country might see the inside of things; and the city that the gridded imagination considered so secure might wobble, groan and slide into the pattern on the flanks of the snake.

None of these marks was legible when I began working on Perth's Yagan Square project in 2013. For the stranger in a foreign country these human accompaniments had to be walked into being; noticed in passing, they were at first like those flocks of pigeons whose spiraling ascents may outline architectural surfaces you cannot see; then the faint traces of the deeper tracks they sprang from began to hum and resonate. Later, the invitation to help the Metropolitan Redevelopment Authority, the architects and landscape architects of Yagan Square find the storylines that might thread the new place led to the idea for an artwork known as *Passenger*. Originally, it had been called *G/host* in allusion to the perennial hosts of the place and to the shadow their presence cast on my approach. The idea developed into a form that hovered between divinity and doorway: a hollowed human figure that combined authority and absence. Impressed into the surfaces of Yagan Square, the seven manifestations of *Passenger* are both a homage to those who have gone before, and, in their resolute disruption of obstacles to passage, a way forward that does not forget the dictum No man can walk abroad save on his own shadow.[5] No woman either.

---

5   Sir Walter Raleigh, quoted by Sir Herbert Read, 'The Personality of the Poet', in *Selected Writings of Herbert Read*, London: Faber & Faber, 1963, p. 81.

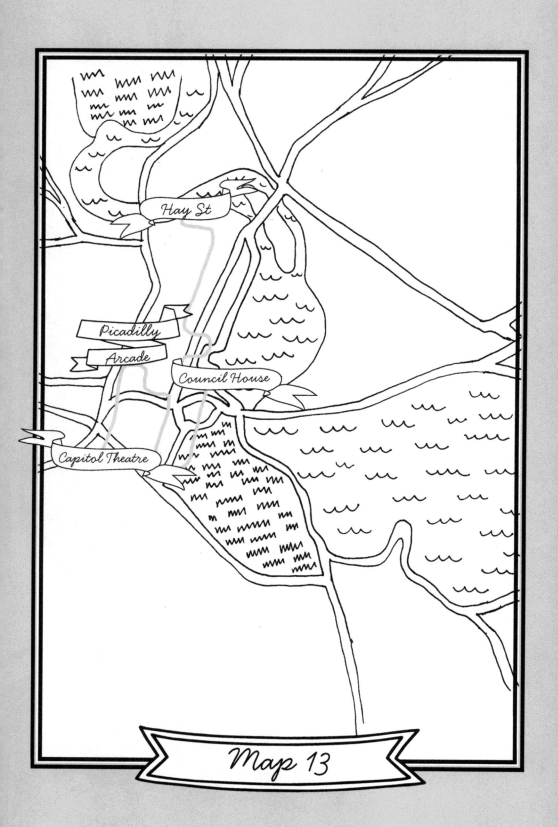

Hay St

Picadilly
Arcade

Council House

Capitol Theatre

Map 13

13

URBAN REFLECTIONS

Geoffrey London

In 2015 the city centre of Perth is undergoing major change and the momentum of this change will continue for years to come. Apart from the bulge of new apartment buildings on the eastern axis of the city, there are three significant current projects: the City Link, connecting the city to Northbridge across a new section of sunken rail; Elizabeth Quay, providing an activated new waterfront for Perth; and Riverside, a revitalised new eastern gateway into the city. These will, together, introduce an unprecedented number of new apartments, new quality office space, new entertainment facilities, and lively street life. They are truly city-changing projects. Perth will be more populated around the clock, more urban, more vital, safer, and offer its residents and visitors a rich variety of uses. In many respects, although at a different scale, this is a return to a previous condition, one that was in place before Perth became, for a period from the 1970s, a business and retail centre and little more. Encouraged by planning regulations and the profit incentives offered by plot ratios, inner-city residents and the amenities that supported them were emptied out in favour of new office space. This is my reflection on a time when I was closely engaged with the city of Perth, from 1966 to 1972, during an earlier period of urban vitality, and was able to enjoy its pleasures.

The central business district of Perth, one of the most sprawling suburban cities in the world, has undergone significant change since the mid-1960s when, as a student enrolled at the Perth Technical College (PTC) to study architecture, I came to know the city well. The PTC sat squarely on St George's Terrace, between William and Mill Streets, a very central city location. I spent two years in the old PTC before moving on to the newly established architecture course at The University of Western Australia. During these two years in the city, I embraced and explored central Perth, becoming a keen student of the city and it's architecture.

It wasn't long before 1966 that our mothers gave up wearing gloves and hats to 'go to town'. 'Town' was that special place for which you dressed up, where you went for a night out, a place of civic and commercial circumstance. It was where the spectacular film theatres were located, in the days when attending a film was afforded a great sense of occasion: among them was the highly decorated Ambassadors with a spectacular interior that simulated the elaborate setting of a Florentine walled garden; the Plaza (then Paris) where, as a younger boy, I had seen *South Pacific* and endured the attempt to create a tropical atmosphere from scents pumped through the air conditioning system; the Piccadilly, the Royal and, to me, the most glamorous of them all, the Art Deco Metro on William Street. The cinemas, convenient to PTC, enabled viewing of newly released films and often the times between, after, and sometimes during classes were taken up by films. To me, there has always been a link between film and architecture – the concept of space, the use of light, the creation of a value-laden constructed world – as attested by the regular presence of architecture students at the city cinemas.

In 'town' was where I saw Bob Dylan for the first time, at The Capitol Theatre. The Capitol was next door to the Embassy Ballroom, where I attended several T-Square Balls, gala events arranged annually by the architecture students' association.

During the late 1960s, between Barrack and William Streets, St George's Terrace still had its stone-clad and stately commercial buildings, many offering a split entrance, down half a flight of steps to a tobacconist, newsagent, tailor, drycleaner or other small services, and up half a flight into the office foyer. These buildings were designed in a rich variety of architectural styles, their decorative details and stonework giving real character to the Terrace. A little further along the Terrace, just beyond Barrack Street, was the new Council House, a blazing emblem of progressive modernity associated with the youthful optimism of the Empire Games held in Perth during 1962.

Coming off that stretch of St George's Terrace between Barrack and William Streets were the two short streets, Howard Street and Sherwood Court, running downhill to The Esplanade. These streets had wonderful examples of how buildings adapted to a sloping street, with quirky and opportunistic responses. Here there were also music venues, jazz and folk, the most memorable of which was the Shiralee, a basement folk club in Howard Street and the epitome of local cool. The gracious Esplanade Hotel was on the corner of Howard Street and The Esplanade, with the Art Deco Lawson Apartments on the corner of Sherwood Court. Under these apartments were the Lawson Tea Rooms and Coffee Lounge, later to become Luis Restaurant, the epitome of fine dining in Perth. This precinct was, and still is, a particularly urbane part of the city.

The Adelphi Hotel, on the corner of Mill Street, half a block up St George's Terrace from the PTC, housed the bar where the architects of Perth met for Friday evening drinks and banter and mixed with the architecture students. I experienced this collegial bacchanalia at the very end of its time, just before the hotel was demolished. The Palace Hotel provided the alternative bar, on the corner of St George's Terrace in the other direction. The basement bar was the haunt of hard-bitten but fun-loving journalists from the nearby Newspaper House. Although the legal drinking age at that time was twenty-one, tolerant bar staff turned a blind eye, perhaps anticipating the change in law in 1970 which brought the drinking age down to eighteen.

Lunch was sought at the various city cafeterias and my favourite was the Cox Brothers Economic Stores, not for the food but for the location, on the roof terrace overlooking the corner of William and Hay Streets. And then there was Graham's coffee shop in Zimpels Arcade, serving the best coffee and the thinnest toasted ham and tomato sandwiches in town. Takeaway lunches were often enjoyed next door to the PTC, on the roof of the WA Trustees Building where we watched, from above, the workings of the Terrace. This was not a publicly accessible nor particularly safe roof, but access to it and other similar off-limits places became part of the local urban lore.

What is now known as Northbridge was for after-hours. There were shady nightclubs, gambling dens, and good eateries. The cannelloni at the old Sorrento on William Street was a late-night favourite and, further up the street, the garlic-laced beef burgers and ćevapčići at a Balkan cafe were great revivers after a big night out.

Walking through the city became more streamlined as familiarity with the arcade system grew. The arcades provided unique refuges from the city streets and useful short-cuts through the city blocks. They also housed a host of small and quirky retailers – the hobby shops, antiquarian booksellers, tobacconists, pen shops – and gave access to the basement billiard halls, another regular haunt for city-based students.

Late-night working stints in the PTC studio would occasionally end in a visit to a DJ at a commercial radio station a block away and a request for a favourite piece of music to be played and heard on the drive home.

Another lure between classes was the stately Supreme Court, to sit in the public gallery and observe trials. This was so different from our educational experiences, exposing us to the highly ritualised workings of the law and, sometimes, to trials that dealt with sensational or grisly matters. The celebrated trial of Eric Edgar Cooke, whose random killings that spread between 1959 and 1963 had terrorised suburban Perth, had taken place only three years before I became a student at PTC.

The old State Library on James Street, a necessary adjunct to the meagre offerings at the PTC Library, was Dickensian in its workings but its interior was a pleasure to spend time in. The nearby library of the Theosophical Society in the now demolished Arundale Buildings on the corner of a section of Museum Street that no longer exists, provided an alluring glimpse of another world, other belief systems, and an enticing distraction from the rational world of architectural studies. The City of Perth Library was on the lower floor of Council House, accessed through the Supreme Court Gardens and always a pleasure to visit because of its modernity and the attention given to design.

At night, music could be enjoyed at numerous venues but my location of choice was the nightclub on Murray Street carrying the unfortunate name of Trendsetters. Its great attraction was their regular band, the Beat'n'Tracks, who did covers of all the good music of the time, Motown, Stones, R&B. Then, after the nightclub closed up for the night, together with the band and its retinue, we would decamp to the hip Hole-in-the-Wall Club on Newcastle Street for more live music and a bar that was open until early morning.

Trendsetters was the location of a great party following the 1966 Australasian Architecture Students Association convention in Perth. That convention, titled Education, allowed Perth to seem, briefly, the centre of the architectural universe, when architectural heavyweights Buckminster Fuller, Aldo van Eyck, Jacob Bakema and John Voelcker all attended as speakers. And there we all were, after the lectures, sitting on the sun-drenched grass at the Claremont Teachers College, talking to these luminaries – heady stuff for a first-year architecture student. It seemed to me then, and still does on reflection, that Perth offered the mix of experiences necessary for all good cities. It provided a great and accessible urban education.

After the two years at PTC my fellow students and I moved to the Arcadian enclave of The University of Western Australia (UWA). We missed the city, our engagement being limited to the odd social event and the gala Prosh Parade on floats through the city. What I remember about this annual UWA student-run fund-raiser for charities was the intensity of atmosphere and noise during the trip down the narrow contained volume of Hay Street, in the section that is now the Hay Street Mall. The handsome Savoy Hotel provided the opportunity, with its four levels of stacked balconies, for a grandstand of sorts, but also a gauntlet to be run, with hundreds of students packed along the balconies, cheering and jeering, dousing the parade with their jugs of beer.

As a fourth-year architecture student in 1969, I moved from the family house in Mount Lawley into a single-storey terrace house in West Perth. The house at 76 Outram Street proved a wonderful location in so many respects. I shared the terrace with another architecture student and there were three others in number 78, with a young couple and their two children in the corner terrace, number 74. We were one block away from Hay Street, a bustling local shopping street serving the West Perth community, then primarily residential. There were many share-houses and student houses, meaning that that there were regular parties and the opportunity to meet all sorts of people. You would learn about the next party at the previous party or at the local wine bar, the Wine Rack, an early version of contemporary wine bars. Up until then, wine saloons were for winos, entered through batwing doors, into what seemed a gloomy dank interior, but this changed with the popular embrace of wine in Australia.

Being on the edge of the city struck me as a wonderful way of living and the terrace house as a flexible ageless housing type that enabled a certain urban intensity. Sure, we had a modest rear yard, but we had Kings Park at the end of our street. The streets were always alive with people, and it was a real mix – local workers and residents – students, families, singles, and the elderly.

Over a period of four years I lived in three shared houses and an apartment in West Perth. The city was just down the hill, an easy walk. There were many flats at the top end of St George's Terrace and more of them on Mount and Malcolm Streets, sharing views over the river and the city with neighboring gracious houses. The local parties extended to these flats and houses. There were flats also at the other, eastern end of St George's Terrace and along Adelaide Terrace. Most of the flats were demolished in the decade to follow and the streets became empty at night.

For a whole variety of reasons cities can lose their urban spark, while at other times, they improve it; cities go through cycles of decay and regeneration. Melbourne is an extraordinary and widely lauded example of a city that changed from a moribund centre, the city of the 'six-o'clock swill' that emptied after working hours and the early closing of the pubs, to become a vitally energised city with a new inner-city residential population serviced by a rich collection of bars, restaurants and other attractions. None of this happens by chance – it is the result of many factors, among which are enlightened planning, good urban design, and a willingness to learn from past mistakes. This is happening now, in Perth. The city's population has grown to the point where a richer diversity of living options is being sought – not to replace the highly successful suburbs but to offer broader choice for an increasingly diverse population. Household demographics in Australia have changed and we now see evidence that the fastest growing household is that of the single person. The inner urban option is again possible and attractive for people willing to trade off private space for urban amenity. And as this amenity grows to service these new inner-city residents – food and drink, entertainment, recreation, culture, education – all residents of Perth will benefit from their availability.

Queens Gardens

Grain Pool

Malcolm St

Map 14

14

METAL MEN

Sarah Burnside

Perth is still under construction, both in the physical and narrative sense: its streets bear the marks of successive building projects and the city has witnessed numerous arguments about its future directions.

In global terms Perth is a young city, and a somewhat unsettled one. Characterised by a peculiar species of cultural cringe in microcosm, Perth is shaped by its isolation from other cities; the sheer size of the state it governs; and cycles of booms and busts. It's a child of capitalism and colonialism: the Swan River Colony was 'a speculative venture',[1] conceived not by the British Government but by the entrepreneurial naval captain James Stirling, who lured settlers with misleading glowing descriptions. Given this legacy, and a political economy in which the mining and pastoral sectors have long been ascendant, notions of heroic pioneers, explorers and chancers have a particular currency here.

The city is routinely dismissed as dull, but it is not silent; it brims with overlapping tales that can be read in both texts and landmarks. Some narratives are hinted at in the statues that occupy the city, which have led to charges that its public art is dominated by "bronze statues of dead white males".[2] It is an eclectic collection. For instance, an upside-down statue of Percy Buttons, a local street performer active from the 1920s to the 1940s, performs an eternal handstand in the Hay Street Mall[3]; a serious-looking and somewhat criticised statue of Captain James Stirling[4] stands next

1   J. Host with C. Owen, 'It's still in my heart, this is my country': The Single Noongar Claim History, Crawley: UWA Publishing, 2009, pp. 78, 85–86.

2   R. Ghandour, 'End of the bronze age?', West Weekend Magazine, 19 January 2008, p. 24.

3   This sculpture, created by Charlie Smith and Joan Walsh-Smith, was unveiled in 2006.

4   This sculpture, by Clement P. Somers, was unveiled in 1979. Writing in 1998, Robyn Taylor cited Stirling's statue as an example of the 'reluctance to "kill" figurative statues', noting that the

to the Town Hall on Barrack Street; a photographer can be found on Malcolm Street[5]; and Queens Gardens contains a replica of Kensington Gardens' famous Peter Pan figure.[6] For the moment, though, let's consider St George's Terrace.

'The Terrace' is a convenient shorthand for Perth's business community, and its physical presence has been derided as soulless, a "glass, concrete and steel wind tunnel".[7] Not generally high on anyone's list of sites to recommend to tourists, it's a place of work, of coffees grabbed on the way to meetings and political or business gossip overheard. There is more than this, though: dotted along the Terrace are plaques and statues that embrace a particular narrative about a colony's growth into a state. Statues, of course, tend not to be erected in the service of critical historical scholarship. Instead, they exemplify the historical perspective known as Great Man History and reinforce elite values. In 1981 historian Geoffrey Bolton wrote that analysts of Western Australian history were confronted by two "modes of perception":

> One is what actually happened and the other consists of what might be called the mythic factors in Western Australian history. The mythic factors are the easiest to identify because they are pre-eminent in much writing

---

statue was 'poorly executed anatomically and technically' and 'perhaps should have been laid to rest after vandals had had a go at it. But the work represents the 150th anniversary of the founding of Perth, there are no other statues of Stirling, and Prince Charles unveiled it amidst much pomp and ceremony'; R. Taylor, 'Public art: when the honeymoon is over', *Artlink*, vol. 18, no. 2, p. 17.

5   The *Unidentified Photographer* was created by Anne Neil (in collaboration with Greg James) in 1996.

6   This is one of six replicas of the original statue, and was created by Sir George Frampton and brought to Perth in 1927.

7   R. Davidson, *Fremantle Impressions*, Fremantle: Fremantle Press, 2008, p. 148.

about the Western Australian past…This view holds that the growth of Western Australia is to be seen essentially as a chronicle of pioneer achievement. Growth was the product of struggle…And in harnessing the energies of the pioneers the wisdom and leadership of great statesmen starting with Sir John Forrest were pre-eminent in giving good guidance.[8]

The statues on the Terrace speak to the 'mythic factors' Bolton identifies, weaving a tale of the different kinds of pioneers who have built Western Australia and leaving notable gaps and silences. The bronze figures are largely unobtrusive, though, and the casual pedestrian may regularly walk past unseeing. Let's look with fresh eyes and make the familiar strange.

We begin where Adelaide Terrace becomes St George's, and a statue of John Septimus Roe[9], the state's first Surveyor-General, stands outside a coffee shop with a thoughtful expression and a map. Fob-watched, waistcoated, Roe represents what for the settler state is the deep distant past: a biographical account written in 1962 and entitled *Amazing Career* states that Roe "lived through the first half century of colonisation to the verge of that golden era which launched the State on its swift-moving periods of development."[10] Exploration is not innocent except in children's stories, and there is an obvious tension in lauding early explorers in colonised states. It is possible to acknowledge Roe's achievements while recalling that

8   G. Bolton, 'From Cinderella to Charles Court: the Making of a State of Excitement', in E. Harman and B. Head (eds) *State, Capital and Resources in the North and West of Australia*, Nedlands: University of Western Australia Press, 1982, p. 29.

9   The statue was created in 1990 by Greg James.

10   F. Mercer, *Amazing Career: The Story of Western Australia's First Surveyor-General*, Perth: Paterson Brokensha Pty Ltd, 1962, p. 15.

the expansion of a new settler society meant dispossession and disaster for a very large population of different language groups of Aboriginal people, but statues rarely offer such nuance. For instance, the 'native guides' on whom Roe and possibly every other explorer relied are necessarily absent and anonymous. A plaque next to the statue eulogises Roe as the state's "finest public servant"; words that sound oddly old-fashioned in our market-driven age.

We continue towards the centre of town, walking with the river to our left; we'll pass by a mob of metal kangaroos[11] posing nonchalantly to the delight of small children and reminding us that despite the kitsch presence of London Court nearby, we are very far from England. Visitors to the Stirling Gardens, more commonly known as the Supreme Court Gardens for the court building that sits behind them, are greeted by a statue of Alexander Forrest.[12] A politician, surveyor and investor, Forrest was known for exploring the Kimberley, a district he later represented in Parliament and where he invested in pastoral station properties. Criticised during his lifetime for successfully combining private enterprise with public service, Forrest exemplified the kind of (ad)venture capitalism that characterised colonial Western Australia.

Writing in 1958, Bolton commented that this "[e]xplorer and politician, pioneer pastoralist and capitalist" was "usually relegated to the obscurity of being 'Lord Forrest's younger brother'"[13], but in 2015, both figures have become somewhat remote. The radical labour historian Brian Fitzpatrick

---

11   *Kangaroos in the City* was created by Charles Smith and Joan Walsh Smith in 1997.

12   The statue, created by Pietro Giacomo Porcelli, was erected in 1903.

13   Bolton, *Alexander Forrest*, p. vii.

discerned during the 1950s that Australian history did not contain "Jeffersons and Lincolns", for nation-builders were regarded "more typically as a byword than as a watchword",[14] and the same could be said of those who built its largest state. The surname Forrest is enjoying new fame via the CEO of Fortescue Metals Group[15] and a large square in the central business district also shares the name, but otherwise it rarely surfaces outside the works of historians.

A statue of the older brother, Sir John Forrest, stands further afield, in Kings Park. A surveyor, explorer and politician, Forrest was the first premier and treasurer of the now self-governing colony from 1890, as well as serving in several Commonwealth governments. Frank Crowley, his biographer, notes that on Forrest's death "he was one of the last surviving heroes of Australian exploration," but the other side of the story is hinted at when Crowley writes that during an 1874 expedition from Geraldton to Peake Hill, Forrest and his companions experienced "some violent encounters with hostile Aboriginals".[16] Further, during his time in state politics, Forrest's government was fiercely hostile to the Aborigines Protection Board, which had been established in 1886 as a condition of the grant of responsible government to the colony and which remained under British control due to Imperial doubts that the colonists

14   B. Fitzpatrick, *The Australian Commonwealth: A Picture of the Community 1901–1955*, Melbourne: F. W. Cheshire, 1956, p. 208.

15   Andrew Forrest is the great-great nephew of both Sir John and Alexander Forrest.

16   F. K. Crowley, 'Forrest, Sir John (1847–1918)', Australian Dictionary of Biography, National Centre of Biography, Australian National University, http://adb.anu.edu.au/biography/forrest-sir-john-6211/text10677, published in hardcopy 1981, accessed online 14 June 2014. See also J. Forrest, *Explorations in Australia*, 'Chapter Five – Third Expedition from the West Coast to the Telegraph Line – Fight With the Natives'.

were treating Aboriginal people humanely. Ultimately his administration abolished the board in 1897. Historian Chris Owen comments that Forrest's government was "sensitive to interference in the treatment of Aboriginal people in WA and resented outside criticisms[17]", and there is perhaps some continuity here: irritation at external scrutiny remains an enduring theme in state politics.

Cross Barrack Street diagonally and continue down the Terrace, and you'll find yourself outside St Martins Centre, possibly feeling dwarfed by the striking *Footprints in Time* sculpture group.[18] A plaque explains that this work commemorates the 175th anniversary of the foundation of Western Australia, symbolising "the businesspeople who have built this thriving CBD". Notwithstanding the careful gender-neutrality of the language used, the figures are all men, and they represent successive eras, beginning with the Dutch exploration of the Swan River in 1697. The modern man at the end is speaking into a mobile phone that already looks dated; were the sculpture commissioned today he'd no doubt be staring intently at a smartphone. His forehead is wrinkled and he appears more anxious than his fairly cheerful-looking predecessors; perhaps he is reflecting on the crowdedness of modern life and the increasingly long hours worked in his surrounds. The tall, commanding presence of these statues draws attention to an absence: it takes more than business acumen and the invisible hand to create a city, but workers are rarely memorialised for

---

17   C. Owen, "'The police appear to be a useless lot up there'": Law and order in the East Kimberley 1884–1905', *Aboriginal History*, 7, 2003, p. 111.

18   The sculpture was commissioned by St Martins Properties (Australia) Pty Ltd and sculpted by Joan Walsh-Smith and Charles Smith. It was unveiled in 2004.

their contributions to state-building. Certainly there is no sense on the Terrace that workers, including convicts and Aboriginal people, were also indispensable to Perth's success, that labour under varying conditions of coercion helped to shape Western Australia. Opposite Parliament, Solidarity Park testifies to some of the struggles of organised labour, but the statues on the Terrace tell a tale of rugged entrepreneurialism.

Continuing on, at the intersection of the Terrace and fashionable King Street, a plaque on the ground plays homage to the twin local deities of mining and commerce, reading:

> To remember our past in mysterious ways.
> Where the river flowed and the swamp sat.
> People lived here in cottages until the boomtown growth.
> The gold changed everything that time. Next time
> nickel. The metals get lighter but the booms repeat.[19]

The importance of gold has long been an article of faith in Perth. Elsewhere in the central business district, the Perth Mint features a monument depicting the discovery of gold near Coolgardie in 1892, and a plaque explains that this event "secured the future of the struggling colony of Western Australia" and "established one of the state's most successful and enduring industries".[20] In his recent book on the "settler revolution and the rise of the Anglo-world" historian James Belich aptly characterised gold as Western Australian

---

19   The plaque is part of a public art installation commissioned in 1994 to celebrate the history of King Street, and created by the artist Malcolm McGregor. The poem was written by Terri-ann White.

20   This monument, 'The Strike', was created by Greg James in 1991.

historiography's "Handsome Prince".[21] There have been other princes since that time, most recently iron ore, which have helped to nurture a comfortable sense that increasing growth is assured: the booms repeat. However, Western Australia is now experiencing a downturn; iron ore prices are buoyant no longer, and headlines warn of the "post-boom economy". In this context, and against the stark reality of climate change, the plaque's cheerful conclusion summons thoughts of hubris.

Further along, a statue of Bishop Matthew Hale[22], the first bishop of the Anglican diocese of Perth, steps into the site of his old school, and if you cross back towards the river you'll find the second statue of one of the school's former pupils, Alexander Forrest. This artwork, entitled *'The Universal explorer'*[23], is tucked away in an office building, the Forrest Centre, and specifically commemorates his 1879 exploration in the Kimberley. A plaque lauds Forrest for his involvement in the "discovery and naming" of this area, words which fairly obviously erase the long human history of this region prior to the 1800s. Such statements also gloss over the way in which territory is claimed: Forrest himself set out this ugly reality in an 1893 speech in which he asked whether "the life of one European is not worth a thousand natives, as far as settlement of this country is concerned".[24] A plaque accompanying the statue describes Forrest as "Father of the Kimberleys": a banal,

---

21 J. Belich, *Replenishing the Earth: The Settler Revolution and the Rise of the Anglo-World*, Oxford: Oxford University Press, 2009, p. 393. Belich was more sceptical of the importance of gold in Western Australia's economic growth, writing that "there is reason to suspect that a forgotten boom caused the gold rush, not vice versa".

22 The sculpture was created by Greg James in 2004 on behalf of the Old Haleians Association.

23 The sculpture was commissioned in 1998 and created by local artist Hans Arkeveld.

24 Cited in Owen, *Law and order in the East Kimberley 1884-1905*, p. 111.

basic tactlessness. Reading such tributes, the observer might wonder: can we honour a multiplicity of stories about Western Australia, even where they might contradict each other? Is there room in our public spaces for voices that are other than triumphal, and stories that don't belong to the conquerors? Would the whole edifice crumble if its origins were laid bare?

This is not to say that Perth is totally lacking in acknowledgements of its Aboriginal past and present; elsewhere, in Forrest Place, large solemn letters on the ground proclaim that "Where you're now standing used to be a lake...Where you've stopped to chat, people always gathered to fish, drink spring-water and talk...For millennia it was a meeting place". In May 2014, Premier Colin Barnett announced that a new square would be named after Yagan, a Noongar warrior killed by a settler in 1833. The Premier was quoted as saying, "We have so many places and monuments to our European leaders like the Duke of Wellington, Lord Forrest, Sir Charles Fremantle, Queen Victoria and Governor Stirling; not one named after an Aboriginal person in the city...I am delighted we can name this important place after a figure like Yagan". Plans for the square were released that November; it was to be "a place to have fun, meet, play, eat and shop from a showcase of WA produce" and would be influenced by 'a strong Aboriginal narrative...exploring themes of place, people, animals, birds and landscape; all of which shape and create a strong sense of place'.[25] There is room, then, for complexity and clashing narratives in our city. How far this room can be stretched, and how the overlapping stories will fit together, remains to be seen.

25 'Yagan Square', Metropolitan Redevelopment Authority, http://www.mra.wa.gov.au/projects-and-places/perth-city-link/places-attractions/yagan-square.

As the end of the Terrace approaches, we encounter Sir Charles Court, Liberal premier from 1974–1982, in mid-stride at the intersection of Milligan Street heading from parliament back towards the central business district. The statue rests on a platform that lists its subject's achievements, including four state agreements in respect of the development of iron ore in the Pilbara. Court still looms large in Western Australian political history, and speeches in parliament on a condolence motion following his death linked him to Sir John Forrest.[26] Today he is known primarily for his support for the resource industry and for 'states' rights'. There are of course many other stories to tell about Court, including that of his fierce opposition to Aboriginal land rights, notably expressed in the Noonkanbah dispute: a short-term political victory with social costs and far-reaching consequences. In short, Court was in his lifetime a polarising figure, and a highly partisan one, something smoothed over in a Labor government's decision to commission a statue on his death.[27]

We've reached the end of our journey and from this vantage point we can look up towards Kings Park and reflect on another statue, which only ever existed in the mind's eye: Lang Hancock. Following representations made by his daughter Gina Rinehart, the Perth City Council gave unanimous support to the proposal to construct a statue of Hancock on Kings Park Road in 2002, but the project failed to proceed. Amid public criticism of the

---

26   Condolence Motion, *Hansard*, Legislative Assembly, 27 February 2008, 391b-403a. The statue was created by Tony Jones and unveiled in 2011.

27   In a speech in Parliament, then Premier Alan Carpenter concluded that "Sir Charles' life and service to the state of Western Australia should be marked with a permanent memorial…A statue will be a fitting memorial to Sir Charles Court's extraordinary life"h; A. Carpenter, Condolence Motion, *Hansard*, Legislative Assembly, 27 February 2008, p. 2.

Council's decision, on grounds including Hancock's involvement in asbestos mining, Rinehart withdrew her application. The legacy of the asbestos industry is far from the only source of controversy surrounding Hancock; he was a right-wing secessionist who expressed repugnant, eugenicist views about Aboriginal people. It seems unlikely that his statue will ever join the city's silent ranks, and the abandoned proposal stands as a reminder, if one were needed, that commemoration is inherently political. Although the statue never materialised, the Hancock family has since contributed to public art in Western Australia: Rinehart has gifted an inner northern suburb with a rock adorned with a poem entitled 'Our future', a strange, didactic homage to capitalism.

This is a good point to stop and reflect on arguments about the past, contested visions of the future, and tales told by the Terrace's metallic men. The statues discussed here have not gone uncriticised. In 2010, Artrage director Marcus Canning was quoted as saying that bronze had become "dull", "twee", and "redundant", arguing that the metal was "really appropriate for sixteenth-century European capitals" and that "our urban environment should reflect" our "fresh, forward-looking culture".[28] This critique has force. Nevertheless, the statues stand as ambiguous yet inescapable representations of our past: reminders of the ways in which this state has been imagined during its existence, and of the deep flaws in these imaginings.

Despite often being conceived of in terms of what it lacks, Perth is full of contested words, the streets overlaid with narratives and peopled by figures from our past. One thing is

---

28   Quoted in K. Bastians, 'Bold blob pointing to bronze bust', *The Perth Voice*. Saturday 13 February 2010, p. 6.

certain: additional layers of remembrance will be added to the city in years to come. Perhaps these will fill some of the gaps in the stories told on the Terrace, making way for challenges to the familiar stories of heroic pioneers and entrepreneurs. What tales will our streets tell in the future, and what silences will lie between them?

The author is grateful to the staff of the Perth History Centre for their kind assistance with multiple statue-related questions, and also thanks Dr Chris Owen and Ms Tessa Herrmann for their thoughtful comments and suggestions.

Map 15

15

DESPERATELY FAILING THE HOMELESS

Conrad Liveris

Homelessness in Perth is not unique. Poverty is a challenge for every city in the world. It is a deep, debilitating and destabilising experience that nobody should suffer. There are two key challenges to the story of poverty in Perth: how we view homeless people and how we support them.

Since 2013 social discourse in Perth has taken some interest in homelessness, but misinformation and negative stereotypes have been perpetuated. This discourse was here when there was a social awakening on begging and street-present in Perth. It focused with a series of news reports around homeless people in Wellington Square, and residents' responses. This ended up being discussed widely on talk-back radio and in casual conversation. Did we have a homelessness crisis? What were these people doing? How did boom-town Perth have rising poverty? Modern Australian poverty is deep and real, it is part of our story as a city, state and country.

There are many examples of a pervasive apathy towards homeless people in Perth. Leading figures, politicians and everyday citizens that beggars should be banned and fined, even though they need the support services that only an urban area can afford. Leaders of local government and society have said that some people are parading as homeless. Others have said that the homeless services aren't doing their job, in spite of the real budgetary cuts that have occurred in the past twelve months. And finally, there has been a rejection of homeless services in certain neighbourhoods because they don't fit with the residents' view of urban life. NIMBYism (Not in My Back Yard) at its worst.

People in Perth, and in the greater world community, should not instigate or propagate these views. I believe we have the capacity for benevolence and compassion to support those in need. Perth has shown itself to be a caring and community-focused city. We have weathered the good and bad times with a sense of conviction that helping those in need wasn't just the right thing to do, but the smart thing too. Yet, there seems to be a current individualist trend to dismiss the travesty of poverty and diminish the circumstances that lead to poverty.

As of June 30 2015, services that support the homeless – such as the Salvation Army, Ruah, Anglicare and UnitingCare West – face limitations in funding from government and philanthropic donations. At this time there are over 10,000 people who are homeless in Perth, and another 7,000 who are in very insecure accommodation, thus flirting with homelessness themselves.

"I don't know why they say this stuff", said a 16-year-old homeless woman to me recently. She was referring to comments made by politicians and social commentators who considered all homeless people to be violent and disingenuous as to their needs. She viewed these diminishing, distancing and unfounded accusations as an attack on her as an individual. It's a sobering moment to explain to a distraught, barely sleeping sixteen year old who is in a toxic environment that the community actually does care for her. Nobody wants to see a teenager with aspirations and dreams feeling isolated and agitated or perturbed for their future. If we cannot give young people a good start in life to chart their own course, then our society has damned limitations.

It's easy to distance ourselves from poverty and think of it as someone else's problem. I didn't understand the reality of homelessness until I went homeless for a week in January 2014 on my own. Before my experience on the streets, I was engaging with homeless people through indirect services, supporting them where I could.

Putting myself in the shoes of those experiencing homelessness shed great light, and aided the way I approach this issue. Homelessness is an exhausting experience. During the day you are actively trying to keep yourself occupied and thinking about what your next meal will be or whether you can get the medical support you might need. By night you are trying to find one spot to stay so as not to disrupt those around you or have to face unwanted attention. At the same time, you want to stay warm and dry, but are facing a reality where there is activity around you that wakes you up every 45 minutes or so: people going for midnight runs, cars going by, sprinklers going off.

While this first effort of being homeless made me reevaluate how I saw the scale of the problem, it was when I went homeless in January 2015 with my two older brothers that I realised we really needed to challenge the issue.
On our first night on the streets my brother Matthew found himself in a situation where he was almost bashed and I was almost robbed. These experiences led to great exploration and discussion amongst us. It was here that we were able to examine and consider situations while being independent people with a similar upbringing but a different lived experience.

When we – being me, my brother Brendan and our friends Sandra De Witt Hemala and Jessica Short – founded Street Smugglers in 2012 we focused it around a vision where homelessness isn't the only option that faces those in need. Street Smugglers operates at the two extremes: with homeless people and with broad-based advocacy. Our interactions with homeless people are through direct conversations to uncover what they need. Over eighty per cent of all homeless people engage with the major service providers, but it takes just one negative interaction for them to avoid one of them. People who experience homeless in Perth are more likely to have been engaged with child protection services during their youth. It's common for homeless people to have a series of interactions with the justice and health systems, which are rarely positive. Because of these negative experiences, they may have a distrustful view of institutions and bureaucracy. Rarely are the police, for example, giving good news.

The police hold a distinctly difficult role on the streets. A senior police officer once told me that "police are great at following rules and orders – it is what we do – so we will always implement the legislation". Any legal scholar will agree that the law should be adhered to without fear or favour, but for those most in need should we ban them from a park or central place of meeting? In Perth, we have.

It was during our fourth night on the streets in 2015 that I started to realise there was a disconnect. We were in a park in the city with a photographer and journalist for the night. We had just been speaking with young homeless people about their interactions with the police. It was clear that rather than homeless people seeking trouble, there was a cultural issue with the police. Every police force ought to consider their interaction with homeless people. The more I talk with homeless people about their experiences with the justice system and police forces, the more I realise that there is a lack of empathy from those enforcing the law. Police are often fulfilling multiple duties, rightly or wrongly, regarding law enforcement and community development.

Our greatest strength as a society is our diversity. We should be utilising this more to solve homelessness. Policy made in a vacuum, without intelligent consultation with those who have first-hand knowledge and direct access to individuals living homeless, is policy destined to fail.

On the whole, I don't find it difficult sitting down with a politician to discuss homelessness. They usually will listen. Rising homelessness is a sign that government, at every level, is failing. We elect people to improve our quality of life; poverty reminds us that, even in Perth, this failure of society is not recognised widely.

Through wide discussion with the experts on poverty in urban areas Street Smugglers see the opportunity for simple solutions to homelessness. Our first aim should be sourcing housing for people and ensuring it is sustainable for their situation. As soon as someone becomes homeless they are likely to be homeless in Perth for about four months and then, should they alleviate themselves of this issue, they are more likely to become homeless again. Evidence is emerging from European and US cities that keeping people housed actually saves money for governments and societies. Beyond this, it provides the stability that is needed for people to pull their life together.

Broadly, relationship breakdown and financial stress are factors that we have found to be the major catalysts of homelessness in Perth. Relationship breakdown is such a prominent aspect in homeless peoples' lives that we believe it is the common factor. A fight with a parent, or a partner, falling out with a sibling or teacher; a relationship event will occur that will cause someone to think "I am not loved here, I am not wanted". Furthermore, when someone lacks financial independence, and often the requisite literacy or support such as employment, then they too may come closer to experiencing homelessness. Achievable solutions for these root causes of homelessness are relationship counselling and financial literacy programs.

Last year homelessness was costed at over $10 billion to society at large. The Chief Justice of WA, Wayne Martin, has remarked that evidence suggests that one-fifth of this cost is found in the justice system – from that first interaction with police through to jail time.

Despite these depressing figures, there's positive news as well. Evidence from the University of Western Australia's Centre for Social Impact found that for every $1 government invests in homeless services there is a $2 net social return. Knowing this, people in Perth, from the everyday citizen to the highest member of government, should begin to think creatively about poverty and support those in need through innovative programs that aim to provide solutions, not perpetuate apathy.

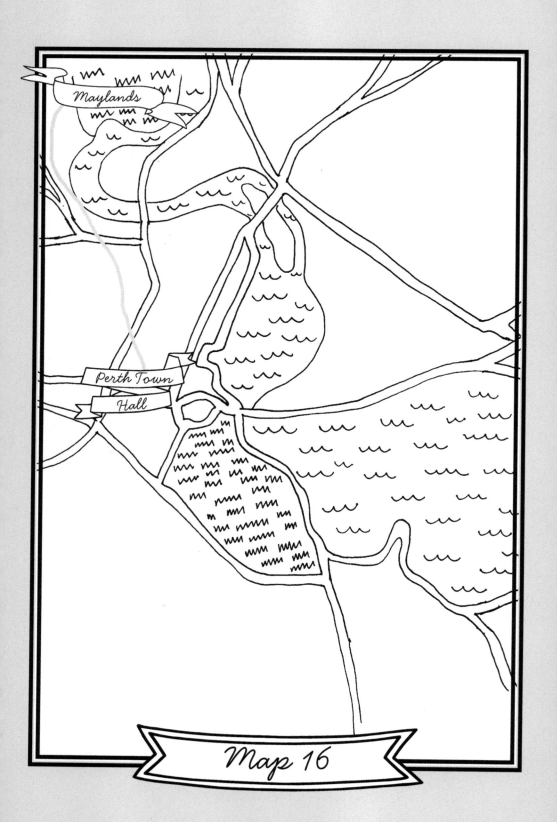

Maylands

Perth Town
Hall

Map 16

16

CREATIVE DARWINISM: PRETTY FLOWERS GROW IN SHIT

Nick Albrook

This is my city and I'm never gonna leave it.
Channel 7 News ad

Writing about my experience of making music in Perth is a strange thing, because as soon as a 'scene' is bound and gagged by the written word it is finished, petrified, swept up into the *Rolling Stone* archives and forever considered 'history'. It might be revered and glorified, but it's still long gone. This could be a very restricting view to take on a community like Perth, which is still just as inspiring and productive as it ever was.

I can't pretend to understand where 'music scenes' begin or end. It seems a futile and narrow-minded pursuit. So before I begin, I want to say that this is merely a reflective exercise. There was never a 'golden age', and if one does exist I can't see it, because it's floating all around, invisible and omnipresent. For years I suffered serious cultural guilt as a Western Australian. The orthodoxy and banality made me feel isolated, relegated to the company of eccentric long-haired ghosts singing to me from inside my Discman. Every birthday and Christmas, Dad would give me a care package of CDs. This blessed nourishment of Jethro Tull, Lou Reed, Led Zeppelin and David Bowie shone a light into the murky tunnels of my future. Playing music and generally being a flaming Christmas fruitcake became my sole purpose, and me and a few other school friends – Steve Summerlin and Richard Ingham of Mink Mussel Creek, and many other brilliant but criminally under-recognised projects – revelled in our little corner of filthy otherness. This outlook was key to our musical and creative development. We railed against the boredom of Perth not with pickets or protest, but with a head-in-the-sand hubris that made us feel invincible and unique. We found more comrades along the way – Joe Ryan, Kevin Parker, Jay Watson – and together we erected great walls of noise and hair and mouldy dishes around our Daglish share house commune citadel on Troy Terrace where we incubated, practised, recorded, talked and grew. A friend stick'n'poke tattooed a spiral shape into my arm to represent that way of life (which I'd lifted from Hermes Trismegistus and other alchemical mumbo jumbo I learned at university). Look inside and the world can be whatever you want. Look out and it's ugly and shitty.

In Perth, use of public space is regulated to the point of comedy, and Orwellian restrictions on tobacco, noise, bicycles, alcohol and public gatherings breed a festering discontent and boredom because no one likes being pre-emptively labelled a deviant. Being trusted enriches the soul – you can see it on the face of the child who leads the family trek. You can see the flipside on the faces of disenchanted detainees. On weekends, this restlessness is unleashed across clubs and pubs in Northbridge and Subiaco in an avalanche of Jägerbombs (a shot of Jägermeister dropped into a larger glass of Red Bull and then consumed with haste) and Midori and violence and cheap sex. When the Monday sun staggers over the horizon, people rub their eyes and heave a great sigh and the city reverts to its utilitarian state – the "bourgeois dream of unproblematic production", as *The 60s Without Apology* (University of Minnesota Press, 1984) puts it, "of everyday life as the bureaucratic society of controlled consumption". That this description of pre-revolutionary 1950s and '60s America is so apt for Perth is damn scary. Or hilarious. I can't decide. I guess it depends on the depth and colour of your nihilistic streak, or if you actually *live* here. Whichever way you look at it, it does not paint a picture of a city conducive to creativity. Art is the antithesis of logic and functionality – it is romance and wonder and stupid, pointless lovelies. As good old Mr Vonnegut so often said, it's an exercise to make your soul grow. So how, in a super-functional and conservative environment whose every will is bent towards digging *really, really* big holes in the ground, have I seen and heard and felt some of the most brilliant, pure and original creativity in the world?

I used to dream about living in a cultural powerhouse like Paris or Berlin or New York, but after spending time in these places I've realised that the emptiness and isolation of Perth – boredom to some – was a far better environment for creativity. The 'cultural capitals' are so rich in art and wonder that it can feel pointless to add to it.

Maybe just being *in* those 'cultural capitals' fills us up with wonder? Strolling through Berlin at night, ducking into a bar with fish nailed to the roof, skipping across the cobblestones for some cheap beers in a record shop in a Russian caravan in an abandoned peanut factory…that kind of stuff fills the romantic void. Having a Ricard and a few Gitanes on the *terrasse* of Aux Folies; stumbling through Camden after a lock-in at the Witch's Tit or the Cock'n'Balls or the Cancerous Bowel or whatever you call it; recollecting a possible conversation with Jah Wobble over a pint…Perth? It has no secret tunnels to romantic fulfilment.

For me, music and art have always been a way to manufacture that romance lacking in upper-middle-class Western Australia. To be honest, if I had lived in New York I probably would've been so damn hungover – or busy ensuring that I would be later – that a whole lot less creation would've gone on. Mundane and discouraging places like Perth create a vicious Darwinism for creatively inclined people, where survival of the fittest is played out with swift and unrepentant force and the flippant or unpassionate are left behind, drowning in putrid mind-clag. You have to *really* need it, and without the mysterious and poetic benefits of a vibrant city culture this has to come from deep inside. Amber Fresh, otherwise known as Rabbit Island, is one person who produces constant streams of music, drawings, essays, poems, calendars, videos and photos from her home. She fills her world with little pieces of home-made, lo-fi, photocopied beauty and magic. They don't have funding or precedent or material ambition – and the result is something fresh and original. Mei Saraswati does the same thing, although with completely different styles of music. She has produced, mixed, mastered and illustrated scores of albums in her bedroom and then released this other-worldly electronic R'n'B brilliance onto the internet with no fanfare, simply to turn around and start making more. These are just two examples. There are many more.

Somehow, by being a cultural long-drop, Perth lit a fire under my arse. In more scholarly terminology this could be called a 'spirit of negation' – a margarine version of the same zeitgeist that has catalysed most worthwhile movements throughout history, from dadaism to punk to all the intellectual and artistic wonders of The Netherlands freshly unchained from their dastardly Spanish overlords.

Being isolated spatially and culturally – us from the city, Perth from Australia and Australia from the world – arms one with an Atlas-strong sense of identity. Both actively and passively, originality seems to flourish in Perth's artistic community. Without the wider community's acceptance, creative pursuits lack the potential for commodification. There's no point in preening yourself for success because it's just *not real*. It's a fairytale, so you may as well just do it in whatever way you like, good or bad, in your room or on the top of the Telstra building, which – as anyone with any common sense will attest – was built for that one potential badass to drop in on a skateboard and parachute off. Growing up in the Kimberley and then Fremantle, the true machinery of the music business evaded me. It was about as real as the Power Rangers and twice as awesome. Led Zeppelin and U2, all the way down to whatever was on *Rage* that morning, was just a pretty dream. But if I grew up in a city where success in music was common and highly visible, I reckon it would have been far more alluring. I would've understood how to go about it, probably before I actually realised how deep my love of music was. With the template for success laid out so precisely – gigs to be got, managers to be found, reviews to be had and the ultimate dream of 'making it' tangibly within reach – Perth would find itself producing far less original art. Because as it stands, it doesn't really matter if you're crap or silly or unbearably offensive, you wouldn't get much further doing something different anyway. This helps to preserve a magical purity because it's executed with love – with *necessity*. And what's more, when these artists keep going and practising and advancing – which they must – somehow their crassness coagulates into something brilliantly individual and accomplished, and you can see it performed in an arena that makes the audience feel truly blessed. I saw Rabbit Island and Peter

Bibby and Cam Avery play in backyards. I saw cease play in a tattoo parlour in Maylands. Me and Joe Ryan were plastered against the wall by their sound, gawking up at Andrew, the guitarist, precariously standing on his enormous amp wearing high heels and full fishnet bodystocking, slowly trying to drive his guitar through the top of his cabinet like some pagan-burlesque reimagining of King Arthur. After hours they slowed to a halt, and the crowd cheered from the stairs and bathroom door and kitchen and I remembered where we were: in a tiny share-house in Maylands, in the flaming cauldron of hell or the halls of Valhalla. Mink Mussel Creek played there a few times and once, in a flash of drunken inspiration, someone turned the only light in the room off mid-performance. I saw the fourteen guitarists of Electric Toad destroy a warehouse art gallery wearing '90s WA football jerseys. Tame Impala and Pond played in Tanya's garage and every time I cried and danced and felt like the breath of God was being embarrassingly saucy all over my skin. We played our very first show in that garage and I can still see Jay demolishing the tiny drum kit – kick, snare, ride, tom – as sparks floated from the forty-gallon drum and lit the faces of the people looking in from the dark. None of us had ever seen anyone play like it in real life, let alone in a garage, sitting on milk crates.

As far as genres go, our music 'scene' in Perth was an anomaly. A mad mosaic of groups and artists only held together by gallant separation from conventional Perth society. Nick Odell, the drummer of cease and Sonny Roofs, still has a poster for a gig at Amplifier Bar that I remember as a kind of microcosmic Woodstock – a tactile realisation of all the beauty and communion we cherished. The line-up included us (Mink Mussel Creek), cease (aforementioned stoner/doom/drone lords), Sex Panther (punk-party queens), Oki Oki (Nintendo synth pop) and Chris Cobilis (experimental laptop noise music). I think most members of the bands ended up on stage at more than one time, wrapped in Cobilis' wires or yelling into a madly effected microphone in front of cease. I certainly did. Nowhere else would such a ridiculously mismatched line-up consider themselves a tight community. We all partied together, played together and are still friends.

I think this spirit is lacking in a lot of the more culturally enlightened parts of the world. Maybe in these vibrant communities the countercultural idea is so entrenched it becomes capitalist orthodoxy and loses its edge. It is subjected to the rationality it once challenged. In the cultural capitals – Paris, Berlin, New York – creativity and original thinking are accepted and valued parts of mainstream life.

In Perth they are not.

Paris has over four hundred streets named after artists and writers, and this honour is not restricted to the most unobtrusive or patriotic. Rue Albert Camus, Rue Marcel Duchamp and the recently proposed Place Jean-Michel Basquiat, for example, show the state glorifying revolutionaries, absurdists, libertines and a gay, heroin-using, Haitian–American graffiti artist. Today we can stroll along the verdant Boulevard Auguste-Blanqui, named after the man who led the uprising of the Paris Commune. A revolutionary, a prisoner, an anarchist. In modern terms: a terrorist.

There, art is a basic fact of everyday life, while in Perth it is an anomaly hidden in garages and living rooms – deep beneath a conservative fishbowl of productivity. So, all things considered, 'cultural capitals' should be havens for art and music, and Perth should not. The romance just seeps into the pores, *ja*?

I always thought this before I left Western Australia, but have since found it to be otherwise. I asked a young photographer and artist in Amsterdam about the music scene there and her reply was wholly negative. A lot of Parisians seem to feel the same way. I look back on my time in Perth and think about the huge number of brilliant musicians and artists who, I saw and knew, often not in official venues but in backyards or sheds or the abandoned entertainment centre (yes, cease). Perhaps with the freedom – almost *expectation* – to create, revel and throw it all around the streets, it all just gets a bit boring.

Like much good art, it doesn't really 'mean' anything, so writing an essay about it is an odd activity. The experience of a city or community varies so much that it can never be defined while it is still occurring. When it's actually happening, a 'scene' is not really a 'scene' – it's completely intangible and only coagulates into a definitive and convenient ball when history puts it in a cage, when someone from the outside looks in and decides there's something shared between a bunch of vaguely artistic fools. I guess that's what I'm doing now, which is pretty ridiculous seeing as nothing is finished and the Perth artistic community is so ethereal that it couldn't and shouldn't be labelled at all.

'*Creative Darwinism: Pretty flowers grow in shit*' was first published in *Griffith Review* 47: *Looking West* edited by Julianne Schultz and Anna Haebich. Available at griffithreview.com.

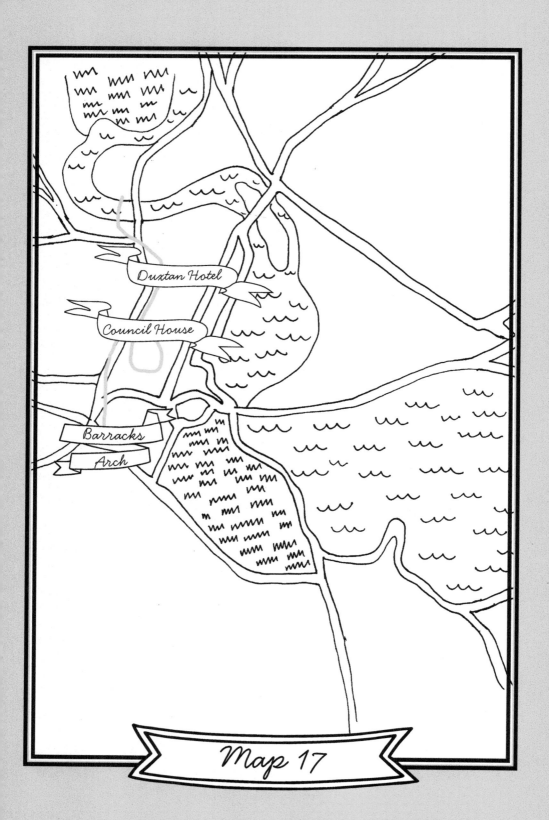

Duxtan Hotel

Council House

Barracks

Arch

Map 17

17

PERTH CITY: LAW AND GOVERNANCE

Antonio Buti

At the fag end of the twentieth century, Australia was engaged in a one-day international cricket match at the WACA ground in East Perth. It was a stinking hot day, the temperature, mid-afternoon, around 39 degrees Celsius. Perth's usual afternoon cooling sea breeze had not arrived, and there seemed little prospect of it doing so.

In the members' stand, the president of the WACA was host to invited guests in the Association's corporate box. In the adjacent corporate box, Channel Nine, the initiator of this modern form of cricket, was hosting its invited guests. The outside viewing area of each box was separated from the other only by a low, waist-high partition. On one side of the partition – the president's side – the managing director of a local bank sat chatting to one of his employees, who was sitting on the Channel Nine side. Wearing a tailored jacket, as attendance in the WACA entertainment suite demanded, the managing director was perspiring visibly. The employee, in t-shirt and jeans, was relaxed. The contiguity in space made the fissure between tradition and new age palpably evident. Eventually, but only after the WACA's guests were showing considerable signs of distress, a WACA executive announced on behalf of the president, with all the dignity that such a moment called for, "Gentlemen, you may remove your jackets."

This vignette is a metonym for Western Australia after World War II. Between 1947 and 1961, the Perth metropolitan population grew from 303,000 to 475,000. With the growth came new challenges for the legislature and local government. There was a need to hold on to tradition; there is security in clinging to what one knows. But, in change lay opportunities. What traditions could we or did we need to abandon to exploit them?

There were new ways of thinking about community, too, as increased migration brought new cultures into the social mix and new challenges for the justice system.

During the early 1960s, a new council house was built directly in front of the Supreme Court, facing St George's Terrace. The thirteen-storey building was opened by Queen Elizabeth II in 1963 and is still home to the Perth City Council. Council House has survived calls, particularly in the mid-1990s, for its demolition and is now a heritage-listed building that has been called the most important modernist icon in Perth, reflecting the confidence of the city to the world. At night, the outside of the building is illuminated by 22,000 LED lights that provide a colourful show.

Buildings of historical significance were demolished to make way for the new council house, including the former Colony's Legislative Council, a post office, and the ABC, the latter of which moved to new purpose-built studios in Adelaide Terrace. Immediately next to Council House is Government House, a beautiful, stone-walled, Georgian two-storey mansion set on 32,000 square metres of manicured gardens. The Governor of Western Australia resides there as Queen Elizabeth II's representative in the state. It has a majestic ballroom that has been used for many official functions, including the presentation of young women to the governor during debutante season, a tradition that enjoyed its pinnacle in the 1950s and 1960s.

The recent occupier of Government House was Malcolm McCusker AC CVO QC, his wife Tonia, and their children. McCusker is a respected philanthropist and leading barrister. Before taking on the role of Governor, McCusker was involved in a number of "wrongful conviction" cases which shook the legal establishment and police force of Western Australia.

This brings us to the Supreme Court, the highest court in Western Australia. The significance of the Supreme Court in the judicial and legal system of Western Australia is enormous. As the current Chief Justice, Wayne Martin remarked in ceremonial sitting of the court on 17 June 2011 to commemorate the 150th anniversary of the Court's creation, "for 150 years this Court has stood at the apex of the systems that have existed within the colony and later the State of Western Australia for the maintenance of law and order and the administration of justice." But, the Supreme Court building, nestled almost incongruously in gardens of traditional contemplative splendour, is not the oldest court house in Western Australia. That claim belongs to the building next door.

Built in 1836, it opened with the Quarter Sessions on 2 January 1837. It has also served as a school, church and concert hall. In 1849 Dom Salvado, a Spanish Benedictine monk walked more than 100km from New Norcia to give a Bellini recital in the Court House to a packed audience to raise funds to develop a mission. It still stands near the current Supreme Court in the Stirling Gardens, just down from the intersection of St George's Terrace and Barrack Street. Now called the Old Court House and being the oldest building within the City of Perth, it serves as a law museum, holding a unique position in Australia and one of only a few such law museums in the world.

The Supreme Court has been in existence since 1861, although the current building was not completed and opened until 1903. The first Chief Justice of the Supreme Court was Sir Archibald Burt, who arrived on the shores of Western

Australia from the Leeward Islands in the Caribbean not long before the first sitting of the Supreme Court on 3 July 1861.

Sir Archibald's great-grandson, Francis 'Red' Burt became a justice of the Supreme Court of Western Australia in 1969, and, following in the footsteps of his great grandfather, he became Chief Justice in 1977.

The Perth legal profession held Red Burt in high esteem. The largest barristers' chambers in Perth bear his name. The Francis Burt Chambers was established in 1962 and was the first set of barristers' chambers in Perth, serving the legal profession in Western Australia, with now more than 100 members. As one would expect, the chambers on St George's Terrace is just a short walk from the Supreme Court building.

Today, on any week morning, just before ten o'clock, the intersection of Barrack and St George's Streets is a scurrying mass of activity. Young, keen-eyed but slightly apprehensive articled clerks and paralegals, sweating as they push trolleys full of files containing important court documents and photo-copies of law cases, wait impatiently for a green pedestrian 'go' sign. Slightly older legal practitioners, in their standard dark conservative court attire, walk in front of the clerks and paralegals, carrying just a few files in their hands.

The barristers, the specialised court advocates, walk behind. Usually, they are talking to their instructing solicitors. They too are conservatively dressed, as tradition deems appropriate for an appearance in court. You may also see the stars of the legal show, the QCs and SCs, or Queens Counsel and Senior Counsel, as they have been called in Western Australia since 2001. Another loosening of tradition's grip, with the removal of implied royal appointment. But a whiff of tradition clings.

SCs are still colloquially called silks. The name derives from the British tradition of the Lord Chancellor awarding deserving barristers the right to wear silk gowns to distinguish them as taking precedence over other barristers in the court. It seems that in law, as in other social spheres, we like our tradition, but only if we can keep it in its place.

For the protagonists in any Supreme Court action, the stakes can be high, as high as their freedom, their wealth, their reputation. Generally the lawyers involved just move on to the next case, leaving the defeated party to the law action to pick up the pieces. Sometimes, however, the outcome can also have consequences for the lawyer involved, but more for their reputation than anything else. This might account for the slightly apprehensive demeanour of those young lawyers scurrying across St George's Terrace on their way to the Court. However, it is unlikely that any lawyer today would be subjected to the treatment one lawyer received in 1838, outside Perth's only Court House, where a Mrs Georgina Collins waited to horsewhip a lawyer who had damaged her reputation. She was fined fifty shillings for doing so. There is no record of whether she thought that was money well spent.

Nevertheless, the Supreme Court is now, as it has always been, a site of bitter legal battles to decide who wins the right to exclaim 'justice has been served'. Nowhere is the battle more compelling than in those cases brought before the Appeal Court of the Supreme Court to right an alleged wrongful conviction. Two of the more high profile wrongful conviction verdicts were in the *Mallard* and *Mickelbergs* cases.

Andrew Mallard was tried and found guilty in 1995 of wilfully murdering Pamela Lawrence in her Mosman Park jewellery store in May 1994. The trial judge, Justice Michael Murray sentenced Mallard to life imprisonment with a twenty-year minimum. However over the next ten years, Mallard's alleged confession was the subject of intense scrutiny as he continued to deny vehemently that he had anything to do with the murder.

In 2003, the then Attorney General referred the matter back to the full bench of the Supreme Court for a new appeal but the Court refused Mallard's appeal, concluding there was no miscarriage of justice. The matter was then appealed to the High Court of Australia, the highest court in the land. In November 2005 the High Court unanimously overturned the WA Supreme Court's decision to deny Mallard's appeal. In a judgment critical of the state's Supreme Court, prosecution office and police, the High Court quashed Mallard's conviction. They ordered a retrial but suggested the Director of Public Prosecutions (DDP) might decide not to proceed on the evidence, given its doubtfulness and the fact that Mallard had already spent considerable time in gaol. The DPP heeded the advice and the State Government awarded Mallard 3.25 million dollars "compensation" for his twelve years of wrongful imprisonment.

The *Mickelberg* case enthralled many in Western Australia for over twenty-five years. It is a saga of Hollywood proportions. On 22 June 1982, the Perth Mint was swindled out of gold worth over half a million dollars. Three brothers, Ray, Brian and Peter Mickelberg became the prime suspects and were convicted in a trial at the District Court, held in the heat of late summer in February 1983. They always protested their innocence, claiming they were stitched up by the police, alleging that the younger brother, Peter, had been beaten by the interview detectives, and that police had fabricated their alleged statements. Moreover, they said, Ray's fingerprint had been imprinted on one of the dud cheques.

Not long after their incarceration Brian was released from prison after successfully appealing his conviction. But shortly after winning his freedom he died in an aeroplane crash, purportedly due to the aircraft running out of fuel. Peter would end up being inside for seven years and Ray a little longer.

They continued their fight to clear their names and in 2002, after many legal and political battles, were rewarded when Tony Lewandowski, the former detective who had interviewed the Mickelbergs, admitted to assaulting Peter and concocting the police interviews with the help of his colleague, Detective Don Hancock. Hancock was not around to refute the admission; he had been murdered a year before when his car was bombed, allegedly as pay back for the killing of a bikie in the goldfields. Lewandowski's confession led to another Supreme Court appeal.

Finally, after many unsuccessful appeals to the Supreme Court and even to the High Court, on 2 July 2004 the Supreme Court of Western Australia found in favour of the Mickelbergs holding by a two-to-one majority that the original guilty conviction was unsafe and there had been a miscarriage of justice.

The pursuit of justice is a cause without end. But, as the volume of work increases, the current Supreme Court building is straining under the pressures of modern demands. The building was designed to house three justices but there are now in excess of twenty Supreme Court justices. Complaints about the inadequacy and poor quality of the Supreme Court building are not new. As far back as 1867, when the Supreme Court sat in the Old Court House, the *Perth Gazette* reported on 7 June 1867: "An unusual sight to be seen on Wednesday in the Supreme Court, a judge presiding on the bench under an umbrella. The roof was leaky and his Honour did not like to suspend the case under hearing."

The State government response to the accommodation and space problems has been to build a multi-storey structure between the Old Treasury Building and the Perth Town Hall, at the spot where the felling of a tree denoted the establishment of the City of Perth. This building, when completed, will provide additional space for the Supreme Court, and the Crown Solicitors will also move in from their current offices further up the Terrace.

The other significant court is the District Court of Western Australia, which was established on 1 April 1970. At first, civil trials were temporarily held in the Public Trust building behind St George's Cathedral and criminal trials continued to be heard in the Supreme Court. But, from April 1982 the District Court was relocated to the Central Law Courts at 30 St George's Terrace, and this is where the Mickelberg trial took place. Their subsequent appeals were, of course, heard in the Supreme Court.

In June 2008 the District Court moved across the road to 500 Hay Street. The new District Court is a much lighter, more modern building with massive window panels at the front. In 2012, the District Court became the stage for the state's highest-profile murder trial. Lloyd Rayney, a former criminal prosecutor working for the State's Office of the Director of Public Prosecutions, was controversially named by police as the prime and only suspect in the 2007 murder of his estranged wife, Corryn Rayney, whose body was found in scenic King's Park.

Given Mr Rayney's prominence in the legal community and the significant media attention the investigation attracted, a judge from interstate and an interstate prosecution team were appointed to manage the case. Corryn Rayney was also well-known in legal circles as a registrar at the Supreme Court of Western Australia. The trial was conducted by judge alone, rather than a jury, as is the procedure for normal criminal trials. But this was at Lloyd Rayney's request, as is his right.

As testament to the inadequacy of the Supreme Court building, the trial was relocated to the District Court building to accommodate the large number of public and media observers expected. In November 2012, following an extensive three-month trial, Mr Rayney was found not guilty by Justice Martin. Justice Martin said that a lack of logic in several areas of the State's case was obvious and that crucial evidence was lacking.

About five minutes' walk from the District Court, where St George's Terrace commences and Adelaide Terrace concludes is the Duxton Hotel, formerly the Taxation Office and before that a Christian Brothers School. Behind the Hotel heading down Victoria Avenue towards the Swan River is the Federal Court precinct. Within that precinct is the Family Court of Western Australia.

The Family Court of Western Australia is a unique court in the Australian Federation. All states and territories of the Commonwealth of Australia, apart from Western Australia, come under the Family Court of Australia. But Western Australia has its own separate family court, even though its laws mirror those of its Commonwealth brother. When the

Family Court of Australia was established after the passing of the *Family Law Act* in the Commonwealth Parliament in 1975, the Western Australian Solicitor-General at the time, Ron Wilson, who was to become Western Australian's first High Court Justice in 1979, was against the idea. Wilson lobbied the WA government against being part of the national family court, his view being: "I think my incentive at the time was pride in Western Australia and the conviction that it was as good as or better than any other State and it could run a State court better than being dependent on the Commonwealth."

St George's Terrace, which is home to many of Perth's major legal establishments, is the main thoroughfare of Perth's Central Business District. In the 1940s and 1950s, it had the ambience of a boulevard, a place to stroll in one's lunch break and enjoy social intercourse with others who worked in the offices nearby. That ambience is gone now, replaced by efficient but unsocial high-rise buildings that have turned the Terrace into a virtual wind tunnel. A lunchtime stroll is now an endurance test rather than a chance for friendly social encounter, which was one of the pleasures of working on the Terrace mid-last century. Nevertheless, it is still the heart – albeit cooled a little in the wind tunnel – of Perth's business and professional activity.

At the Western end of St George's Terrace, the Barracks Arch stands a rather out-of-place structure. In 1966 the wings of the barracks were demolished to make space for the new Mitchell Freeway heading from the City to the northern suburbs. But some wanted the whole edifice demolished, with the Premier of the time, David Brand saying: "Down with the thing". But forces wanting the Arch to remain mounted an effective campaign through lobbying Perth City Councillors and State politicians and holding day and night vigils at the Arch. During Parliamentary debate, one member loudly remarked: "Just look at the bloody thing. Is that what you want to keep?" Another member responded to laughter from the chamber: "What would you look like from the rear with your pants down?" Over time there have been other politicians who have wanted the Arch demolished as it obstructed their view down St George's Terrace from the House on the Hill. But, like it or not, the Arch is a link with tradition. It is also a reminder to those who work in the House on the Hill – the Parliament of Western Australia – that they are there at the pleasure of the people they represent. It is the place where the laws of Western Australia are made. But, as Premier David Brand realised when voters threw his government out, the Barrack Arch stands there as a reminder that, when making the laws, they ignore the voices of those people at their own peril.

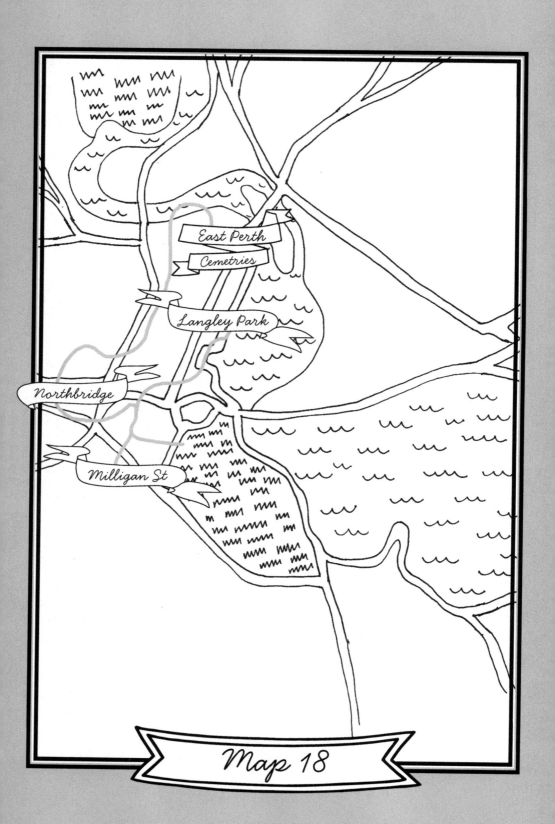

East Perth
Cemetries

Langley Park

Northbridge

Milligan St

Map 18

18

A WALK DOWN FOUR STREETS THAT DON'T EXIST

Beth George

The stories collected here imagine a Perth that is parallel to the one we know. They are based on the findings of my own research into the city's cartography and structure and on work produced through architecture studios, run between 2010 and 2014, which make an inquiry into the city. They are walks down streets that don't (quite) exist – or ones that *want* to exist. The basis of what my students and I do in speculating on Perth is to imagine into being certain desires that are embedded in the city's memory – its physical makeup – that are nascent.

We are compulsively drawn to the anomalies to the city's rectangular grid. They are the vestiges of pre-existing streets, the snapped-off axes from neighbouring morphologies that run counter or angular, which have found their way into the grid, the ones that emerged through some sort of necessary tweaking of the order of the city proper – a subversion of its neutrality. We are obsessed, as well, with those sites that have become the city's whipping boys and fed a culture of complaint.

From American urbanist Mario Gandelsonas we have learned that patterns found in a city's plan are not just shapes – their stories do not end there – they often have implications, and are tied to histories that have great and opportune meaning for the continued development and architectural inscription of a place.[1]

What underpins these studies is the notion that a city's story is written in its layout – that scratching away at the city's morphology and delving into its plan can be deeply revealing.

---

1 M. Gandelsonas, *The Urban Text*, Cambridge, Mass: MIT Press, 1991. Gandelsonas' morphological drawings reveal poignant civic narratives, particularly in Chicago where his "invisible wall" studies that connect the edges of broken streets coexist with socio-cultural borders. The notion that a city might hold "desires", as implied by such abstract readings, is largely owing to Gandelsonas' work.

Collected here are some useful fictions that value the anomalies, the hidden histories and the flaws of our town. From these, I wish to construct an image of Perth that amplifies its own truths and looks inward, not across the sea or the desert, for its urban curation.

ANOMALY 1: FORREST AND HILL

Forrest Avenue runs at an angle, bisecting two grid squares from corner to corner. It is the only diagonal street in central Perth and exists at a rare high point of the otherwise low-lying city. The

monument of the Don Aitken Centre — a lug of a building, solid and slab like — marks the termination of the street. Beyond that lies the dry and crackled East Perth Cemetery.

From these facts — the steep hill, the city below and the cemetery above — we now see the explanation for this anomaly: the welcome relief from the slope must be the very motive for the orientation of Forrest Street and the reason for its singularity. This is where the bodies would have been pulled, initially by cart and probably in exhaustingly hot weather, from the city's centre to its burial ground. While the north-south streets run directly against the contours of the hill, the oblique path offers some amelioration. It is likely that it was trodden into being before it was gazetted and made visible on a map.

Forrest Avenue now pulls back from the corners, its longing connection truncated by dead ends. It is severed from the cemetery, marooned as a strange, seeming accident.

The buildings that line it don't know what to do. Face the grid or face the diagonal? They do a little of everything – some belonging to the grid and leaving a cake-slice of verge along their edge, some aligning to Forrest Avenue and forming a triangular garden, some jack-knifing to maximise their plot-ratio. The buildings flanking this unique piece of city do not engage with it.

Ringing the cemetery, medium-density houses stand facing the verge as any house would, addressing the street with open frontages. But the curtains are drawn – there are no neighbours, nor a normal park. There is the cemetery, neglected and fenced in to safeguard it from a degree of vandalism that once brought bones to the surface.

These two territories – the cemetery, whose rugged surface is in complete contrast with the manicured and thirsty Gardens down the hill, is deliberately dry, populated with carefully selected trees, a truly elegant if unusual landscape; and Forrest Street that slices across the knoll toward it – contain the rich possibilities of living closely and beautifully with the dead, with civic memory. A messy planning history has left bodies interred in land adjacent to the cemetery, unmarked and lost, under car parks and verges. These might be exhumed and gifted the construction of a strange and nameless memorial – an ossuary, a marker.

We'll walk from that marker, embedded in the dry ground, cool concrete to the touch, fringed with lichen, connected with both the hill and somehow with the river. The ossuary contains mollusc shells from the middens overturned nearby in the residential developments around the Claisebrook inlet. It will be shaded, floored with leaves, scratching and quiet. We'll walk from here across the cemetery. Small lights will mark each grave whose timber crucifix rotted away years ago, knowing where to step. As we walk up the hill, the Don Aitken Centre looms like another tombstone, stretching up out of the hill, its friends, the WACA flood lights, constituting a family of urban monuments joining it to ring the scene. The cyclone fence can stay. It is suitably humble for our purposes.

And down we will walk to Cemetery Road. Here, now, the architecture swells to the edges of the boundary, reinforcing the legibility of this one oddity in the city's layout. Two sharply triangular buildings announce its angular presence, their skin-niness telling you that something is different here. The austere and elegant facades along Cemetery Road will stay the same height at the top, forming a datum. You can measure with your body the degree to which you are sinking down into the city proper, the buildings growing up around you.

Or perhaps not. Maybe all of the buildings around Cemetery Road will cling to their regular, grid-like edges, leaving a striking negative space through the middle. And the diagonal street will not be reconnected with the grid, the cul-de-sacs will remain and their edges will be walled. The whole site and its four vestigial parcels of land will become cloistered. Only on foot will you pass into and through this rich, deep garden. It will have tall edges that show you where the grid is, but its interior will be oblique. Here, along its central axis, everything will sit oddly – street benches, bollards, kerbs – they all will belong to the diagonal. The ground will intersect them – it will not be flattened and tidied but remain a perfect articulation of its topography, and it will exacerbate the diversion of these objects from the grid and from the architecture around the periphery of the block that wants to belong to it. Here you might stop, for a moment, feel a strange breeze, feel the grass, feel tied to something, to simply stop and not know why.

ANOMALY 2: PIER STREET

Pier Street punctures into the city proper, sitting at the slightest odds with the grid around it. A look beyond the city shows you that it is in fact a rogue piece of Northbridge. Now disconnected from the Northbridge grid by the rail reserve, which at this point can be crossed only on foot, the street has merely a visual connection with the morphology it belongs to.

The capacity for Pier Street to become a limb of Northbridge within the city is great. The main streets that form (literally) a bridge between the two sister pieces of city are William and Beaufort – the positioning of the Cultural Centre is no doubt a catalyst for this connection, as is the well-trodden path from the train station into the shopping arcades of the city proper. William and Beaufort have long been making the traverse. And after a long duration of being the seedier limbs of the city, they are now squeaky clean and rife with development.

If you have ever walked down Stirling Street, you will

notice that it is bizarrely wide. It is a street many would have missed, as the other two will more often be used. Felicity Morel identified through her mapped studies of the city that Stirling was the intended boulevard.[2] At a time when the city's northern environs were wet with swamps, Stirling traced the driest path and could have been the very street on which Northbridge clung to pivot away from the angle of the city by degrees. Stirling, though, has no enduring presence in the city proper – it breaks and disappears at the rail reserve.

Historically, the city and Northbridge were never aligned: the wetlands caused their crank, a road reserve squeezed between them and finally the railway cemented the divide. In the city's infancy, as Perth became the hub of commerce and the home of the wealthy, Northbridge came to house its bars, brothels, restaurants, and market gardens. The recipient of the city's shadier functions, it was referred to as Perth's 'nightsoil'.

As William and Beaufort have lately tidied themselves and become the stomping ground of developers and speculators, the grimy stuff, as it does, must step further outward.

With William and Beaufort becoming civic avenues, and Stirling lopped off and left to obscurity, the attention might turn to Pier Street – that one moment where Northbridge's grid infiltrates the city. This could be not only a morphological pricking of the city, but an enduring embedment of Northbridge's historically seamy character into the city's ordered one. Here, those disparate and strange functions (gentlemen's club, dive bar, print houses, backpackers') that cling to the rail reserve

---

2   F. Morel EdnieBrown, "the Swamp Stealers: topography, settlement and the evolution of Northbridge, an inner urban area in Perth, Western Australia, using geographic information systems," PhD thesis, University of Western Australia, 2006.

might begin to leak into the city to dance with the Chinatown restaurants, small hotels, theatres and heterotopia of Pier Street.

THE VOID OF LANGLEY PARK

Perth's foreshore is a construction site, and not for the first time. It was first a reserve, then it was built out. Then it was missed and reclaimed from the river to be a park at the foot of the city again.[3] It has been firmed with gabions, thickened and padded for the freeway, been played with like sand in a playground to create motorways and return again to grass. But it is, for the first time in a lifetime, a construction site for buildings – for that long-anticipated bringing of city to river.

Let's stand at the freeway interchange – gaze at the earthmovers, the cranes, the trucks, the dredgers creating Elizabeth Quay. You can see the river changing shape, you can see the skeletons emerging of towers to stand beside it. You can see the wiggle in the road that previously ran, straight as a die, punctuated only by palm trees in Los Angeleno style, from the city's east to its west.

But look beyond this to the expanse of windswept lawn – the space where nothing is – the city's doormat. This is

---

3   G. Stephenson, *The Design of Central Perth: some problems and possible solutions*, Perth: University of Western Australia Press, 1975. Pages 1–9 show various mappings of the city's grid and the foreshore between 1833 and 1955.

another kind of construction site – one that is built and rebuilt constantly without leaving so much as a mark.

There, at the foot of Barrack and William streets, lie the Perth baths in 1884. Despite the provision of a shed for changing in, a group of young men take a good old-fashioned nudie-run onto the mainland for a hoot.[4] A clap-trap solution, the baths have little more than a shed and timber jetty to define them.

Later, in the 1920s, White City's fairground spills over the same location. A fairground that began as 'ramshackle' grows more sophisticated – its gates glittering in the warm night air.[5]

Marches, soapbox speakers, light aircraft – all traverse the site over the years.

In the twentieth century, the annual Autralia Day fireworks become a larger attraction. The shores are swamped with people gazing at the spectacle of the sky lit up and the bridges spraying sparks. And each year the grass is deserted again.

The circus comes to town and great tents populate the gardens and lawns. Theatres are erected and come apart again. The motorway carves up the earth, sends cars spinning along tracks, pours infrastructure and dollars to convert the lawn into a rally track and return it again unscathed.

In the course of 100 years countless projects have been conceived to develop the foreshore and improve the city – to connect its physical structure with the river. A competition in 1991 generates some fabulous scenarios for the creation of a

---

4 *West Australian*, 7 February 1884. An article documented the unruly behavior of young men at the jettys: "Aware that their appearance, ungarmented, is objected to by persons whose reasons for doing so they are unable to appreciate, they take particular delight in issuing from the screening walls of the bathing house to cut capers on the bridge and pay uncostumed visits to the mainland…".

5 J. Gregory, *City of Light: A History of Perth since the 1950s*, Perth: City of Perth, 2003.

new, peripheral city centre. Hundreds of students in planning, architecture, and landscape architecture cast their imaginings upon the site. But, having been empty for so long, the grass seems to reject any finite proposition. While it has been reproached all of these years for its emptiness, its emptiness has become somehow valuable.

And so, gazing at the lawn, we can see not just the grass but the traces of all of these acts. It continues to house temporary and transient functions – structures of all scales and of any duration but permanent – and remains the primary site of celebration, spectacle and wonder in Perth.

And all the while it fuels debate, it captures the imagination of the brightest minds in our city and continues to make them churn. It is not a void. It is not a negative space. Its absence is its presence. It is a machine for ideas.

A FUNERAL FOR MILLIGAN STREET: A PLAY IN FIVE ACTS

Act I: in which the buildings remove their awnings as mourners remove their hats

Slowly the change begins. First, the fabric awnings are removed, laying bare their frames. Canvas falls and crumples on the pavement. Next, the awnings lined with cladding. Fibre cement sheeting is pulled off, whole cantilevered shade structures lowered and pulleyed to the ground.

Beneath the signage, the tin, the cladding, lie flimsy and ad-hoc structures pegged to the masonry walls. These seem too small and slender to have held all that weight.

Detached save for one bolt, a naked bracket swings.

All loose fittings – flags, buntings, signs, come down one after another. Names, logos, sale banners. Anything extraneous, anything light or superficial. With them comes away time: the rudiment of the original bricks and mortar are undressed.

Finally, the brackets and frames themselves are removed, leaving only holes and puckers in the cement render where the bolts and screws were fixed.

The faces of the masonry buildings, raw and stripped, with blanched and weathered paint marking where their attachments left off, now hold fast and face the sun. In the afternoon glare they stand, bare.

Act II: in which the doors stop working

Enter Man

*{**Man** approaches a door. A usual haunt. He is holding a shirt on a hanger – he wants to get it laundered. The door does not open. He shakes it by the handle. Looks around, tries another. Shut.}*

Man: Hello?

There are people inside They don't seem to recognise him or hear him tapping on the glass. It seems business-as-usual inside, lights on, but the locks

are latched and bolts dropped.
*{**Man** walks away, befuddled and cross, holding his shirt.}*
From inside the shop, a roller door is shut, a curtain pulled-to.
*{**Man 2** parks a ute on the kerb, removes a sheet of plywood from the tray and walks it toward a shopfront}.*

Act III: in which a veil is drawn

After a time, materials arrive. Lengths of steel tube, braces, shadecloth. Steadily, a scaffold is erected. It runs unbroken along the entire length of Milligan Street. It presses up to the facades, marching its way down the footpath. Strung along it, bolts of draped fabric. The structure shrouds the faces of the mourning buildings.

A construction site is forming.
*{**Construction Workers** busy themselves behind the veil}.*
Late afternoon, the site is still. A wind disturbs the fabric.

Act IV

Silence.
The veil becomes tattered, develops holes where it clings to the scaffold and rubs against the joints. Curious fingers and pocket-knives have opened eyeholes along the ground level.
The veil is replaced several times over. Each time the effort is spectacular: the fabric is perfectly meted out and hung afresh to ripple in the wind.

Twenty-seven years pass.

Act V: in which the buildings form an orderly line

Approaching Milligan from Hay Street, light spills from the corner where the veil ought to be. The veil has dropped from the facades along Milligan Street and, at the juncture where the facade would meet an adjoining wall, there is instead a gap. This is where the light is emanating from. As if by some tectonic act, the buildings have distanced themselves, and stand free, from their facades.

With the veil removed, one can see that the faces of the build-ings along Milligan have been plugged – their entry thresholds bricked and permanently sealed. The facades are otherwise as they were – still weathered, still denuded, still bearing the marks of their old clothes. And older now – peeling and crumbling a little.

Those facades now form an unbroken wall, lining Milligan Street from north to south. They stand as one monolith, buttressed and patched, seamless and heavy.

Behind this wall, the buildings have retreated. There is a canyon now, a passage between the ageing wall and a new skin that forms the boundaries of the tenancies that once abutted it. Each building has distanced itself from the wall, forming a perfect line.

The newly created void wedges itself between the hard, masonry line of the Milligan Street Wall and the light-filled interiors of the spaces crouched behind it.

Epilogue
Nobody will enter the City Proper from Milligan Street again. Access will permanently be made from its flanking streets.

The wall itself will be carefully maintained. Its structural viability regularly tested, and any works to bolster it undertaken expediently.

It will bleach, but it will stand. It now shades the new territory beyond – protecting it from the wind and sideways westerly sun.

Never beautified, but not allowed to disintegrate, the wall will remain.
END

NOTE

Milligan Street forms the westernmost boundary of the Prohibited Area, a territory that Aboriginal people were denied entry into for twenty-seven years. Those Aborigines who worked in the City Proper held a permit that allowed them entry during business hours, after that they might be forcibly removed. According to Jenny Gregory, a brawl which broke out at White City – a semipermanent carnival site that stood at the foot of Barrack Street in the 1920s – marked the beginning of a series of events leading ultimately to the permit legislation and the drawing of this invisible line.[6] Our fairground, it seems, possessed a sad and ironic name.

From 1927 to 1954, this legislation remained. It is not a truth well known.

ACKNOWLEDGEMENTS

For Milligan Street – thanks to Lola Sheppard who brought the map of the exclusion zone to the studio discussion. I had known the story, but had not seen the line.

For Langley Park – thanks to my teammates Rene Van Meeuwen and Jon Tarry with whom, through our Venice Biennale proposition "speciation city" the idea of valuing the state of reserve was elevated to the necessity of the reserve as a generator of ideas.

For Forrest Avenue – thanks to the National Trust of WA's Phil Palmer for the guided tour of the cemetery and the stories of its past.

---

6   J. Gregory, *City of Light: A History of Perth since the 1950s*, Perth: City of Perth, 2003, p. 6.

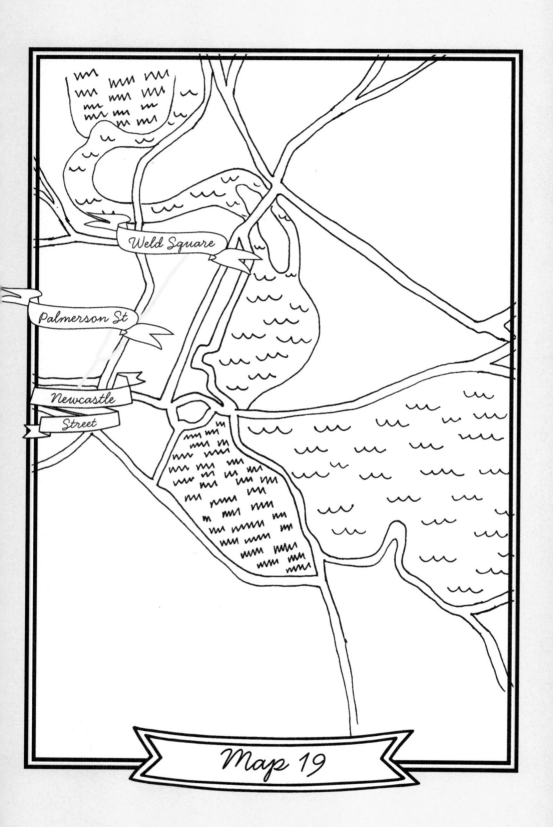

Weld Square

Palmerson St

Newcastle
Street

Map 19

19

DEVELOPMENT AND PLANNING

Alannah MacTiernan

Despite nearly 190 years of displacement, it is a cause for celebration that we have a real Aboriginal presence in the Newcastle Street precinct. It is brilliant to have Aboriginal businesses, a training centre, representative bodies and media operations collect around Weld Square, a park still popular with our Indigenous brothers and sisters. This is not a chance location, but a remnant of living history that demonstrates the resilience of Aboriginal Australians and how they manage to maintain a community in the face of harsh and contemptuous policy.

In 1927, the central area of Perth became prohibited to Aboriginal people. Even those given a pass to work in the city had to be out by 6 pm. The northern boundary of the prohibited area was Newcastle Street. Not surprisingly, Aboriginal people from across Western Australia: Nyoongah, Yjamatji, Wongi and others from further north, congregated on the city limits in Weld Square and created an attachment to the area that endured well beyond the repeal of the legislation in 1954.

The fabulous Coolbaroo Club opened its doors in 1946. It was a mecca for an Aboriginal population with a renewed postwar pride and insistence on civil rights. The area became a natural location for those early organisations fighting for Aboriginal equality. The Aboriginal Advancement Council has been entrenched there for over fifty years. Even ten years ago Aboriginal people arriving in Perth from around the state would still head to Weld Square to trade stories and track down friends and family. Mobile phones have probably seen the networking function of the park decline, but it still has a place in the heart of the Aboriginal community – and that connection is now officially acknowledged.

Perth expanded slowly over its first fifty years. In 1881, the rail link from Fremantle to Guildford was built to serve the three original settlements of the Swan River Colony. The railway cut Northbridge from the CBD and caused it to develop in a different way. I seem to be alone in thinking this was not all bad. It created in Northbridge that character of a quarter – an entertainment precinct, which is the one place in Western Australia you still can bop till you drop.

But the big changes really began in the late 1880s when gold was discovered in the Coolgardie region and money and people poured into Perth. It helped that Depression struck the Eastern states at the same time, bringing lots of skills into Western Australia. The architecture of this period still forms a significant part of today's landscape in the area.

But by the 1950s, the gloss was wearing off. Around Australia, post–World War II inner-city suburbs were being hollowed out with affluence and widespread car ownership, and the suburbs beckoned with their promise of a better lifestyle, cleaner homes with more bedrooms and shiny bathrooms. Our postwar European and Anglo-Asian migrants moved into the vacated city, driven not just by price, but a desire not to be buried alive in suburbia. They created the Northbridge scene.

By the 1970s, more Perth people were beginning to understand the appeal of the inner city, which had come a decade earlier in other Australian cities and abroad. But the Newcastle Street precinct was subject to planning blight. Still on the books from the car-oriented 1960s was the Northern City Bypass, a large highway planned as part of a bigger bitumen collar around the CBD. And the local authority wasn't complaining. 'Your car is as welcome as you are' was the defiant stance of the City of Perth throughout the 1980s. The establishment of Perth was not going to have any of this 'new urbanism' nonsense with its focus on pedestrians and inner-urban residential development. The City mascot of Herbie, a little, repulsively cute, pink polka dot car, incited the population to bring their car into the city. Besides, vehicle parking was a great little earner and councillors on the vehicle parking committee got the best junkets.

It was the mid-1980s when the ByPass project came to the head of the Main Roads priority list, and a road and bridge proposed around the Parry Street alignment. The politically aware renovators who had gradually moved into the area over the past decade organised against this project. At the same time, the Labor Government broadened the franchise for Council elections and activists, including me, started to penetrate the corridors of Council House. CBD businesses were also beginning to appreciate that a high speed by-pass separating them from their customers might be a second-rate idea compared to actually trying to rebuild a residential inner-urban base for their business.

The State Government backed down and some of the planning blight was reversed. A whole streetscape of feder-ation houses and some very different Art Deco townhouses were restored and dedicated to public housing. Just as impor-tant as conserving the architecture, this maintained some of the social diversity and the energy that is generated by that diversity.

But the road would not go away – and a new government revived the plan in the mid-1990s. This time it was to be a tunnel, its alignment on the northern side of Newcastle Street.

Regrettably, the construction technique was trenching, so heritage was again under the hammer. Another campaign was waged – this time the opposition focused on priority being given to investment in roads over rail in the metropolitan area.

Some extraordinary remnants of our history emerged during the campaign. We discovered that behind the buildings that fronted onto Newcastle Street were much earlier, street alignments of a pre-goldrush Western Australia. Along these huddled lanes were the vestiges of long-gone trades as well as remains of a local evergreen industry, the knocking shops. This time the campaigners didn't win and the ancient houses of ill-repute and candlestick makers went in the construction of the trench. With them went the landmark pub, the Beaufort, a source of lots of local colour. The tunnel opened in 2000 and certainly proved to be an effective and popular addition to the transport infrastructure.

The next challenge was to reinvent the area over the tunnel and the adjacent streets where the WA Planning Commission and Main Roads had acquired significant property over the decades. This new Northbridge task was added to the charter of the East Perth Redevelopment Authority (EPRA). It was with some karmic pleasure that I found this authority in my domain when I became a minister in the new Labor Government in 2001.

The first battle was to reorient the plan to demolish dozens of heritage buildings that had survived the trench construction. I spent many weekends working Newcastle and Aberdeen Streets with heritage activists and EPRA officials. The EPRA was right in seeing that the rejuvenation provided great opportunity for large-scale modern buildings that would bring people and businesses back to the area. But a city is not interesting without surprises. Weaving the past into the present makes that quality of surprise far more likely. Empowered by the extraordinary knowledge of amateur historians, I reversed the decision to knock down some great little architectural gems that have now been incorporated in the new re-development. The guiding principle was if it was nineteeth century or had a startling form, we would keep it. My particular favourites were three federation bungalows designed and built by Talbot Hobbs on Newcastle and Palmerston Streets. They now house active businesses and form a little precinct where we celebrate the life of this Western Australian soldier architect.

The project led to a new focus on Weld Square, bringing us back to the beginning of our story. Half the Moreton Bay figs were removed for the tunnel construction. The shallow soil over the tunnel drove the replanting of the southern end in small Western Australian flora – a nice reference back to the park's native history. Now the park is surrounded by apartments and office blocks. It not only provides for the biophyllic needs of city dwellers but is a playground for the old and new community. The basketball half-court would have to be one of the best value-for-money infrastructure investments by the City of Vincent because of the constant use by locals.

Change is the constant in these precincts on the fringe of the CBD. They are places where we see the rich tapestry woven by waves of migration and evolving aspirations. It is not always painless, but if we insist on blending the old with the new – punters and buildings – we get the best the city can offer.

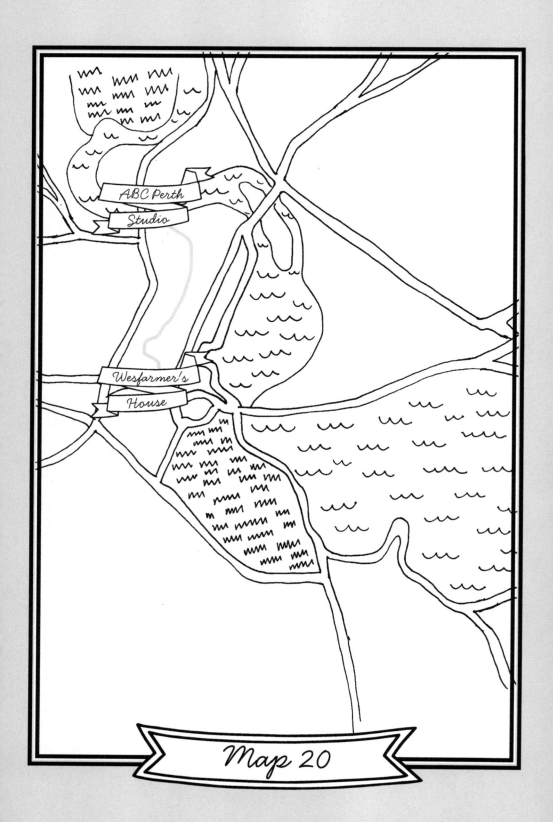

ABC Perth
Studio

Wesfarmer's
House

Map 20

20

PERTH IN CONVERSATION

Gillian O'Shaughnessy

Just over the road from Claisebrook Railway Station you'll find the East Perth headquarters of the ABC and the home of 720 Local Radio. The ABC has been broadcasting the voices of Perth people for almost 100 years now, first as 6WF, from a small studio within the Wesfarmers Building in the heart of the city, then from the sprawling Adelaide Terrace offices of ABC radio, television and the state orchestra, WASO.

I've worked at the ABC since the mid-1990s. I started in a very junior role for radio news having tussled my way into a two-week tryout and from there, a short-term contract. It was very competitive. I worked hard for a chance, but I was also lucky and I knew it. Often in those early days I felt so overwhelmed that my heart would beat violently inside my chest and I felt sure it was visible. It was surreal. Every day to start work, you would walk in off Adelaide Terrace, past the big blue ABC logo sign at the entrance, through the glass double doors and down the corridor, then down several flights of stairs to the radio newsroom. It was enormous. Occasionally you'd catch the orchestra tuning up on your way. There's something about hearing an off-key cello being tuned up alongside a grand piano with the occasional clash of a cymbal that made me feel wonderful. I loved walking down that corridor.

Like so many others, I'd grown up with the ABC, and radio felt like home. My mother, Pieta O'Shaughnessy, was one of the pioneers of community radio in Perth in the early 1970s. Community radio was all about niche markets, giving parts of the community that didn't have a mainstream voice on TV or radio a place to have and hear conversations that were familiar to them. Community stations in Perth broadcast Aboriginal radio, ethnic programs, shows for retirees, for local original music, for non-mainstream sport. Radio helped reflect the voice of Perth back at itself. It was a conduit, so that those who might otherwise feel locked out could find a place. My sister and I spent a lot of our childhood out at 6NR (now Curtin FM) and running around UWA at 6UVS-FM (now RTR-FM), poking through the record library and playing with old reel-to-reel recorders. Radio was familiar, and comfortable, and there were plenty of people with something to say.

I had been inside the ABC only once, when I was fifteen and at drama school. I got a part in a radio play recorded in the ABC studios. I was given the small but deeply thrilling role of an 'expressive dog', and I took it very seriously. We recorded it at the ABC studios for Radio National, I think, from memory. We took a taxi from school, which was exciting in itself, and pulled up at the front entrance. My drama teacher led us into the building, pretending for a lark to shield our faces with a newspaper from a non-existent crowd of autograph hunters. He knew we felt we were somewhere special. Five of us stood around a microphone in the WASO studios to perform. I don't remember anything about the play at all, except for my part. I had no actual words in the script aside from various cues to woof in a way that would reflect an emotion. I think the script went something like this:

Dog: woofwoofwoofwoofwoof (with surprise!)
Or,
Dog: woofwoofwoofwoofwoof (exasperated!)

I'm not sure I quite pulled it off, but I gave it my best. I felt like I was in the Goon Show being inside that building making a radio play. I wanted to be back there.

It was another fourteen years before I picked up a two-week work experience gig in news as a tryout with a view to a short-term position. And I nearly lost it as soon as I started.

I'd yet to receive an actual contract with ABC News, and was desperate for one, as were hundreds of other young would-be journalists behind me. If you didn't get it right the first time, there were plenty of people to take your place and there were very few opportunities for a start. Interestingly many of those opportunities came through a long stint in work experience in Perth's community radio newsrooms, but I went straight for an ABC cadetship and came second. Not enough to get me a permanent job, but enough to convince them to take a closer look at me. So there I was, hopeful, inexperienced and overwhelmed.

Early on, I was assigned a shadow shift, a shift where I wasn't required to do anything, interview anyone, write anything or record anything, just watch and learn from the senior police reporter. I was to accompany him to a police news conference, which was being held not at the main East Perth Police head-quarters, the horseshoe shaped building you can see on the eastern side of the city overlooking Burswood and the river, but in West Perth, in a random nondescript block, several flights up, in a beige office.

He leapt in the car, I scuttled in behind him trying not to get in the way, and off we sped. The police did their thing, he did his, and we shot back to office to file a story. Then he realised he'd forgotten his notebook, so he threw me the car keys and told me to go back and get it.

What I hadn't mentioned in any of my cadet interviews was that I had no driver's licence. I was still on my L-plates and some months off sitting my test, but I wasn't about to mention it. I thought it might affect me getting a job. It would have.

It was a horrifying moment, but I didn't have time to react. I caught the keys. I imagine I stared at him for longer than was appropriate, then I said, "Ok," because there was nothing else to say. I strode off fast towards the doors that led to the news car garage, then took a sharp left at the last minute and out the double glass doors at the front. I couldn't tell you if the orchestra was tuning up then or not. I found a bus outside and got on it; it carried me about two blocks up the Terrace before turning in the wrong direction. I got off. I found another bus heading in my direction, I got on, I got off. And so on I went. I didn't have the money for a taxi.

It was raining. And windy. Perth is one of the breeziest cities in the world and the Terrace can be one long wind tunnel.

I bussed, ran, ran and bussed all the way from East to West Perth, located the missing notebook, and bussed and ran, ran and bussed back to the ABC studios. It was sheer fear that kept me moving. I could feel my new world falling about me. I could feel panic hovering.

It took me about 45 minutes to get there and back and I was dishevelled. But I made it. I handed the notebook to the Police reporter.

"You took your time," he said.

"The traffic was awful," I replied.

He probably thought I was a weird one, but he took the notebook and I didn't get caught.

I got a job a few weeks later and had to come clean eventually, but it was too late by then. I have noted since that any job application at the ABC Perth offices will include a question about your driver's licence.

The ABC moved to the other side of East Perth in 2005 to brand new offices at the corner of Royal and Fielder Street, near the Health Department and TAFE and City Farm, an old scrap metal yard that's been transformed into an urban community garden and cafe. The Claisebrook Cove end of East Perth was still very new, now a model of urban renewal, then still a bit toy-town. Everything was there, shops and houses, street art and man-made lakes and waterbirds, but there weren't many people who were there outside of work. They were yet to move there in any sort of numbers.

The new building looked glorious. We went from an immense rabbit warren of a building to a tight, well-equipped, light-filled modern studio. The old building was aging, with carpet that had been badly re-dyed rather than replaced so often that the dingy colour ran a little into the walls. It lurched over the space of a large city block, from the Esplanade next to Riverside Drive to the Terrace. It was not a building that fostered close ties. You could quite literally work on air, studio to studio, with a colleague you would never meet in person from one year to the next.

The new ABC offices were glass and steel and filled with Perth light. There were great flat metal louvres across the west-facing windows to moderate the afternoon sun and tall plane trees that lined the streets outside. It's small, much smaller than the old place, although just ten years later it still feels too big for a shrinking media landscape. Then, it was cutting-edge architecture.

I felt more connected with the city and its people there, and I was a much more confident journalist by then, although I suspect it's the kind of job you never really feel you have mastered. I moved from news to a job in Local Radio, my new desk literally a 30-second walk from one side of our floor to the other. I took on the afternoon shift, broadcasting a talkback radio show to Perth and Western Australia between 1 and 3 pm.

At first it was uncomfortable, not working in news, and I felt out of place. News is a very precise medium. It's today. It's factual. It's concise, and there is no place for winding colourful prose in a news script. It's not focused on being friendly or inclusive. It's not a chat. In news you turn your microphone on to tell people what's happened and then you turn it off. In local radio, you turn it on and invite them to tell you and then maybe you'll both start talking to each other like normal people do. You might not know where it will lead, and it may not be about anything important by news standards. A colleague once described it to me as 'the stuff of life'. At first, I had no idea what that meant or what to talk about without something concrete and absolute 'happening'. But that comes, as the city and its people begin to tell you their stories and you realise it's all just about having a conversation.

A city like Perth is made up of millions of small happenings. It is a product of its infrastructure, its architecture, its history and its landscapes, and its people, past, present and future. Their stories are absorbed into it and resonate from it, constantly evolving, like a conversation in itself.

Radio reflects that in a way nothing else can. It is the original social media. It's a series of tiny snapshots, conversations and stories and voices that in some aspects will be the same anywhere you go, but at the same time will be entirely particular to Perth.

I love to hear those stories. They're everywhere. They're in the most surprising places and also exactly where you'd expect to find them.

Take the train for example. I catch the train from Fremantle to Perth City, and I carry on two stops to get to East Perth. It's like a microcosm of the bigger city experience. There're lots of different people who you can assume are basically the same as people anywhere, or you can assume that each of them has their own story that's important to them. We all have stories that are as individual as we are yet also as universal as love or sorrow or shame or joy. Sometimes people will tell you their story.

Like an elderly man I sat next to from Fremantle to the City. We got off the train at the same time and I made way for him. He moved slowly and with some trouble like an old man might do. He wore trousers with pleats at the front and a pale checked short-sleeved shirt. It was the kind of shirt with wide sleeves that don't hug the arm and are ironed flat. His hair was grey and not quite neat, as though he didn't get it cut as often as he once used to. He was pushing a stroller that held a small boy who was maybe two or three.

He looked slightly startled.

I assumed he was a grandfather from a generation who was not familiar or completely comfortable being in sole charge of a child who might do something unexpected or difficult to deal with in public. I smiled at him, so he might feel reassured.

"What a sweet little boy," I said.

The old man looked at me and clutched my arm very briefly and then let me go fast, as if he had not meant to do that. "He's mine," he said, a little desperately. "I'm seventy-two years old.

I didn't even know it was possible."

And he moved away before I could respond. I didn't get a chance to ask him how his life turned out that way. I really wanted to know. The experience stuck with me – that man, who looked like so many other older men but whose life had not evolved how he expected, who had a story that was his own.

There's another man who travels to Perth every morning in the same carriage at 6 am on the same line. He likes to strike up conversations. He asks people about their day, shows an interest in whatever part of their life they want to share. He's worried too many of us spend our train trips looking at our phones. Only connecting with our own small groups of people, family and select friends. He's right, we do. But he's developed a small informal club of like-minded people who commute to work in Perth, and they now go out of their way to catch the same train. They like to talk to strangers.

We invited him on to the program to talk about his experi-ence. He was slightly surprised we wanted to interview him. He didn't think he was important enough, or that he had anything important to say. He was concerned he'd need notes or that he might ramble. He didn't, and the last thing you want from a guest with a story is a stilted, nervous recitation from a list of notes. You're really looking for the essence of the story, the essence of them. He just said what he did, how one day he was traveling on the train feeling disconnected and he started to talk to the person next to him. A stranger. And they wanted to talk back. And it grew. He felt good that he was building a small community.

A lot of listeners called in that day, or later, because they connected in some way with him. They said things like, his story made them look around them a bit more than they had before. Maybe now in a small way, they might put their phone down for a minute and just look at a view, or they might say hello to a stranger in passing. They liked it. They talked about conversations they had struck up in the queue at the supermarket, or a stranger who had helped them. They talked about a time they noticed something, and did something about it. They talked about small connections that they remembered.

Stories don't have to be big. But they work best for Perth radio when they're Perth stories. It takes those millions of small happenings and begins to connect them into a picture of our city. They lift our city into more than a collection of buildings and traffic and busy people. There are people who are tired, people who are lonely, people who have passion, people with vision, people who have given up or would like to, people who are quiet, people who have come here from another place or who have always been here. There are people who are hopeful, or afraid, or filled with great grief or immense joy.

Perth people.

Their stories are who we are. Radio's beauty and its constant endeavour is to tell those stories.

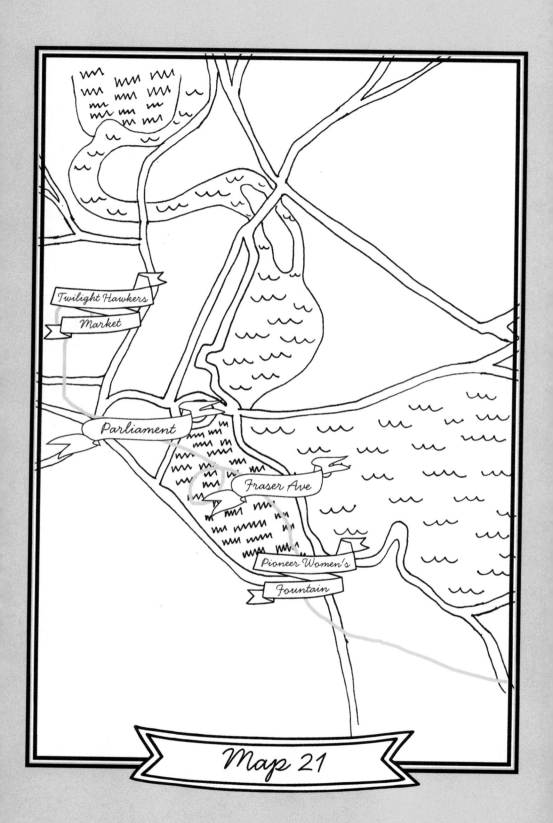

Twilight Hawkers Market

Parliament

Fraser Ave

Pioneer Women's Fountain

Map 21

21

PUBLIC ART IN PERTH:
A PERSONAL VIEW

Andra Kins

What always interests and excites me about public art is the potential it holds for the creation of artworks that engage with their environment and their public in such a way that something new emerges. This can be a new intellectual insight or emotional response that nudges us to think more about where and how we live, visually delights us and inspires a new appreciation of form and beauty, or calls us to physically interact with the work. All of this contributes to an exploration and expression of what it means to be living at the start of the twenty-first century.

Art is an aesthetic endeavor alongside architecture and landscape design. Public art expresses, through the creative work of individual artists or those in collaboration with other design professionals, the underlying and overt interests of our culture. Often we think that art is just about the individual artist and his or her personal concerns, but with public art there is more complexity in the process, more demand for an authentic relationship with the context of the artwork. The artist's relationship to the site will either reflect to a large degree existing aspects of the community's relationship to a particular place or it will stretch and expand that relationship by introducing something new. Conscious engagement with context is necessary for public art to achieve its maximum effect.

I was the child of Latvian World War II refugees and grew up in an old weatherboard house at 58 Alma Road in North Perth. My parents were both painters – my mother an artist, and my father a house painter. They were typical Europeans and walked a lot before they saved enough money to buy their first Holden station wagon. My mother and I would catch the bus that ran along William Street to central Perth to go shopping at Boans and Bairds. I grew up very much with a sense of the difference between public and private realms. Essentially the private personal realm of home was rooted in Latvian culture, and the public sphere was about places and institutions outside the home and located within Australian culture.

My parents were used to making the most of public space. At a very young age I was taken to Hyde Park and Kings Park. There are photos of me in my pram gazing intently at the ducks in one of ponds in Hyde Park, and then another where I'm enveloped by the twisted sculptural trunk and roots of a huge old Moreton Bay Fig tree. This is the same park where I rode my bike with my school friends from North Perth Primary, and where my husband and I had photos taken on our wedding day by a tipsy Latvian photographer.

Kings Park is the green heart of Perth, combining gardens and the largest area of natural bushland in a capital city. I have always loved banksias and the two seating areas, created by artist Philippa O'Brien for the Banksia Garden, incorporating marble mosaic paving, steel and Banksia wood seats are a delight to visit. It also has playgrounds, memorials and public facitilies. The playground I find the most inspired and attractive is the Rio Tinto Naturescape, completed in 2011. Here children can enjoy the natural environment and learn about it in a very hands-on way. Artist Jon Tarry has created a vibrant contemporary entrance sculpture for the area. It's like an assemblage of pick up sticks that you walk through to find hidden thickets, a creek, lookouts, a cubby building area, upside down trees, and a wetland. It's a place to take your shoes off and wade into the cool creek water.

The memorial I find the most moving in the park is the series of Honour Avenues with each tree bearing a small plaque at its base dedicated by family members to Western Australian service men and women who died in World War I and World War II. The trees form a large-scale sculptural element winding through the park, symbolizing vigorous life rising from the sacrifice and loss of death. Fraser Avenue, the main entrance avenue to the park at the top of St Georges Terrace, is lined with towering lemon-scented gums and is one of the most visited sites in Perth. These trees with stunning white boughs were planted in 1937 and form a cathedral-like entrance, each one having a centenary plaque to acknowledge prominent Western Australian citizens commemorated in 1929.

As a Public Art Consultant I have facilitated many public art selection committees. Often there is a pull towards the 'already known' safe option that supports the status quo rather than provoking and pushing the public to contemplate more openheartedly and with more genuine curiosity the meaning of an artwork. Margaret Priest was the first woman to undertake a public art commission in Western Australia and it was the largest single bronze cast in Australia at that time, in the late 1960s. The bronze sculpture of mother with child for the Pioneer Women's Memorial in Kings Park was commissioned by the Country Women's Association and the artist had to contend with mutterings about "the baby not wearing nappies and the woman not wearing stays".[1] The sculpture is set in a pond with a large fountain shooting up jets of water, which was designed by architect Geoffrey Summerhayes. I remember

1   From a letter written by Margaret Priest in 2000 to her friend Joan Youngberg where she describes her experiences while creating the Pioneer women's sculpture for Kings Park.

my mother muttering about conservatism in Perth in relation to press reportage of this sculpture when it was installed in 1968. But times have changed, thank goodness, and today we are able to commission artworks that will not necessarily please everyone, but they may push the boundaries of our understanding.

Adjacent to King Park, and located in the river at Matilda Bay, is another bronze sculpture of a woman poised to dive into the river. *Eliza*, by Tony Jones and Ben Jones, is a robust woman in a swimsuit and bathing cap commissioned by the City of Perth in 2007 to commemorate the old Crawley Baths. I remember going to swimming lessons and school swimming carnivals at these baths from North Perth Primary School in the days before the Beatty Park Complex was built for the Commonwealth Games. My memories are of brown murky water with huge man-of-war jellyfish floating by and scaring us stupid. Amazingly, *Eliza* has come alive through a heartfelt connection with the Perth community. Unidentified people dress her up during the night, and every time I drive into the city from Fremantle along Mounts Bay Road, I look to see what outfit she is wearing, or what cause she is championing.

In the parliamentary precinct, within the newly refurbished Office of the Premier and Cabinet Room, is Monique Tippett's stunningly beautiful *Wandoo Country*. This wall artwork, commissioned through the Percent for Art Scheme, was created using recycled Wandoo timber from the original seating from Perry Lakes Stadium, where together with my fellow students from Mt Lawley High School, I fervently cheered on our competitors at interschool athletics carnivals. When the artist started work on this project she had to peel away chewing gum still adhering beneath the slats!

Brought together in fifty separate panels and hung on two levels of the building, this artwork evokes in the viewer the grandeur and scale of a Western Australian wandoo landscape with its variety of textures and colours. It brings the contemplative aura of the natural environment into a busy office space expertly designed by Cox Howlett & Bailey Woodland.

When I drive into the city centre I almost always park under the Alexander Library – a habit from the time when Nic Beames and I occupied the little Urban Thresholds office in the old Perth Central School Building that now houses the Blue Room Theatre. The entry statement to the performance space is a fabulous floor to ceiling mural painting by Tom Alberts completed in the late 1980s.

As I emerge from the carpark and enter the Perth Cultural Centre, I pass *Gateway 2: Coalesce*, a black and white striped sculpture by Akio Makigawa, which has become a Perth landmark and meeting place. Makigawa explored the idea of a gate as a symbol of passage or development from one state to another. It's a contemporary version of the traditional Japanese *torii*.

The Blue Room is located at the western end of the Perth Cultural Centre, a gateway to James Street and Northbridge, Perth's nightlife and entertainment district. Nearby is the award-winning State Theatre Centre of Western Australia, designed by Kerry Hill Architects and opened in 2011. In the evenings you can walk across Matthew Ngui's complex interactive artwork *falling from heaven to earth; the shooting star* on your way to a show. It's like walking a celestial red carpet pulsating with light, colour, and dazzling comets.

The Metropolitan Redevelopment Authority (MRA) is currently revitalizing the cosmopolitan inner-city neighbourhood of Northbridge. It's an interesting area of Perth, having been home to waves of migrants and refugees, in particular Italians, Greeks, Chinese, and Vietnamese. My grandparents rented rooms in a house on Newcastle Street when they first arrived as displaced persons after the war. Recently, some seventy significant heritage buildings have been retained, restored, and recycled and William Street has received a new lease of life with a vibrant mix of restaurants and quirky boutiques moving in. This spirit of rejuvenation has included the commissioning of a number of murals by the City of Perth, and my favourites are Laurel Nannup's *White Tailed and Red Tailed Cockatoos* on the corner of William and Aberdeen Streets, and emblematic horses in Audrey Fernandes-Satar's *Border Wall* on the side wall of Connections nightclub and viewable from the No 2 Roe Street carpark. Laurel is a Noongar artist celebrating the natural heritage of this landscape, while Audrey hails from India and Mozambique and explores in her artwork the themes of migration and diaspora. If you go up close to *Border Wall* you will find scripts traced from her grandmother's handwritten recipe books.

In 2012, an unusual new public artwork entered Aberdeen Street, not far from the little Lutheran Church where I was married. It's a series of three sculptures, *Baba Yaga Houses,* by then Central Institute of Technology School of Art and Design student Marwa Fahmy. This was a joint project between the East Perth Redevelopment Authority (now MRA) and the Central Institute of Technology. The sculptures are strange, chicken-legged houses from the story of Baba Yaga, a witch in a series of Eastern European cautionary fairytales. Marwa is the child of Egyptian migrants, and like the murals, the *Baba Yaga Houses* are visual markers for the area's cultural diversity.

The latest wave of major public artworks to arrive in the city centre, implemented with bigger budgets, are bold, iconic and larger scale. Some have been developed and modelled in a digital environment utilising contemporary materials and new fabrication methods.

The first one, commissioned by the Anglican Dean and Chapter of St Georges Cathedral through their Foundation for the Arts and funded by successful local prospector and mining investor Mark Creasy, is *Ascalon*, an abstract interpretation of the story of St George and the Dragon. The artists, Marcus Canning and Christian Vietri, have created a dynamic sculpture that captures the billowing movement of St George's white cloak and the focused intensity of the trajectory of his lance. This one-pointed intensity speaks directly to the essence of the St George mythology and what intention and effort it can take for good to triumph over evil. At night a light shines up through a crack at its base illuminating the billowing form in a way that increases its dramatic spatial effect. This stunning sculpture is located next to St George's Cathedral, on St Georges Terrace in central Perth.

Forrest Place is historically Perth's most well-known public square. When I worked at the Craft Council that was housed upstairs at the Perth Railway Station in the late 1980s I used to look out of my office window onto Forrest Place and see the old Boans building being demolished to make way for Myers and the new Forrest Chase development. Up until then Forrest Place had big old shady trees with seats beneath them and the steps of the GPO were used for political speeches and public demonstrations. My mother went to Forrest Place to buy a copy of Philip Roth's banned book *Portnoy's Complaint* in 1969 when it was sold clandestinely from the back of a truck!

As Perth continues to grow and change, Forrest Place continues to evolve with the addition of new public artworks. Commissioned by the State Government together with the Perth City Council, James Angus's *Grow Your Own* has been colloquially termed 'The Cactus' by the people of Perth because its three-dimensional biomorphic form cast in aluminium and painted bright green does resemble a cactus. Its colourful, joyful presence animates the space both visually and spatially. Perth City Council's commissioning of Jeppe Hein's *Water Labyrinth* has introduced into the city centre a highly interactive water feature that is a magnet for children in Perth's hot summer months. Jets of water shoot up twelve metres into the air creating a series of rooms that disappear as quickly as they emerge from the ground. The sounds of water rising and falling mingle with squeals of delight as children play in this cool, constantly changing 'labyrinth'.

Commissioned through the State Government's Percent for Art Scheme, *Totem* by Geoffrey Drake Brockman sits next to the new Perth Arena in Wellington Stree. The predominantly bright yellow artwork has been referred to as 'The Pineapple', 'The Corn Cob' and 'Banksia Cone', highlighting to me how much we want to see something familiar, something that we already know when we look at an artwork. Six years in the making, *Totem* is a high-tech version of an origami paper tower with moving panels programmed to open and close like flower petals in response to people walking past. It also shoots geometric laser projections onto the Arena at night. The overall form of this interactive public artwork complements the aesthetics of the Arena building. They look as if they belong to the same family.

The Perth Arena building, an aesthetic exploration of the eternity puzzle, is an entertainment and sporting venue designed by architectural firms Ashton Raggatt McDougal and Cameron Chisholm Nicol, and replaces the old Perth Entertainment Centre where together with many other Perth baby boomers I attended rock concerts by groups such as Dire Straits, U2, Bob Dylan, Talking Heads and Simple Minds. It is part of the first stage of the Perth City Link project, a 13.5-hectare urban renewal and redevelopment project that will reconnect the city centre with Northbridge. Another urban renewal project underway is Elizabeth Quay. Both Perth City Link and Elizabeth Quay were developed and guided by the MRA, and will create new public spaces for Perth, the largest being Yagan Square, in the Perth City Link area. Yagan Square is named after the local Noongar leader and warrior who died in 1833 resisting harsh colonial rule.

The MRA has a long-held commitment to incorporating public art into new public places in Perth. It is a pleasure to be involved with the development of public art for Yagan Square, and to be working closely with visionary project director Reid Ballantine. The Design Team (Lyons, Iredale Pedersen & Hooke and Aspect Studios) includes an artist team: Malcolm McGregor, Jon Tarry, Jeremy Kirwan-Ward and Helen Smith, Paul Carter and Shaun Gladwell. Paul Carter, after consultation with Richard Walley OAM, developed a creative template drawing on Indigenous and settler histories of the site, to guide the design development of the Square. Local Whadjuk artist

Sharon Egan is working with the design team to develop integrated artworks for the space. More Indigenous artworks are planned. This is a truly inspiring example of creative collaboration between the client (planners, place makers, and managers), architects, landscape architects, Indigenous advisors, and artists. I can't wait to see Yagan Square completed in 2017!

Private developers, responding to MRA's statutory planning requirement for public art, are also commissioning public artworks in the city centre. Fraser Property's Fraser Suites development in Adelaide Terrace so far has two new artworks – *Venation – twin patterned,* an intricately patterned decorative wall piece based on eucalyptus leaves by Stuart Green and Jennie Nayton, and *Patterns of Movement,* an abstract sculptural composition of aluminium circles and ovals inspired by Swan River jellyfish by Anne Neil. A glass artwork, *Swan River Life* by the Kidogo Artists Team, comprising Wendy Hayden (Noongar), Deborah Bonar (Yamatji/Gija), and Joanna Robertson is also in the works.

Public art, in its various different forms, contributes to the creation of a vibrant and liveable city – one that embraces diversity, values imagination and innovation, and cares about the quality of its public spaces. Perth is a city on the brink of more development, and public art is an inherent part of the design equation that will put Perth on the map as a truly cosmopolitan city. In addition to the public artworks mentioned in this chapter, there are many more public artworks in the Perth city centre, in particular along the length of St Georges Terrace, in the gardens next to Council House, in the Perth Cultural Centre, in the railways stations, and in Northbridge. I hope you enjoy discovering them all as you explore Perth!

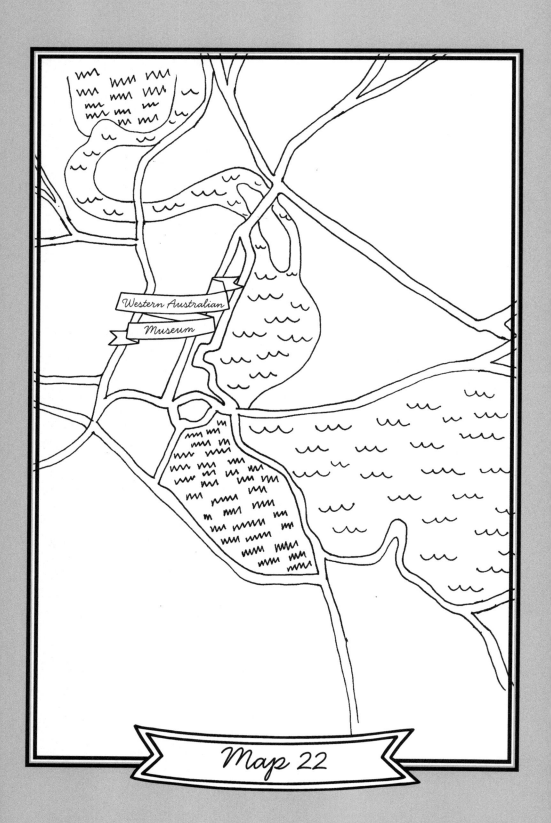

Western Australian Museum

Map 22

22

CRIMINAL PERTH

David Whish-Wilson

In all my years teaching poetry in the prisons around Perth I only ever asked after one man's crime. It was a rule of mine not to ask, to commit to the present and ask my students to do the same. Defined by the crime that led to their incarceration, most of my students, most of whom were lifers, were happy enough to leave their reputations at the door. The classes then became about exploring those parts of their experience, in language and narrative, that they carried most quietly within themselves. One of my students, I'll call him P, was no exception. An enthusiastic writer and reader, P worked in the Casuarina library, making the most of his life sentence. He was smaller and less overtly masculine than some of the other men, but I noticed they were wary of him. One day, a day like any other, he was fixing his manuscript together with a blue plastic paper-clip, and the clip snapped. So did he. Or rather, imploded. He didn't move, or make a sound, but the current of blood that flooded his face amid the terrifying stillness caught me off-guard. I looked at him and he looked at me, and as his fury subsided what remained was an obvious shame that I had witnessed his loss of control. The following day I asked, discreetly, another inmate whom I knew well and respected, about P's sentence and crime. As a teenager, P had been subjected to terrible physical and mental abuse by his father and elder brother, with whom he lived in a shack on the rural fringes of the city. It was P's job to hunt in the nearby Banksia scrub and shoot rabbits for dinner. When he didn't shoot any rabbits, there was no dinner, and he would receive a savage beating. One day, a day like any other, P was walking home through an ordinary suburban street when he saw a child playing innocently on a driveway; innocent and happy. The child's innocence, an innocence he had never known, was the trigger, and P was overwhelmed by fury. He entered the driveway and murdered the child.

As shocking as P's crime is, in its randomness and ferocity it has always acted as a metaphor for me, a reminder of the way Perth can turn, in an instant, into something unrecognisable. The veneer is so calm that the regular punctuations of rage I witness never fail to take me by surprise. Except that I shouldn't be surprised, knowing what I know. The surprise itself, it seems to me, is something characteristic to Perth. After all, I have lived in cities where it was wise to go armed in public, to project an aura of confidence, where the likelihood of assault and robbery was part of life. People were naturally wary, and took precautions, were on their guard. And I have lived in one other city, namely Tokyo, where there was little to no violence and negligible street-level crime. But Tokyo is an exception, and the majority of crime in Perth is no different to that of any Western city where inter-generational poverty, a culture of heavy-drinking, a lively prohibition drug economy, simmering racial tensions and a culture described by Tim Winton as involving "a kind of hardness and blindness that comes with an invader's ethos" intersect.

Sometimes these rips in the fabric of normality can be absurd. One night in 2013 I was entertaining an out-of-state friend in a Fremantle restaurant, when it came time to return home. He suggested a taxi, and I was initially reluctant to drop him at the local taxi-stand, where I've witnessed so many fights over the years. But it was, after all, a Monday night, my Melburnian friend reminded me, and it was admittedly quiet as we pulled alongside the stand. There were only two men waiting alongside one another, and they looked to be friends. But no sooner had I said my goodbyes and driven away when I looked in my rear-vision mirror and saw the two men laying into one another with vicious and audible blows. I reversed my car and collected my friend. They were fighting over who was next in line, still fighting as we drove away, and I ended up driving him back to his hotel.

A friend of mine has a saying about Perth, only partially tongue in cheek: "The taste of the lash is still fresh on the back." This is his explanation for the enduring feral spirit in Perth's streets, outside of the gentrified suburbs, the reflexive anti-authoritarianism and readiness to use fists to settle disputes, the traditional mongrel attitude towards bouncers and public officials at the football and other places. It's also his paradoxical explanation for the fact that Perth seems massively over-regulated, with laws and prohibitions governing everything from street drinking to wearing hats in certain pubs and waving wooden spoons at footy derbies. Absurd laws and prohibitions; not the product of a wowser or nanny state, but in his view a reflexive tendency due to an anxiety that has its origins in the convict era. The feral attitude and the over-regulation are two sides of the same coin. It's certainly true that Perth was the last Australian city to accept convicts, right up to the 1870s and well after other Australian capitals had striven to move on from the 'convict stain'. The large percentage of Perth's populace made up of convicts, and the widespread poverty of the majority of Perth's citizens resulted in a situation where, according to historian Geoffrey Bolton, in one year alone, one quarter of the male population of Fremantle was locked up for drunkenness and other petty crime. Perth allegedly had a crime rate seven times higher than that of Adelaide, and the incarceration rate for Perth's 'fallen women' was also very high. The lateness of Perth's convict period also meant that up until the 1930s, and in some cases beyond, there were men walking Perth streets who had been tied to the frame and flogged with the cat-o-nine tails; the grandparents and great-grandparents of my own generation.

The crucible for this attitude, and in many cases the site of its inception, was Fremantle Prison, a place that to this day feels haunted by the stories of the generations of men and women incarcerated there. There remains a "stern reminder of reality" still locked behind the high limestone walls, described by Fenian convict Joseph Boyle O'Reilly above the "green shoal-water, the soft air, with a yellowish warmth, the pure white sand of the beach…in the centre of the houses, spread out like a gigantic star-fish…a vast stone prison." O'Reilly's first impression of the Swan River colony captures something representative of the atmosphere of Perth, as it relates to the 'stern reminder' of crime and punishment in the city outside the prison walls. Leaving aside the various traumascapes that to Nyungar residents describe the sites of murder and massacre within the city limits, engendering an eternal haunted air, there is also something of O'Reilly's observation mirrored in the impressions of many Perth residents, suggested by what I've described elsewhere as the double-effect of a scalpel-sharp light and the general impression of space and silence and stillness – the strange marriage of a realist vision with an absurdist tone. The heart of this layered atmosphere is present in writer Elizabeth Jolley's wonder at a vision of Perth that "lies in repose as if painted on a pale curtain…it has a quality of unreality as if no life with all the ensuing problems could unfold there." And yet, one constant in many narratives written about Perth is the presence of what might be described as a gothic undertone, the idea of a surface beauty floating mirage-like upon an undercurrent of aggression, or weirdness. For many Perth residents, this is an atmosphere inscribed most forcefully by personal memories of crimes that have occurred, and perhaps are still to occur. As a crime writer, and someone with an interest in Perth's history, some of these crimes are specific to my own experience; the little pangs of adrenalin and remorse when I pass the site of fights, thefts, a suicide; but the majority belong to communal memories of the city; the enduring ghosts of crimes past. It's impossible for me to traverse the city without calling to mind some of the characters and crimes from long ago; the colourful exploits of bushranger Moondyne Joe and more recently of local boy turned bank-robber Brenden Abbott, for example, and there are others that recur with the force of personal recognition. Many of these relate to Perth's early colonial history: the hanging of Nyungar elder Midgegooroo's body from a tree outside the Perth lockup, left for three days; the image of Calyute's relatives whispering to him through the walls of the roundhouse prison in Fremantle before he was flogged; the tragic end of fifteen-year-old John Gavin, the first white man hanged in the colony, carried down the roundhouse stairs to the makeshift gallows that awaited him; the children of Perth's Boy's School being taken to watch the hanging of murderer James Malcolm in 1847, and meeting him on the Guildford Road beforehand, sitting on his own coffin. For my mother's generation, the sites of serial killer Eric Cooke's eight murders and fourteen near-deadly assaults linger upon the landscape, and still haunt the night with childhood fears. For others, it's the impossibility of driving past the Gnangara pine plantation without recalling the stories of the bodies buried there over the years, particularly those associated with the terrible murders by David and Catherine Birnie. Similarly, driving past the Continental Hotel in Claremont is to always be reminded of the three young women murdered by the 'Claremont Killer'.

Every city has such sites of horror and outrage, made worse when a killer or perpetrator isn't identified. My own personal involvement with the investigation and writing of my second novel, *Line of Sight*, exploring the murder of Perth broth-el-madam Shirley Finn in 1975, means that Fairway Seven of the Royal Perth Golf Club, where Finn was executed in Perth's first major gangland slaying, is on my mind long before I pass the site, and is especially vivid when I'm nearby. It's even worse for her children, of course, who have had to live in a community knowing that her murderer(s) live alongside them.

Researching the novel taught me something else significant about Perth. While it's the sensational crimes that are at the forefront of the public mind, there is a longer and more endur-ing history of violence associated with organised crime that largely goes unreported, and therefore unrecognised. Finn's murder at the hands of corrupt CIB detectives – and later the murder of ex-CIB Chief Don Hancock, by car-bomb, who was one of the detectives involved in the flawed investigation into Shirley Finn's murder – represent the two major irruptions of the previous decades, but scratching at the surface of the silence associated with the policing practices of the seventies and eighties and the organised crime figures who maintained the prohibition economies of gaming, vice and drugs, reveals a terrible catalogue of beatings, rapes and alleged murders that remain unrepresented, but can be sensed in the faces and inflected voices of the men and women from the period. It's this silence that is the larger subject of my crime fiction, a silence related to what I see as the atmosphere of Perth reflected in its crime – the sense that outside the clear demarcation between brightly lit centre and darkened suburbia, there are stories of this city's light and dark that remain to be told.

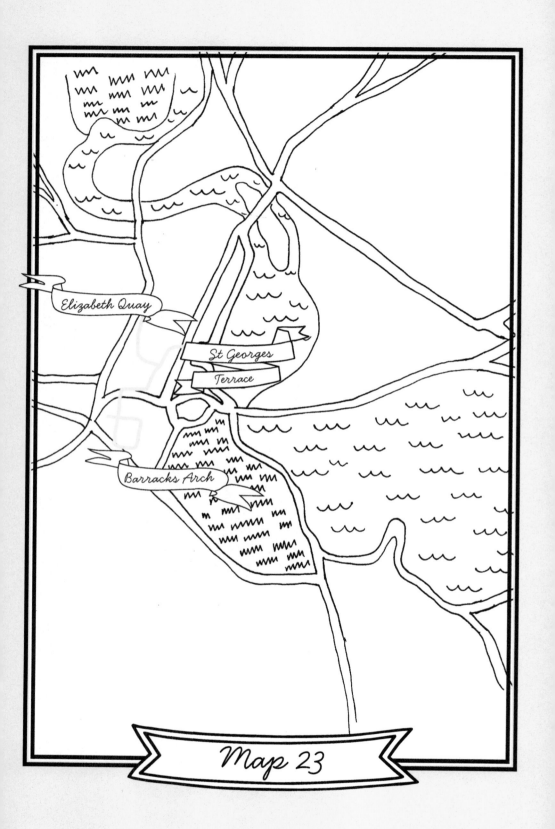

Elizabeth Quay

St Georges

Terrace

Barracks Arch

Map 23

23

CITY CENTRE BIG PROJECTS

Craig Smith

My father was a pilot and mum taught in the city. We grew up in the post-war paradise that was the garden suburb of Floreat Park. It was an all-new world, relatively affluent and with enough kids to overflow both local primary schools. As youngsters we roamed far and wide and the only constraint was that we had to be home for dinner. There was no fear of the unknown, no political correctness, and no sense of the pain that our parents had been through during the war. While Perth was purportedly a city, we may have well been living in the sticks as we wandered as free spirits in our suburban wilderness. There were kangaroos, snakes and goannas, two swamps, a lake, a dump and endless acres of bush around us. We played cricket in the summer, football in the winter and spent the rest of the year halfway up a tree, observing the world around us.

Dad had bought an Avro Anson after the war and my older brother went flying with him. Unrestrained, my brother would peer out the barely modified and open bomb doors as a camera quietly recorded the changing face of Perth below. That change came in what seemed to us almost imperceptible increments as new photos to replace the old. To our grandparents who came from a time before motor cars and aeroplanes, the changes must have appeared as a cultural onslaught conducted with unseemly haste.

As a small child my paternal grandmother lived in St Georges Terrace, her parent's house next door to the Cloisters. The house fronted the Terrace and the stables on Hay Street. Later they were to move "further out", to fashionable Adelaide Terrace. In a letter written in 1909 by my grand aunt to her fiancé, she bemoans the fact that he was living on a farm in

Applecross, about eight kilometres away and it was unlikely that she would see him for weeks on end. As young married women, she and my grandmother moved to the remote wilds of Mill Point Road in South Perth, which was then aptly named Suburban Road. Separated from the city centre by the expanse of Perth Water, their homes reached down to the river where the Kwinana Freeway now dislocates the South Perth peninsula from its tranquil past.

Our perceptions of time and space are so strongly influenced by our childhood experiences. My own suburban life was modified by time spent at our holiday house in Mandurah, where the node between river and ocean and the curiosities of nature played compelling roles, but it was more so in the city centre, where both my parents worked, that my spatial and social understanding developed. As a schoolboy I explored every lane, every shop and basement and in particular the then numerous live theatres in the city. Two of my favourite places were the basement of Foy and Gibson's store (sporting goods and hardware) and the laneway next to newspaper house where the smell of newsprint prevailed and the Bays trucks, in their bright red livery, lined up to deliver the afternoon Daily News. There were very few locked doors.

I grew up in a city that was in a state of constant growth and change. For me, Perth was a wonderful place to grow up, and it remains so today. In the years that I spent at school, the population of the Perth metropolitan area doubled from 350,000 to more than 700,000 and the city evolved through two of the many cyclic boom and bust periods that are crucial to understanding the process of its development. To some extent my comfortable relationship with change has moulded me as an optimist and I like to think that many important processes can be distilled into simple concepts, such as the realisation that great cities don't just happen; that people make decisions about the design of cities, and that consistently good planning and design decisions can transform a city's overall appearance and function, as well as the more intimate places that people enjoy.

Some folk seem to think that cities exist as a casual by-product of commerce and that they are driven by commercial activity alone, but civilised places are actually forged by the parallel imperatives of social and cultural need.. Prior to federation and during the reign of the Public Works Department, Perth gained many projects that built up the cultural and physical heritage of the city, as evidenced by how many of these buildings now grace our heritage inventories. But as our city blossomed outward, growing as it did along the lines of public transport, the architectural, engineering, planning and urban design outcomes of large projects instead gave us a lot to learn from, particularly in the city centre. Rather than simply accumulating the cultural layers of successive generations, a series of unrelated and disjointed projects lurched across the landscape like a cluster of inebriated youths. I see the visual and physical dysfunction of these transformations as blips on the cultural horizon that are entirely curable, and in an odd way, building blocks for creating a better Perth.

In the 1950s there emerged worldwide an apparent clarity of thinking in town planning as new theories swept aside centuries of ad hoc European development. Functions needed to be codified and separated into hermetically sealed silos. It was a theme that ran through the now rather quaint land-use planning policies that were advocated for more than forty years. Various functions had to be isolated from each other, regardless of obvious synergies that had brought them together for the previous millennium or so. The result was that by the end of the 1970s the office buildings of St Georges Terrace stood like a giant monoculture, devoid of cultural imperative. The people of Perth had to go to Fremantle to take in the pleasures of urban places, while in Perth we have had to spend quite some time incrementally piecing the functions of the city back into to a more pluralistic and complex beast, though some significant challenges remain.

The Perth Convention Exhibition Centre is by most measures an urban design disaster. It is arguably in the right functional location, but the simplistic brief issued for the building meant that the inevitable outcome could never relate properly to the city, the river or adjacent transport links and, however well designed, that it would be encapsulated in an entirely inappropriate suburban building, like a very large fish out of water. But for me it remains an opportunity, a valuable land bank that we should plan around and utilise more profitably in the future.

The freeway cutting in front of the parliament is a project of its time; a triumph of transport planning over urban design. It bifurcates the city and sets the parliament buildings apart, looking across the abyss to the CBD. Few will remember but Paul Rigby, the cartoonist for *The Daily News*, campaigned with others for the Barracks Arch to be retained at the top of St Georges Terrace, when the freeway was built at the end of the 1960s. The campaign wasn't, as those who don't know their history might say, a tokenistic heritage gesture, but rather a delightful two-fingered salute to our political masters that blocks the view from the parliament down St Georges Terrace. Though the campaign didn't stop the freeway blitzing a large portion of the western end of the city, it was a turning point.

Should the cutting be seen now as a planning blunder or is it an opportunity? The closing of this scar remains an exciting challenge. Surely no government could ever convince the public that spending money fixing up the front yard of the parliament is worthwhile, but perhaps a city that wants to set itself higher expectations might. By combining a range of planning objectives, including light rail, peripheral parking, a changed emphasis on freeway access, and commercial development, the much needed provisions of parliamentary offices, a civic place and a city re-joined to West Perth and Kings Park could happen. Personally I say, let's bring it on.

To the east there is more stitching to be done. Unlike the railway to the west, there is no need to sink the line. All you need is to imagine that a small hillock once ran through that part of town, a simple viaduct covering the rail that could form new sites and connections in one of the few places where the cost of construction might be offset by the value of the land produced. The drawbacks are few and the benefits to that part of the city, which is currently subject to unprecedented growth, are many. The *What If* project looked at the connection east in 2010 and explored the proposition that neglected eastern parts of the city could be transformed with a Rambla-like boulevard that stretched from the city station all the way to the river at the old East Perth Power Station. It would have been, in *Yes Minister* terms, a brave decision to push on with this concept, but to me it is critical that we continue to explore such game-changing ideas as they have the capacity to cultivate and enrich our city.

As we await the fulfilment of the Link Project, Elizabeth Quay and Riverside and to a lesser extent the new stadium, public debate continues. These projects, and in particular Elizabeth Quay, have collected some pretty vitriolic, and at times mendacious, comment. But at last urban design is on the table and emerging as the key means of integrating large projects into the city fabric as urban rather than suburban developments. Large projects have the capacity to achieve outcomes that are not possible in smaller developments, and yet they have often occurred in our city without due regard to their impact or potential. The measure of these factors, from both economic and urban design perspectives, is fundamental to creating great outcomes.

Perhaps there is a conceptually simple solution to this and other problems facing the planning of the city, and that is to recognise that they are planning issues; issues that transcend the boundaries of existing silos of government and issues that require overarching strategies and direction that better define roles and shared goals, within a defined development framework. The planning of Perth, like many other cities, suffers from having too many jurisdictions holding sway over isolated planning controls. The Council and a plethora of State Government organisations work on the design of the city and despite the talent and best intentions of their respective staff, each organisation pursues independent objectives for the city that never quite fit into a coherent whole.

Did I say a simple solution? Well, the concept is simple enough and there have been moves in recent years to establish a framework for city development in the City's *Urban Design Framework* and *What If* and the State documents *Capital City Framework*, *Directions 2031* and the *State Planning Strategy*, which cast wider nets over our future. But however good or well intentioned these documents are, we will never have the city we deserve until there is a calm and guiding hand that oversees and directs the inputs that affect development of the city. A Capital City Act should indeed be beckoning and perhaps then we could better deal with large projects and develop a planning and economic city strategy that transcends the limits of the political cycle.

I see numerous aspects of city design that need to be addressed if we are to consistently achieve good results. First cab off the rank should be defining the need and then intended outcome of the project. Capital cost and economic impact over time should combine with assessing the leverage the project can provide for other desired planning, social, cultural and economic outcomes. Standards of design should be set and their achievement guaranteed. The project should integrate into the city to enhance and add to the quality of life and over a given period. Strategically we should ask if the project is a good fit for its time and place within the city's development framework and if it isn't, then can it be made to be a good fit? That is, can the framework successfully accept the level of change proposed or be modified to embrace it, or is the project simply a bad idea?

There is an understanding in design circles that good clients create good projects and that well researched, properly briefed and funded projects are invariably better than those that are not. Examining our less successful major projects reveals the common factor: they all had inadequate or flawed briefs. Sometimes the failure to set up a brief correctly stems from a desire to execute programs within inadequate time frames, or to achieve one outcome at the expense of others that are of considerable or greater importance. Regardless of the reason, a major part of being a good client in design is to ensure that the brief meets the aims of the project and the planning framework in which it sits, or as the old British Army adage goes, proper prior planning prevents a certain type of poor performance. Similarly, you don't get an exciting and vibrant city if the effects of economic development are not considered in detail, just the propensity for projects to go off the rails. Indeed, light rail routes should not be ruled out without an examination of the long-term economic impacts, both from transport and city development perspectives.

Some projects have been badly briefed due to budgeting "errors", which, more often than not involved the hiding of real-istic budgets in order to get projects up and running. Fortunately this problem is now so well tagged at state level that expensive blowouts are unlikely to rear their heads again in the near future.

One of my university lecturers once said that in Europe developers spend more time and money on the design phase of projects to get a better result, and in Perth they put marble in the lobby. Project budgets have two bedfellows that go cheek by jowl: quantity and quality. Cost, quality and quantity, of which the client can only control two or project management becomes impossible. I'd like to introduce a design excellence process that aims to bring quality to the fore, without neces-sarily changing the overall cost.

Good design transcends cost or utility. It integrates function, appearance, materials, longevity, history, a sense of place and social outcomes. We should look for buildings and spaces to work at various levels: on the macro scale they need to perform as a part of the cityscape; technically they need to respond to environmental and other performance objectives. At street level, projects need to engage with the activities of the ground plane, just as internally they have to respond to the needs of the individual users and for the developer they need to make money.

Whether we like it or not, cities attract big projects and in order for them to excel we need to think differently about city design. West Australians embrace huge mining ventures, but shy away from great engineering or public works, in much the same way that we tend to take down tall poppies. It is important that we overcome this recoil and start to embrace change with more confidence. To achieve this it is important that we bring all aspects of city design on to the one page. This approach may still result in failure or limited success from time to time, but the more we pursue good design, the more often we will succeed; in the end, a design-savvy community will demand better and better places in a city that we can all enjoy.

Cities are not the work of an individual or the expression of a single project, but an accretion of the actions of many people that gradually moulds the shape of our place in history.

Map 24

24

LEAVING PERTH

Ruth Morgan

In June 2012, I packed my bags and headed east. The enormity of my decision only sank in as I passed through the X-ray machine at the airport, leaving my parents, my partner and Perth behind.

It wasn't a decision I'd made lightly. I knew that academic positions were as rare as hen's teeth, and with the ink yet to dry on my PhD thesis it was an offer too good to refuse. When I received the offer, I had immediately said, 'Yes!' And as I hung up the phone, the doubt and the guilt set in. What about my partner? Could he move? Would he move? Should I wait and see if another opportunity would arise in Perth? From all reports, the latter happening any time soon was unlikely. I could hang around, hoping a morsel of work would be thrown my way, or seize this chance to forge an academic career in Melbourne. "But…what about him?" This was the question that hung in the air as my friends, many of whom had settled down with partners and husbands and wives and babies and mortgages, looked at me with concern written all over their faces.

Of course, he hadn't wanted me to go. He kept asking, "Why are you rushing into it?" I wondered the same thing myself. Because I have to, I told him. And myself. But I was still asking that question when I went home for Christmas.

I'd been home before then and he had visited me. We'd also travelled overseas together and I had no doubts that we would forge on, somehow, despite living on opposite sides of the country. Maybe it was because I was home for a long stretch over summer, where I could relax into old rhythms again. Somehow I was home but still homesick – I just couldn't shake the dread of leaving again.

Quitting wasn't an option. That much I knew. And I would be better for the experience. Stronger, more independent. I had barely strayed from the nest – I hadn't lived away from Perth before and I saw my parents all the time. I had to persevere, even if it was just pigheaded pride.

Moving away from Perth had always been on the cards. I had just never expected to do it alone. When I first contemplated postgraduate studies, a Canberra academic warned me of the perils of Perth's isolation. If I wanted to seriously pursue my studies and a research career, I would have to travel far and often. So I did. I do. More than ever. Now it's not just for work, but to see my partner, to see my parents, to go home. My suitcase is never entirely unpacked; I'm always on the move, never still. It's exciting and exhausting and essential – it's just the way it is. At least for now.

"We'll just see how we go." I've said it so often, it's become a mantra. I envy my friends who have more conventional arrangements, who can come home at the end of the day and relax with their partner or pop over to mum and dad's for dinner. I do and I don't. But it can be lonely. It occurs to me that we live a FIFO existence – just without the red dust, fluoro vests and steel-capped boots. Is this how a twenty-first-century romance is supposed to be?

Before I left Perth, I hadn't dared to think too far ahead about the new life, the 'other' life, I was about to begin. Although I had visited Melbourne on holiday, everything felt new, vast and overwhelming. A new job, new flat, new routine. More people, more traffic, more responsibility. And it was cold. Bloody cold. And wet. My new colleagues apologised for the weather – it's not usually this bad, they assured me. At least my welcome was warm – friends from school and university had already crossed the Nullabor, seeking opportunities in the arts or looking for a change of scene. And I've discovered more and more people who spent their formative years in Perth, only to drift away or escape, as some have described their experiences. To be from Perth in Melbourne is to feel like you're part of some kind of a diaspora, a community of émigrés and exiles in the east.

Having only just left, I've felt obliged to defend Perth's honour when others have drawn it into question, which has been often. It's either Dullsville, where we refuse to turn our clocks forward in summer and the shops never open, or it's Boom Town, where the likes of Gina and Twiggy rule the roost and the streets are paved with gold. Worse still, they say, it's far away and in the middle of nowhere. Yes. Maybe. But... it's still home.

It's where I grew up and went to school. It's where I went to university and met my friends. It's where my mum grew up and met my dad. But it's become more than a family connection. Researching the history of the place and its people has brought another kind of attachment, wrought through knowing Perth beyond my kith and kin. It's a familiarity that comes from grasping why Perth is the way it is, what might have been, and how it's seen itself over the years. Digging deeper into Perth's past by sifting through the archives and touching its history has made me feel as though I know Perth in a different way, my own way – as if I might know some of its secrets. Writing about Perth and its water histories over the last decade or so, I feel a kind of responsibility when it comes to speaking about its past – a protectiveness about the West, a mix perhaps of parochialism and pride that simmers just beneath the surface.

Three years on, my partner has just moved to Melbourne and at last it feels as though I can put down roots there. Finally, we can start planning our futures together. As he settles in, I am remembering and reliving my own move east – the adjustment, the adventure, the anxiety of starting afresh. We can't help but compare the two. On the one hand, Melbourne is Perth writ large – a city straddling a river, a north-south divide, an urban sprawl; but on the other, they couldn't be more different – Melbourne, so self-confident, so self-assured, while Perth seems more nervous, more flighty, more concerned about its future.

And yet I still feel Perth's pull. Our families and friends are still in the west, growing older and settling down. So while our future seems to lie in the east, our past and roots remain in Perth and there's a sense that we are missing out. The Nullarbor is vast and the distance between Perth and Melbourne seems to grow with every trip home. How quickly we lose our way on the streets of Perth, how soon we lose track of where we are going, how much we feel like strangers in our own town. Now we see the city from the outside, and while there are plenty of things to rib and ridicule, we know just how far it's come. Perth may still have a long way to go, but it's definitely going.

And so I pack my bags and board the plane again, flying in, flying out, going home.

BIOGRAPHIES

Nick Allbrook grew up in Derby, Western Australia. He made music in the accidentally popular Daglish bogan-ascetic commune that spawned Mink Mussel Creek, Tame Impala, Pond, Space Lime Peacock, Allbrook Avery and a sack of other near-saleable art/products.

Clarissa Ball is the Director of the Institute of Advanced Studies at the University of Western Australia where she is also an art historian in the Faculty of Architecture, Landscape and Visual Arts. She has a wide range of art historical interests including late nineteenth century English painting and documentary photography from the 1860s to the late 1930s. More recently she has developed an interest in the role and representation of women in the establishment of urban settlements in nineteenth century Australia.

Julian Bolleter is an Assistant Professor at the Australian Urban Design Research Centre (AUDRC) at the University of Western Australia. His role at the AUDRC includes teaching a master's program in urban design and conducting urban design related research and design projects. Julian is an awarded landscape architect and urban designer and has worked in Australia, the USA, the UK and the Middle East on a range of major projects. Julian has completed a PhD and published three books: *Made in Australia: The future of Australian cities* (with Richard Weller), *Take me to the River: A history of Perth's foreshore* and *Scavenging the Suburbs*, a book which audits Perth for ~1,000,000 possible urban infill dwellings. In 2014 Julian was awarded the Australian Institute of Landscape Architects WA gold medal award (in conjunction with Richard Weller).

Clint Bracknell is a Senior Lecturer for the Sydney Conservatorium of Music and Division of Architecture and Creative Arts at the University of Sydney. His major research focus centres on Aboriginal Australian song and languages, emerging technologies, contemporary music and Indigenous creative futures. A musician and composer, his Nyungar cultural elders from the south coast of Western Australia use the term 'Wirlomin' to refer to their clan.

Sarah Burnside has lived in Perth for most of her life, where she has worked as a native title lawyer and in policy. The views expressed here are her own. She has an abiding interest in history and politics and her writing has appeared in outlets such as The Guardian, Overland, The Griffith Review, Arena, New Matilda, Crikey and The Baffler.

Antonio Buti MLA is the Member for Armadale in the State Parliament of Western Australia and Honorary Fellow at the Law School, The University of Western Australia. He was educated at The University of Western Australia, Australian National University, Oxford University and Yale Law School. Dr Buti has written books, articles and other publications on a wide range of issues. His biography of Sir Ronald Wilson, A Matter of Conscience (UWAP), won the 2007 Premier's Non-Fiction Award and the overall Premier's Book Award.

Marcus Canning was born in Perth in 1974. He graduated from the University of Western Australia School of Architecture, Landscape Architecture and Fine Arts in 1997. Following the establishment of Jacksue Gallery (1995-2000) and work with the Awesome International Festival for Young People (1998-2001), Canning became CEO of Artrage in 2002, the year he created The Bakery music venue (2002-2015) and Breadbox Gallery (2002-2008). In 2010 he created Rooftop Movies and in 2011 launched the Fringe World Festival, which officially became the third largest Fringe in the world in 2015. He has sat on the Australia Council's New Media Arts Board, Theatre Board and Inter-Arts Panel and has chaired the federal Festivals Australia committee. Large-scale public art commissions include 'Ascalon' with Christian De Vietri at St. Georges Cathedral in 2010, 'Onward! Onward!' at the Treasury Buildings and Cathedral Square in 2015 and 'Rainbow' for the City of Fremantle in 2016.

Paul Carter is a highly acclaimed writer, artist and interdisciplinary scholar. His book *The Road to Botany Bay* and his artwork *Nearamnew* (at Federation Square, Melbourne) are particularly well-known and acclaimed. He is Creative Director of the design studio Material Thinking (established 2007), and Professor of Design (Urbanism) in the School of Architecture & Design, RMIT University.

Len Collard is an Australian Research Council, Chief Investigator and Professor with the School of Indigenous Studies at the University of Western Australia. Len has a background in literature and communications and his research interests are in the area of Aboriginal Studies, including Nyungar interpretive histories and Nyungar theoretical and practical research models. Len's research has allowed the broadening of the understanding of the many unique characteristics of Australia's Aboriginal people and has contributed to improving the appreciation of Aboriginal culture and heritage of the Southwest of Australia. Len is a Whadjuk Nyungar and who is a Traditional Owner of the Perth Metropolitan area and surrounding lands, rivers, swamps, ocean and its culture.

Beth George is a lecturer in Architecture at the University of Western Australia. She is a teacher, practitioner and researcher. She has been teaching for over ten years in WA, at both UWA and Curtin University, in architectural design, design communication and urban and regional architecture. She is a cofounder of Post-Architecture and Spacemarket and is now running a sole practice. Her PhD was completed at RMIT in 2009. An investigation into Perth through the medium of mapping, it is a study in urban curation that the work herein continues to explore.

Kate Hislop is an architect and academic at The University of Western Australia where she teaches in architectural design, history and research methods. Her research is predominantly in the areas of Australian architectural history, suburban theory and colonial studies and particularly in the intersections between Nineteenth Century colonial values and the suburban paradigm. These interests informed her PhD entitled 'Sketches in the Sand: Speculative thought and the aesthetic foundations of the Swan River Colony 1826-1839' which documents the impact of speculative thought and practice upon the colonising, planning, spatializing and building of early Perth. She has published numerous scholarly as well as creative works in Australian professional and academic journals.

Peter Kennedy is Perth born and educated. His affinity with Perth's central business district began in his primary school years in the 1950s when he made the daily return tram trip through the city from the family home in Subiaco to Christian Brothers' College Perth at 1 St Georges Terrace. Much of his working life has been spent either at Newspaper House in St Georges Terrace with The West Australian, or in nearby Adelaide Terrace with the ABC. This has enabled him to closely observe both the changing character, and characters, of the city over sixty years. He is the author of *Tales From Boomtown* (UWAP 2014).

Andra Kins was born in Perth, Western Australia in 1952, the child of Latvian refugees. She is passionate about creativity and cultural development. She holds a degree in architecture and a postgraduate diploma in creative writing. Working as an independent public art consultant she has developed and co-ordinated numerous public art projects, large and small in many different contexts, and has written about contemporary public art for various publications. Her memoir *Coming and Going* explored the lives of four generations of women in her family and was published in 2004. Currently she is spending time every year both in Australia and Latvia.

Michal Lewi AM is a retired lawyer who now spends his time applying his life-long hobby of photography to his enthusiasm for architectural history. He has long advocated the conservation of heritage places, including both historic and modern heritage, has served twice as chairman of the National Trust Council, and received the award of AM for his heritage work. When he first moved from London to Western Australia in 1961 he could see little heritage significance in the built environment of Perth; since then, however, he has come to recognise that Perth has its own special and precious heritage values which are of great importance to its citizens.

Conrad Liveris is an advocate, adviser and researcher on the politics and economics of diversity. Advising some of Australia's leading companies and executives on workplaces and productivity, focusing on inclusion, he has also written for the Sydney Morning Herald, Financial Review and West Australian, amongst many others. His research has been featured in The Australian and by ABC News, and he has presented to leading Australian and international universities and institutions on topics including corporate governance, superannuation and political leadership. In 2012 he co-founded, a homeless education and advocacy organization and is its general manager.

Geoffrey London is the Professor of Architecture at The University of Western Australia and a Professorial Fellow at the University of Melbourne. Over an eleven year period he served initially as the inaugural Government Architect in Western Australia and then as the Victorian Government Architect. He is a past President of the Western Australian Chapter of the Australian Institute of Architects, and a Life Fellow of the Institute. He has acted as a consultant on numerous architectural and urban design projects and has served on and acted as chair of a number of competition juries.

Malcolm Mackay is a UK registered Architect of over 20 years experience. He practised architecture for many years in Milton

Keynes and London before deciding to heed the call of urban design. After four years as a Senior Urban Designer in State Government in Western Australia, Malcolm returned to private practice and formed mackay urbandesign. A talented all-rounder, Malcolm has a particular interest in town centre design, the relationship between land use and transport, and the sustainability of places.

Alannah MacTiernan is the Federal member for Perth. Her public life began in 1988 with a five-year stint on the Perth City Council, followed by 17 years in the State Parliament. From 2001-2008, she was Western Australia's Minister for Planning and Infrastructure – implementing a triple bottom line agenda and making many infrastructure changes to the metropolis of Perth. Alannah was Mayor of Vincent for two years before standing in the federal election of 2013. She has always believed that in a democracy you can't just wait for someone else to do something – and has always been active in community and politics since her teenage years.

Felicity Morel-EdnieBrown has a PhD from the University of Western Australia exploring the development of Perth's history, heritage and cultural development. She is interested in the planning and symbolism of cities; the reading of authenticity; architecture and spatial relationships to humanity; urbanization as a physical and psychological process; and, the interaction between culture in cities, interpretation and new technologies. With a professional background in history, heritage, interpretation, cultural tourism and conservation, she works alongside planners and architects on projects affecting the city. She is currently Director of strategic consultancy Culture+Context, an Honorary Research Fellow at the University of Western Australia and an expert Member of the ICOMOS International Scientific Committee on Interpretation and Presentation.

Ruth Morgan completed her PhD at The University of Western Australia in 2012 and took up a lecturing position at Monash University in the School of Philosophical, Historical and International Studies the following year. Her doctoral thesis was awarded the 2013 Margaret Medcalf Prize by the State Records Office of Western Australia for excellence in reference and research, and shortlisted for the Australian Historical Association's Serle Award for the best postgraduate thesis in Australian History. Her first book, *Running Out: Water in Western Australia*, was published by UWAP in 2015. She has been a visiting scholar in the USA and Germany. Ruth coordinates the 'Making Public Histories' seminar series, a joint initiative with the History Council of Victoria and the State Library of Victoria.

Gillian O'Shaughnessy is a Perth journalist with 20 years experience. She did her cadetship in radio news with the ABC in Western Australia, and has since worked presenting and reporting for radio and television news and current affairs. She has presented radio news, and the former ABC state based tv current affairs program, Stateline. She was one of the first senior editors of the ABC online news site. Gillian filled in as a presenter on the ABC Morning Program and Breakfast shifts, before making the permanent move to Local Radio, to host the Afternoon show between 1pm and 3pm on 720 ABC

Perth. Gillian has lived in Fremantle most of her life furthering her passion for good food, good coffee, average to fine wine and the Fremantle Dockers.

Angela Rooney is a Research Associate at Curtin University Sustainability Policy (CUSP) Institute. Her research explores the investigation of themes of revolving around Indigenous place name meanings, sustainability, heritage, mapping and connection to country. Born in the Southwest of Western Australia within the Bibulman area of Nyungar country, she has built a professional work career spanning from UK, France and Singapore. Angela is qualified in Cartography, holds a Bachelor of Commerce and achieved Masters in Sustainability and Climate Policy.

Craig Smith is the Perth City Architect and principal of Craig Smith Architect. He advises on all new development proposals in the city as well design reviews on government projects including Elizabeth Quay and the Old Treasury redevelopment. His private work ranges through commercial, transport, schools, industrial and housing to mining, master planning and urban design. In practice since 1980, he also taught at UWA till the 1990s, where he established the Housing Research Information Centre. Craig has represented the Australian Institute of Architects at national level, in public affairs, membership and education and on the Federal Government's Development Assessment Forum.

Diana Warnock AM, a former newspaper and radio journalist, State politician and university tutor, has lived in Perth's CBD for most of her adult life. She and her late husband Bill, a former advertising executive, novelist and playwright, enjoyed a close relationship with the city, working and walking in it, eating out, serving on committees, and constantly attending films, plays, ballet, opera, concerts, book launches and art exhibitions in the heart of Perth.

David Whish-Wilson's first novel *The Summons* was published in 2006. His second novel *Line of Sight* (2010) and its sequel *Zero at the Bone* (2013), concerned with the mean streets of Perth from the 1970s, have been acclaimed. David's most recent publication is *Perth* in the New South Publishing city series, which was short-listed for the 2014 WA Premier's Book Awards. David has taught in the prison system in both WA and Fiji, where he started the country's first prisoner writing program, which now operates in all Fijian prisons. He currently lives in Fremantle and teaches creative writing at Curtin University.

Helen Whitbread is the Manager of Sustainable Initiatives and Adjunct Senior Lecturer in Architecture Landscape and Visual Arts at the University of Western Australia. In 2014 Helen was awarded an Honorary Fellow Australian Institute of Landscape Architects and has written and illustrated two children's books, *The Stone Swan* and *Idjhil*, which was the 1996 winner of the Western Australian Premier's Prize for Children's literature.

Terri-Ann White is a writer, former bookseller and currently the Director of UWA Publishing.

First published in 2016 by
UWA Publishing
Crawley, Western Australia 6009
www.uwap.uwa.edu.au
UWAP is an imprint of UWA Publishing
a division of The University of Western Australia

National Library of Australia Cataloguing-in-Publication entry
Title: Perth: a guide for the curious / edited by Terri-ann White.
ISBN: 9781742587554 (paperback)
Subjects: Perth (W.A.)--Anecdotes.
    Perth (W.A.)--Description and travel.
Other Creators/Contributors: White, Terri-ann, editor.
Dewey Number: 994.11
Typeset by Alissa Dinallo
Cover and internal design by Alissa Dinallo
Printed by Lightning Source

Thanks to the following people for their support in the preparation of this book:
Craig Smith
Simon Anderson
Adrian Fini
And the team at UWAP

IMAGE CREDITS

p.5 Photo by @attic.salts

p.112 White City, William Street, Perth with view to Mount Eliza, Courtesy of the State Library of Western Australia, 012321D.

p.115 A White City attraction. Jim, the flying greyhound, who nightly clears the 12-foot jump for the benefit of White City patrons. Courtesy of the State Library of Western Australia, 047484PD.

p.129 Portia Bennett, *Perth Town Hall*, 1935. Watercolour on paper, 59.0 x 42.0 cm. State Art Collection, Art Gallery of Western Australia, purchased 2005. © Portia Bennett, 1935.

p.130 Harald Vike, *Perth Nocturne*, 1934. Oil on canvas on board, 49.5 x 59 cm. Janet Holmes à Court Collection.

p.132 Guy Grey-Smith, *View from Kings Park*, c.1949-1954. Oil on canvas, 41.0 x 51.0 cm. © Mark Grey-Smith, Sue Grey-Smith.

p.139 Thomas Hoareau, *Lovers (Business As Usual)*, 1988. Oil on linen, 127.0 x 156 cm. S and K James Collection.

p.139 Tom Alberts, *As the Crow Flies*, 1989. Oil on canvas, 81.0 x 71.5 cm. The University of Western Australia Art Collection, University Senate Grant, 1989

IMAGES COURTESY OF THE CITY OF PERTH

p.6 Aerial View of Perth looking South-West 1933, C AD42.

p.9 T.G.A Molloy Mayor 1908-09, A-1 (2) L60.

p.17 St George's Terrace 1950's ,C-4 DG60.

p.47 Colonial Mutual Life Building 1939, B-7 AK44.

p.71 St George's Terrace near to the National Mutual Arcade 1970's, C-4(1).

p.103 The Town Hall Corner 1950's, B-1 V47.

p.159 North up London Court 1958, C-9 AJ46.

p.217 Town Hall after Renovations 1948, B-1 (1) V46.

p.241 Visit of the Duke and Duchess of Cornwall and York- Chinese Arch 1901, E- 1 (5) AP50.

p.253 Aerial View of Perth 1930's, C(2) CE54-.

p.275 Sydney Stubbs Mayor 1906-1907. A-1 L56.

p.287 Visit of the Duke and Duchess of Cornwall and York- Timber and Coal Arches 1901, E-1 (6) P57.

INSTAGRAM IMAGES

p.18
1 @_jackiewong
2 @alistair_2262
3 @amyer
4 @attic.salts
5 @benn_tudor
6 @attic.salts

p.19
1 @benstieger
2 @champagnesailor
3 @champagnesailor
4 @coffeyandtea
5 @dani_egloff90
6 @date.with.a.plate

p.184
1 @dewianggraenip
2 @ezinwonderland
3 @gordon_cheok
4 @jessxmadeira
5 @jooey
6 @lavinia.w

p.185
1 @laviniaw
2 @lina.ltg
3 @lina.ltg
4 @lizinspired
5 @luitedotnet
6 @mhlava

p.294
1 @mr_p_c
2 @mr_p_c
3 @nathanlaw
4 @nathanlaw
5 @nathanlaw
6 @nathanlaw

p.295
1 @perth_hues
2 @photobyto
3 @rgimagery
4 @rgimagery
5 @rgimagery
6 @luitedotnet

CPSIA information can be obtained
at www.ICGtesting.com
Printed in the USA
BVOW11s0837200316

3961BVAU00002B/2/P